DOMINUS MUNDI

This monograph makes a seminal contribution to existing literature on the importance of Roman law in the development of political thought in Europe. In particular it examines the expression 'dominus mundi', following it through the texts of the medieval jurists—the Glossators and Post-Glossators—up to the political thought of Hobbes. Understanding the concept of dominus mundi sheds light on how medieval jurists understood ownership of individual things; it is more complex than it might seem, and this book investigates these complexities. The book also offers important new insights into Thomas Hobbes, especially with regard to the end of dominus mundi and the replacement by *Leviathan*. Finally, the book has important relevance for contemporary political theory. With the fading of political diversity, Monateri argues 'that the actual setting of globalisation represents the reappearance of the Ghost of the Dominus Mundi, a political refoulé—repressed—a reappearance of its sublime nature, and a struggle to restore its universal legitimacy, and take its place.' In making this argument, the book adds an important original vision to current debates in legal and political philosophy.

Dominus Mundi

Political Sublime and the World Order

Pier Giuseppe Monateri

•HART•

OXFORD • LONDON • NEW YORK • NEW DELHI • SYDNEY

HART PUBLISHING

Bloomsbury Publishing Plc

Kemp House, Chawley Park, Cumnor Hill, Oxford, OX2 9PH, UK

First published in Great Britain 2018

A catalogue record for this book is available from the British Library.

Library of Congress Cataloging-in-Publication data

Names: Monateri, P. G., author.

Title: Dominus mundi : political sublime and the world order / Pier Giuseppe Monateri.

Description: Portland, Oregon : Hart Publishing, 2018. | Includes bibliographical references and index.

Identifi ers: LCCN 2018013678 (print) | LCCN 2018013821 (ebook) | ISBN 9781509911769 (Epub) | ISBN 9781509911752 (hardback)

Subjects: LCSH: Roman law—History. | Law—Philosophy. | Political science—Europe—Philosophy. | Roman law—Reception—Europe.

Classification: LCC KJA147 (ebook) | LCC KJA147 .M66 2018 (print) | DDC 340.5/4—dc23

LC record available at https://lccn.loc.gov/2018013678

ISBN: HB: 978-1-50991-175-2
ePDF: 978-1-50991-177-6
ePub: 978-1-50991-176-9

Typeset by Compuscript Ltd, Shannon

ACKNOWLEDGEMENTS

There are many people I wish to thank. My first tribute must undoubtedly go to Geoffrey Samuel. This book originates, indeed, from the table talks we regularly had in Paris. We sat in his favourite *bistro*, midway between the Pantheon and the Sorbonne, and it was his idea to confront the *Dominus*. His were the first and deeply remarkable suggestions. From there our conversations often slipped among velleities and Latin fragments, and a first part of this book was eventually discussed at the seminar organised in his honour by Simone Glanert and Pierre Legrand. To Geoffrey I owe a deep debt of gratitude.

Another person to whom I owe so much is Horatia Muir Watt. She has been a great friend and a mentor, and I could not have worked without her deep insight on every subject, her strong support and her eager wit. She has those qualities upon which friendship lives, and I would say that without these friendships—life, what *cauchemar!*

A special mention is due to Gunter Frankenberg. We met by chance in the Arabian Desert and since then his inspiration has always been particularly relevant for me. His works have illuminated my path.

A great help has come from Gary Watt, who I once saw performing Shakespeare in Verona, and who wasted his time in giving invaluable suggestions and remarks.

The ideas contained in this book were publicly discussed for the first time in an advanced writing workshop during the Conference of the Institute for Global Law and Policy (IGLP) organised at Harvard by David Kennedy in 2015. I wish to thank all the participants whose interventions have shaped my research: Dennis Davis, Zoran Oklopcic, Antonio Marzal Yetano, Gleider Hernandez and Nahed Samour. I also cannot forget Luca Siliquini-Cinelli who, though living in Australia at the time, was the first to encourage me to develop my ideas into a book.

Many others I must thank, and I am deeply grateful to them all. But I must especially thank Roxana Vatanparast who has been the 'perfect editor'. We regularly met to read and correct the manuscript and developed those hours of work into a real intellectual encounter. Her suggestions have all been of remarkable and outstanding importance.

There are two other young scholars without whom this work would never have been finished. If this book exists it is because of Davide Gianti and Mauro Balestrieri. They worked hard to check every aspect of the manuscript. They have been wonderful, learned and patient. I cannot thank them enough for all that they have done.

I would like to thank my wife and my daughters who constitute the enduring stuff of my life. Maria Letizia (ML) has been patient beyond limit in tolerating all my whimsy and intemperances: the wife of my youth to rejoice with. My daughters, Francesca and Valentina, whose intellectual development has been the greatest thing I have seen through all my life, have been wonderful in shaping arguments, inventing replies, giving insights and correcting misjudgments.

All errors, of course, are my own.

TABLE OF CONTENTS

ABBREVIATIONS

Auth	=	Authenticum
BCE	=	Before Common Era (used only when needed to avoid confusion)
CCSL	=	B Jannsens, L Jacqué and P Sartori (eds), *Corpus Christianorum Series Latina* (Turnhout, Brepols, 1953–ongoing)
CE	=	Common Era (used only when needed to avoid confusion)
CJ	=	Corpus Iuris Civilis
clm	=	Column
Cod	=	Codex
Coll	=	Collectio
Comp	=	Compilatio
Const	=	Constitutio
Dig	=	Digest of Justinian
Dist	=	Distinctio
Feud	=	Libri Feudorum
IGRR	=	G Lafaye (ed), *Inscriptiones Graecae ad Res Romanas Pertinentes Auctoritate et Impensis. Academiae Inscriptionum et Litterarum Humaniorum Collectae et Editae*, (reprint Paris, Leroux, 1906–1927)
ILS	=	H Dessau (ed), *Inscriptiones Latinae Selectae* (Berlin, Weidmann, 1892–1906)
Instit	=	Institutes of Justinian
fol	=	folio
JGR	=	KEZ von Lingenthal (ed), *Jus Graeco-Romanum* (Leipzig, Weigel, 1856–1884)
KJV	=	King James's Version of the Bible
l	=	lex
Lib Aug	=	Liber Augustalis = Constitutions of Melfi (1231)
MGH	=	GH Pertz and G Waitz (ed), *Monumenta Germaniae Historica* (Munchen-Hannover-Berlin, 1826–1886)
MIC	=	*Monumenta Iuris Canonici: Corpus Glossatorum* (Città del Vaticano, Biblioteca Apostolica Vaticana, 1969–ongoing)
Nov	=	Novellae constitutiones
PL	=	JP Migne (ed), *Patrologia Latina* (Paris, Garnier, 1844–1855)
qu	=	quaestio

Sept	=	Greek version of the Bible known as the Septuagint = A Rahlfs (ed), *Septuaginta, id est Vetus Testamentum Graece Iuxta LXX Interpretes* (Stuttgart, Deutsche Bibelstiftung, 1935)
Syll	=	W Dittenberger (ed), *Sylloge Inscriptionum Graecarum*, 3rd edn (FH von Gaertringen ed, Leipzig, Herzel, 1917–1920)
TAM	=	E Kalinka (ed), *Tituli Asiae Minoris: Tituli Lyciae Linguis Graeca et Latina Conscripti* (Vienna, Hölder, 1920–1944)
v	=	sub verbo, gloss to a phrase in a law or decretal
Vulg	=	Latin version of the Bible known as Vulgata = R Weber Osb (ed), *Biblia Sacra Iuxta Vulgata Versionem* (Stuttgart, Wuertembergische Bibelanstalt, 1969)
X	=	Decretales Gregorii IX

Given the many textual variants existing in different editions, when not otherwise specified comments of medieval glossators will adopt the form: Author [commented legislation]. Examples: Bartolus [Dig 6.1.1], Bartolus [Const *Omnem*].

All Biblical citations follow the standard form. Examples: 2 Corinthians 3:1 (Second Letter to the Corinthians, chapter 3, line 1); Ecclesiastes 3:6 (Book of the Ecclesiastes chapter 3, line 6).

1

Master of the World and the Law of the Sea

I. The *Dominus*, Carl Schmitt and Beyond …

A. Apocalyptic Politics and the Parable of the *Dominus*

In his theory on the *nomos* of the earth, Carl Schmitt declared that our times will witness the last round of the terrible struggle for a law of the planet, and the winner will become the master of the world.[1]

The winner will take possession of the whole globe—land, air and sea—dividing and assigning it according to his will and pleasure. But the sea, vast and void, will not last in the new order. Schmitt himself links his theory to the theology of the *Revelation* (21:1):

> Then I saw a new heaven and a new earth, for the first heaven and the first earth had passed away, and there was no longer any sea.

According to this vision, then, as long as the Leviathan is the Sire of the Sea, the definitive unit of the globe under its Lord will be eventually reached through its taming. And since the domain of Satan—Schmitt adds—is a unitary empire, as Jesus acknowledged speaking of the 'Lord of Flies', the new master will take in hands a globe already assembled by the Enemy.

In this way, Schmitt's embarrassing theory of law is strictly connected to his theory of *political theology*, which in turn is directly linked to his conception of sovereignty and exception. If the 'sovereign' is he who decides on the state of exception, the latter represents in political theory the same thing as the miracle does in theology. At this point, the concept of the 'political' as a decision between friend and foe also assumes a theological and ontological trait, and we face a number of nested conceptions evoking the dark side of political philosophy.

But, we must question, are these ideas right or wrong? Where did they come from? What, indeed, were their origins? What is their genealogy? And where do they lead us to? What is, for instance, the sense in the insistence on the concepts of

[1] C Schmitt, *The Nomos of the Earth in the International Law of the Jus Publicum Europaeum* (GL Ulmen trans, New York, Telos Press Publishing, 2006) 354.

'Empire' and the 'state of exception' rebooted by some of Schmitt's contemporary epigones like Hardt and Negri,[2] or Agamben?[3] And if this narrative is a form of knowledge about political and juridical forms, what kind of knowledge is it?

It is in the text of Justinian's *Digest* (14.2.9)—never cited by Schmitt—that we find the 'revelation' of the existence of a *Dominus Mundi*. The original of this passage is in Greek, here followed by its traditional Latin version:

ἐγὼ μὲν τοῦ κόσμου κύριος, ὁ δὲ νόμος τῆς θαλάσσης[4]

Ego quidem mundi dominus, lex autem maris.

This can be translated into English in two rather different ways, as '*I am the lord of the world,* and *the law of the sea*', or alternatively as '*I am the owner of the earth (lands),* but *the sea is governed by the law*'. This striking difference is due to the ambiguity of the original wording, the difference between the Greek term '*kurios*' and its Latin translation '*dominus*', and by the more than astonishing variance between the Greek '*kosmos*' and the Latin '*mundus*'.

What is at stake here is, of course, the ideal of a single, and legitimate, world rule. The everlasting nature of this ideal was well witnessed by Kissinger when he recently stated that our age is insistently—at times almost desperately—in pursuit of a concept of 'world order', and, as in the apocalyptic scenario envisaged by Schmitt, 'chaos threatens side by side with unprecedented interdependence'.[5]

This grandiose prose marks an enduring paradigm of Western political thought, constituting a form of philosophical occultism that was cultivated by such different and influential authors as Schmitt, Kantorowicz[6] and Bloch,[7] and which is still haunting our political models. Their works point unequivocally to the mystical nature of sovereignty, the magic of monarchs, and the 'miracle' of exception. The comprehensive paradigm centred on this mystical idea is often referred to as 'Political Theology'—a rather vague, and somewhat elusive and multifarious label constantly being reshaped,[8] and quite certainly at the root of the 'Italian Theory'[9] based on the emergence of terms as 'bare life'[10] or 'uses of bodies',[11] and

[2] M Hardt and A Negri, *Empire* (Cambridge, Harvard University Press, 2001).

[3] G Agamben, *State of Exception* (K Attel trans, Chicago, The University of Chicago Press, 2010).

[4] A classical transliteration of Greek could be the following: 'Egò mèn toù kòsmou kùrios, ho dè nòmos tès thalàsses'.

[5] H Kissinger, *World Order* (New York, Penguin Books, 2014) 2.

[6] E Kantorowicz, *The King's Two Bodies: A Study in Mediaeval Political Theology* (Princeton, Princeton University Press, 1998); E Kantorowicz, *Frederick the Second: 1194–1250* (EO Lorimer trans, New York, Frederick Ungar Publishing Co, 1957).

[7] M Bloch, *Les Rois thaumaturges. Études sur le caractère surnaturel attribué à la puissance royale, particulièrement en France et en Angleterre* (Paris, A Colin, 1961).

[8] PW Kahn, *Political Theology: Four New Chapters on the Concept of Sovereignty* (New York, Columbia University Press, 2013).

[9] R Esposito, *Living Thought: the Origins and Actuality of Italian Philosophy* (Z Hanafi trans, Stanford, Stanford University Press, 2012).

[10] G Agamben, *Homo Sacer: Sovereign Power and Bare Life* (D Heller-Roazen trans, Stanford, Stanford University Press, 2004) 55.

[11] R Esposito, *Persons and Things: from the Body's Point of View* (Z Hanafi trans, Cambridge, Polity Press, 2015).

other intriguing investigations on the emblematic nature of the *flesh* of political entities;[12] a theory rendering the political discourse decisively theological in its own linguistic premises and practices. It is hard not to see at work in this paradigm a 'fascination for the extraordinary'[13] leading to prophetic-like questions such as '[a]re we facing a period in which forces beyond the restraints of any order determine the future?'.[14]

This attitude has been perfectly captured by critical author Koskenniemi in describing our time as one in which even international lawyers are 'losing faith in the secular', and in which the ideal of the world order can always be described in the 'messianic' language of present imperfection merely highlighting the brightness of law's promise: an international law as a self-correcting, secular project whose meaning would *nonetheless* be given by a horizon of transcendence.[15]

Our standpoint, here, lies on the need to investigate the origins of this paradigm, starting from its beginnings in the imperial Roman revelation of the presence of a universal 'Master of the World' that strongly influenced the *exotic* and *heterodox* evolution of political modernity. Our main theory is that, to a large extent, the intellectual and political history of the West has been seasoned with magic and occultism, which contributed to defining and developing the concept of sovereignty as we know it today. From the narratives of ancient Roman law to the specific emblems of the English Renaissance, and the famous frontispiece of Hobbes's *Leviathan*, our investigation will unveil the occult prerogatives of the 'political'. As far as the origins of theological and political modes of thought are concerned, it is precisely in the historical and ideological vicissitudes of the passage of the *Digest* on the *Dominus Mundi* that we may encounter the two most impressive icons of our political conceptions: on one side the continental land-based emperor, and on the other side the English sea monster, the Leviathan. On the one hand we face a *Dominus* that could also be an *Antichrist*[16]—a sovereign who could be at the same time within and without the law—and on the other hand we meet the Old Serpent, that could become a Saviour.

The double nature of the *Dominus Mundi* produced many romanticisations of the global power. The awing duplicity and ambiguity of the English Leviathan has never ceased to be at the heart of its spell, as the most influential and powerful image of the political. Our task will be to investigate these exotic ambiguities of the modern political discourse, starting from the very possibility of a legitimate world order, to eventually dismantle the Schmittian paradigm at its root.

The aim of this book is, then, to investigate the parable of the *Dominus Mundi*, from its beginning to its contemporary remnants. Now, the basic point in building

[12] EL Santner, *The Royal Remains: the People's Two Bodies and the Endgames of Sovereignty* (Chicago, The University of Chicago Press, 2012).

[13] G Frankenberg, *Political Technology and the Erosion of the Rule of Law: Normalizing the State of Exception* (H Bauer and G Frankenberg trans, Cheltenham, Edward Elgar, 2015) 114.

[14] Kissinger, *World Order* 2.

[15] M Koskenniemi, 'International Law as Political Theology: How to Read Nomos der Erde?' (2004) 11 *Constellations. An International Journal of Critical and Democratic Theory* 492–511.

[16] Kantorowicz, *Frederick the Second* 385.

a model of world order and universal rule is to investigate the hegemonic devices by which the world is divided into spaces and jurisdictions.[17] As it has brilliantly shown, the neoliberal paradigm is not purely an economic order or based on rational choice theory, but has many geopolitical aspects governing spaces through exception and exclusion.[18] This contributes to defining a new, mutable experience of law that challenges traditional territorial boundaries and self-defined political entities in global times. As a consequence, a concept of a world order, making sense of global and anti-global movements, must cope with three basic elements: space, transcendence, and exception.

Accordingly, the plan of the book can be summarised as follows.

In the *Digest* we find stated that the Roman Emperor is the Master of the World and the Law of the Sea. This passage, though contested and in need of philological investigations, would imply that there is a single legitimate universal authority. Our first aim, then, would be that of investigating this proclamation, its problematic origins, its contested formulation, and the different and incompatible meanings that it acquired through the ages.

A pure model of the *Dominus Mundi* would, in theory, allow no fracture, resulting in a strong and compact spatial construct where there is no possible distinction between an inside and an outside, and the world is conceived of as a unique spatial entity whose government is concentrated in a single *locus* of authority. This model would be the icon of the frightening and sublime ideal of a united government extended to the whole *cosmos*. Undoubtedly the European world order became eventually fractured after the outburst of the Thirty Years' War (1618) and its end at the Peace of Westphalia (1648), a compromise inaugurating varieties of 'world order conceptions'.[19] Modern sovereignty became grounded upon a widespread acknowledgement of the impossibility of world dominance by a single entity[20] and imagined the kings as Leviathans who did not recognise any legitimate superior authority. This *normative inversion* founded the legal theory upon which the sovereign territorial state of early modern times later developed. The main feature of Westphalia, according to many, including Kissinger,[21] was the acceptance of 'political diversity' and the formal coexistence and equality of different sovereign powers. In this sense, with the rise of the new Westphalian order, the parable of the *Dominus Mundi* came to an end. But what is the most striking for us is the contemporary transformation of the Leviathan from a symbol of the Old Serpent

[17] T Zarmanian, 'Ordnung und Ortung/Order and Localisation' in S Legg (ed), *Spatiality, Sovereignty and Carl Schmitt. Geographies of the Nomos* (London, Routledge, 2011) 294.

[18] A Ong, *Neoliberalism as Exception: Mutations in Citizenship and Sovereignty* (Durham, Duke University Press, 2006).

[19] Kissinger, *World Order* 23.

[20] See WG Grewe, *The Epochs of International Law* (M Byers trans, Berlin, Walter de Gruyter, 2000) 47; W Ullmann, 'The Development of the Medieval Idea of Sovereignty' (1949) 64 *English Historical Review* 1.

[21] Kissinger, *World Order* 23.

into the emblem of the modern political saviour. As the Roman emperor, after the conversion to Christianity, changed from a figure of Satan into that of a representative of God, assuming a proper theological dimension, so conversely the modern sovereign assumed the form of a demonic monster incarnating the ideal of political salvation. From this standpoint Westphalia was a meeting of Leviathans, of heterodox monsters. These new creatures, so different from ancient empires, free cities, bishoprics, princedoms, and so on, started to share the common traits of all the Westphalian creatures: they came to possess a flag, an anthem, an army, a treasury, a police force, and a well-defined territory. They accepted the existence of other similar monsters on the earth, having the same right to legitimate jurisdiction and power, no matter how different they were, protestant, catholic, socialist, liberal or despotic. This was a peculiar and exotic European adventure, which universalised itself through the—now trembling—categories of international law and international politics. From this perspective, we can see this parable of the *Dominus Mundi* in its entirety, because we are experiencing the dissolution of its dissolution, in other words, the end of the Westphalian world order.

First of all, the world is becoming populated with non-Westphalian creatures: the European bloc is not purely Westphalian, the World Trade Organization and the World Bank are not at all Westphalian, and certainly Isis and other terror networks are completely different from the Westphalian state, whatever name they may claim for themselves.

Secondly and most importantly, the acceptance of political diversity is fading away. Both the theory of universal human rights and conceptions of a universal caliphate can no longer accept the idea of the legitimacy of political diversity, and so they are producing a global clash of ideas and a disruption of the formal legal categories of international law, causing a strong reaction and resistance. Humanitarian intervention is certainly the most striking example of a departure from the purely Westphalian international law, though it operates within its framework.[22]

Our theory is, then, that the current context of globalisation represents the reappearance of the ghost of the *Dominus Mundi*, which lies dormant as a repressed political figure, a *refoulé*. The spectral reappearance brings with it the sublime and, at the same time, rotten nature of the Master of the World. From this standpoint, the clash that we are currently experiencing between populism and globalism could ultimately be seen as two sides of the same spectral form, since the *Dominus* was both a national sovereign and a global Lord. But what is more important is that the sublime-kitsch-rotten nature of the political has been left to wander about and must be 'recaptured' in its proper significance, superseding the neoliberal dream of a totally depoliticised world.

[22] N Rengger, 'On Theology and International Relations: World Politics Beyond the Empty Sky' (2013) 27 *International Relations* 141–57; see also M Barnett, *Empire of Humanity: A History of Humanitarianism* (Ithaca, Cornell University Press, 2011).

Given this background, we shall articulate our aim in more detail in the next section. First, we shall give the reader an account of Schmitt's main theories, and their influential impact. Next, considering the demonological turn which brought the Leviathan into the place of the *Dominus*, we shall propose a model to cope with the global discourse on the origins of the sovereign with the precise aim of shedding new light into the 'intangible side of power'[23] which still inhabits our present political imagination in all its ineffability.

B. Messianism and the Theological 'Ghost' of Decision

Since one of our aims is to bypass the uncomfortable presence of Schmitt's thought, and undermine his, and his epigones' paradigm, we summarise here for the reader the major tenets of his conceptions, maintained by the structural connection that he posed between legitimacy, sovereignty and the exception, and that may be found closely compacted, on a global scale, in the grandiose figure of the *Dominus Mundi*.

One of Schmitt's most famous definitions is that of the 'concept of the political' as a choice, a decision between friend and foe. His formulation is probably derived from Álamos De Barrientos (1555–1640)[24] and is mainly a reflection on the Westphalian world and its existential characters. We mean here the birth of sovereign political units that could freely decide between war and peace against other parallel, identical, pure political units.[25] This paradigm is, in a way, 'existential' because Westphalia represented a real situation concerning political existence: the impossibility of terminating the lengthy religious conflict, and the reality of the power equilibrium between fighting units, realised in a legal compromise which gave birth to what we today call international law and international relations. Westphalia represented the outcome of a stalemate, and it is from the compromise reached to cope with this stalemate that the apparatus of modern juridico-political concepts was produced, *including* the concept of the political.

As Koskenniemi notes,

> Schmitt modified his discussion about the limits of the 'political' between the first (1927) and the second (1932) editions of *Der Begriff des Politischen*. In the first edition, the 'political' had existed alongside such other realms as economy, morality, law, culture, etc. in an apparently equal position as one of the aspects of a community's life, distinct from

[23] HJ Morgenthau, *Politics among Nations: the Struggle for Power and Peace* (New York, AA Knopf, 1948) 121.

[24] G Maschke, '"Amigo y enemigo": Kautilya y Álamos de Barrientos, anticipadores del criterio schmittiano' (2017) 1 *Carl-Schmitt-Studien* 111–20. Baltasar Álamos de Barrientos was a Spanish scholar and an important jurist of Salamanca who wrote *Tácito Español illustrado con aforismos* and probably also *Discurso del gobierno*.

[25] M Fichera, 'Carl Schmitt and the New World Order: A View from Europe' in M Arvidsson, L Brännström and P Minkkien (eds), *The Contemporary Relevance of Carl Schmitt Law, Politics, Theology* (London, Routledge, 2015) 168.

> its other aspects. In the second (and third) editions, the political stood out, however, from such delimitations so as to potentially encompass all of them. Now politics had no intrinsic limit: every aspect of life could manifest the friend-enemy opposition and thus transform itself into political struggle. Politics has no substance, it describes the 'intensity of association or dissociation of human beings'.[26]

A second main theory developed by Schmitt is that of 'political theology'. It assumes that all the concepts of the general theory of the state have previously been theological concepts. In this way, he implied that the theological dimension decayed into the realm of pure politics, even if it is still operating and directing our thoughts implicitly—almost in a subliminal way. State and politics have then replaced God but not eliminated theology: we still live politically in a hidden theological setting.[27] Secularisation was, for Schmitt, concretely, the fading power of the pope to ex-communicate a king and transform him into a tyrant. Such papal jurisdiction transformed into the purely political practice of state recognition in international affairs.[28]

The third main focus of Schmitt is on the 'state of exception'. This focus derives from his studies on Roman law and the difference between a commissarial and a constituent dictatorship. The point is that Roman law included the possibility of a suspension of the law for the *salus rei publicae*, the salvation of the state. In this respect, also extremely relevant in analysing Schmitt are the influences that these Roman models exercised on the French revolutionaries, and on Robespierre and Napoleon in particular, in creating the sequence: *état de siège—état de siège fictif—état de siège politique*,[29] that is to say, the passage from the actual situation of being assaulted by an enemy to the pure political decision of its occurrence. It is one thing to *declare* the state of exception in front of a real threat to the State; it is another to have the power to declare its occurrence independently from any real existential threat, as the pure power of decision about the political opportunity of using emergency powers for governmental purposes, which constitutes the basic ground for Agamben's analysis of the state of exception.

The fourth main enduring point is Schmitt's theory of the world order. He offered in his *Nomos der Erde*[30] a picture of the ending of the juridico-political order that regulated the world for the last 300 years. Of course, in our view this world law should be appraised as the bequest of the death of the *Dominus*. The term *Nomos* is adopted by Schmitt to signify not a simple formal frame of rules,

[26] M Koskenniemi, *The Gentle Civilizer of Nations: the Rise and Fall of International Law 1870–1960* (Cambridge, Cambridge University Press, 2004) 436.

[27] Santner, *The Royal Remains* 8.

[28] Fichera, 'Carl Schmitt and the New World Order: A View from Europe' 17; C Schmitt, *Dictatorship. From the Origin of the Modern Concept of Sovereignty to Proletarian Class Struggle* (M Hoelzl and G Ward trans, Cambridge, Polity Press, 2014) 35.

[29] F Saint-Bonnet, *L'état d'exception* (Paris, Presses Universitaires de France, 2001) 286.

[30] Schmitt, *The Nomos of the Earth*, 140. See also Koskenniemi, 'International Law as Political Theology: How to Read Nomos der Erde?' 493.

but a substantive or concrete spatial order derived from an original act of land-taking. Schmitt argued that this concrete order collapsed between 1890 and 1918 in the face of a sea-based, economically driven, Anglo-American universalism that was slowly doing away with earlier spatial distinctions and the centrality of sovereignty.[31] For Schmitt, European lawyers had completely lost any consciousness about the concrete spatial order, starting to speak in increasingly abstract and universal terms to the point that international law had been reduced to an empty formalism of rules.[32] Schmitt envisaged three alternatives for the coming global order. One was a universal empire under one great power—likely to be the United States. A second alternative was for the United States to take over England's place in the old territorial equilibrium as the 'balancer', the external guarantor of Europe's internal peace, accompanied by unquestioned primacy in the Western hemisphere, something as a revival of Mackinder's geopolitics of balance between sea-powers and land-powers.[33] The third alternative—clearly preferred by Schmitt and perhaps seen by him as the one most likely to emerge—was a structure of territorial division between a limited number of large blocs (*Großräumen*) that mutually recognised each other and excluded external intervention. Clearly a reinvention of a Westphalian compromise, no more between states but between great spaces. And clearly again, a solution strikingly parallel to that recently purported by Kissinger.[34]

What unifies each of these theories?

The *nexus* is offered through a major *coup de génie* by Schmitt in his expression that 'the state of exception is to Jurisprudence what miracles are to theology'.[35] In this way, the political actions of Augustus or Robespierre are one with the sublime appearance of a super-human dimension in political affairs. If the parallel is to be taken seriously, they were *not* looking for supernatural justifications: they *represent* the intrusion of transcendence in world affairs. If the state of exception is a miracle, then the sovereign is a priest-king and the political is theological in itself. For us, the major point here is the revelation of a sublime side of politics, in the sense of a transcendent value of the political, that *in Schmitt* is captured *as* political theology. The bulk of Schmitt's theories consists of the creation of a specific paradigm which captures the ineffable, intangible side of law and politics within the theological framework as its background.

It is on these bases that we can try to grasp the intellectual performance of Agamben.

He moves from Foucauldian premises concerning bio-power and bio-politics to offer a theory of bare life (*homo sacer*) as produced in the paradigm of the

[31] Koskenniemi, *The Gentle Civilizer of Nations* 416.

[32] C Schmitt, *Political Theology: Four Chapters on the Concept of Sovereignty* (G Schwab trans, Chicago, The University of Chicago Press, 2010) 36.

[33] H Mackinder, 'The Geographical Pivot of History' (1904) 23 *The Geographical Journal* 421.

[34] Kissinger, *World Order* 371.

[35] Schmitt, *Political Theology: Four Chapters on the Concept of Sovereignty* 36.

concentration camp, ie, the inclusion of life into the state of exception, and of the state of exception within the domain of the legal. In this respect, Agamben is uniting Foucault and Schmitt in a new scheme. His main critique is that, under the surface, liberal democracies are reproducing the paradigm of the camp and that this paradigm is inscribed from its beginning in the very structure of the law. In his theory, Western law, prevailing in modern liberal democracies, is centred upon the *void* space of the state of exception, and it is destined to become a killing machine, the opposite of a liberal democratic order. At the heart of the law lies a lawless space which tends to reproduce the paradigm of the camp:[36] a trap where 'bare life'—a life divested of legal form—is subjugated to the direct discipline of pure domination. These lawless spaces of dominion are still *within* the legal framework, but are now—in his terms—legitimised places of *extra*-legal disciplinary powers.

Moreover, for Agamben, this is true not only where the theological apparatus is more evident, as in the law and the state, but also in the domain of economics as the production of a particular form of life, one that increasingly deprives life of its dress towards a final bareness. In his recent publications, Agamben showed a method for genealogical inquiry as applied to the notions of 'office' and '*oikonomia*' which can hardly be ignored.[37] He reconstructs the deep layers of our modern words to their past archeology in order to activate a revolutionary messianism from below. If law is destined to be a killing machine, then only a messianic movement out of the law can save us.

In order to avoid the destiny inscribed in Western law and economics, he proposes the development of forms-of-life that can eventually disrupt such a frame and provoke an exit from the legal cage in which we are captured. A form of life, like, for instance, that of the medieval monks,[38] not regulated by the law but constituted as an *habitus*, a way of life so internalised that it does not need rules or enforcement and escapes the legal framework dominating our conceptions of the societal order. From our standpoint, Agamben's claims seem to reactivate St Paul's opposition to the Law (Romans 1:1–4). If without the law there could be no sin, then also without law there can be no state of exception. In other words, it is the law, by its device of inclusive exclusion that is producing the possibility of the state of exception. As a consequence, if we abolish the law we free ourselves from sin and if we dismantle the law we can overcome the exception. Only a move away from the law can assure salvation. The mission of the Messiah is, then, to fulfil the law in the sense of bringing the law to its end. In our secularised world this task can be performed by lay subjects transforming their forms-of-life to remain

[36] Agamben, *Homo Sacer: Sovereign Power and Bare Life* 166.

[37] G Agamben, *Opus Dei: an Archaeology of Duty* (A Kotsko trans, Stanford, Stanford University Press, 2013); G Agamben, *The Kingdom and the Glory: For a Theological Genealogy of Economy and Government* (L Chiesa trans, Stanford, Stanford University Press, 2011).

[38] G Agamben, *The Highest Poverty: Monastic Rules and Form-of-Life* (A Kotsko trans, Stanford, Stanford University Press, 2013).

outside the reach of the law. This can be considered, indeed, as a messianic move to bypass the law *through* theology; but a theology from below against the theology from above which is sustaining it. In this way, Foucault's 'archeology' can happily marry Schmittian analysis in a revolutionary as well as a messianic stance.

C. Legitimacy, Hegemony and Transcendence

A vision of the *Dominus Mundi*, a unitary and legitimate world government, faces, as we said, three main questions concerning space, transcendence, and exception. Since these are terms strongly present both in Schmitt and his epigones, it is necessary to provide here an introductory clarification about these general concepts and the way in which they will be employed in the course of the next chapters.

For space and location we mean both the creation of an inside/outside dimension as well as a placement within the *locus* of authority and power. Such an inquiry into the *locus* of difference and power and its consequences may be needed to provide a different vision of the 'political', as well as a new arrangement of law and its categories.

Typically in the vision that can be associated with a *Dominus Mundi* there is no longer any outside, as the monarch is located within his city, or palace, as it operates directly or indirectly all over the world. The lack of an outside renders his instantiation even more inaccessible as it pervades all the territory under its rule.

By transcendence we mean that which goes beyond words, that which defies our lexicon, but to which reference is made to supply justification for legal or political action. There is no need here to presume that the term is religious; it can be mundane, as a kind of a *surplus* of immanence.[39] It vaguely represents what we feel when we say that 'there is more to it than that' in a legal text or in a political fact.[40] It is something like the hidden, never fully verbalised background notions, such as legitimacy or hegemony. It does not matter, of course, whether we believe in the existence of a transcendent plan in itself or not. It only matters whether it has been influential in political history, and as such remains in our time, even, and especially, in secularised discourse. It is not something metaphysical or superhuman. It is basically that which exceeds our *linguistic* capacities to cope with law and legitimacy.[41] It is the unspeakable character of the law, its *uncanny* presence.[42]

We cannot easily dismiss this presence in law and politics as long as we consider to what extent we are still coping with invisible but strongly operating forces. The

[39] Santner, *The Royal Remains* 27.

[40] Du Kennedy, 'Antonio Gramsci and the Legal System' (1982) 6 *ALSA Forum* 32.

[41] G Watt, 'Hard Cases, Hard Times, and the Humanity of Law' in J Bate (ed), *The Public Value of The Humanities* (London, Bloomsbury Academic, 2011) 197.

[42] See also RK Sherwin, 'Sublime Jurisprudence: On the Ethical Education of the Legal Imagination in Our Time' (2008) 83 *Chicago-Kent Law Review* 1157.

law itself is something invisible, which can be rendered visible only by its traces: fences, signatures, seals, courtrooms, etc, but which always supersedes its traces. Transcendence, in this context, is not identified with or equated to a belief in a superhuman entity or a god. Rather, it refers to the fact that human institutions have dimensions which cannot be completely captured in words, and which are actually giving a meaning to words and objects. After all, a corporation is also a metaphysical entity in this sense, without which a huge number of actions, meetings, and rooms would have no meaning at all. If the law did not have a transcendence of its own, a judge's gavel would merely be a little wooden hammer. The problem is where this uncanny transcendence can be located. In our theory, transcendence is part of the over-meaning of objects and institutions. It is the invisible part, connecting a given set of actual facts and objects and forming an institution. It would be simply absurd to support the idea that a corporation does not exist only because our social ontologies are too poor to give a good theoretical account of the fact that corporations really possess assets and operate in this world.[43] If we use the trivial formulation of John Searle for social ontology saying that *x* values as *y* in *S*, and that something assumes the quality or the substance of *y* in the cultural social system *S*,[44] we can say that transcendence corresponds to the 'in' of his formula. After all, there is nothing so transcendent in transcendence. Rather, it is the never completely transparent side of an unlimited *semiosis* in the interaction of meanings in social communication. Theology is thus only one of the many possible places to locate the uncanny side of human institutions: that which is always beyond words, the 'more to it than that' which operates in political, as well as in economic or legal, institutions.

As used in this book, exception represents the *locus* of manifestation of this surplus of immanence as an exercise of 'bare power', as the expression of secret, unknown or undefined, unpredictable or unspeakable powers. In a state of emergency, the legal and moral ontology of the world collapses into exceptions, displaying the inner transcendence of the political as that which can never be completely ontologised, that is, something not made of fixed stuff. Moreover, the real matter is never exception per se, but the way it is located in the discourse and in a given political order.

This said, such an excessive nature of the law and the political leaves us with the problem of '*surplus of immanence*' in the domain of legitimacy that *can* be developed under the rubric of political theology or in other forms. One form of this *surplus of immanence*, as far as international relations is concerned, may be traced back to Morgenthau's insistence on the 'intangible side of power politics' and his opposition to the pure scientific treatment of international affairs. Another

[43] G Watt, *Trust and Equity* (Oxford, Oxford University Press, 2016) 55: 'in the world of law there is no person more real than the corporation, for the corporate person is wholly law—it lives and breathes legality'.

[44] JR Searle, *Making the Social World: The Structure of Human Civilization* (Oxford, Oxford University Press, 2010) 42.

instance—as strange as it may appear at first glance—can be found in the field of economics in Hayek's pro-market approach, in his theory of the ineffability of the overall global order of society, as something which is always superseding our capacities of verbalisation.[45]

This approach reflects the limits of our language to cope with the law and its notions. If our language is limited in describing legal and political relations, it follows that there is an *excess* that our words cannot capture without a *residue*,[46] and that the political world remains partially unfathomable. Such a residue is that which is always beyond words: fear and awe as much as excitement and attraction. For these reasons alone this 'too-muchness' of the political can be defined as *sublime*. This is not a neutral label. Rather, it consciously represents the establishment of a parallel with the language of witchcraft, spell and magic. In this sense, the world has not been disenchanted, nor has theology survived in political and legal concepts. Rather, the old political theology has been reversed into the heterodox political form of modernity.

Through the vocabulary used by Agamben consisting of *signatures*, *captures*, *residues*, *thresholds*[47] and of the dialectic of visible/invisible that characterises the ambiguity pervading human institutions, we want, then, to highlight their 'too-muchness'; in other words, to show that there is always more-than-that in law and politics, and that the semantics of political action *transcend* our capacity to capture it entirely.

The *Dominus Mundi* is the perfect paradigm of what could be defined as the inner ambiguity of human institutions, due to the encounter of classical political theory with the Christian revelation. The *Dominus Mundi* displays in its multifarious characterisations the unfathomable threshold of what is godly and what is demonic in the world order. The entire construction of the *Dominus Mundi*, with its claim to govern the whole world under the strict categories of law, hides a concrete ideological assumption that emerges from every attempt to actualise it. Indeed, the very idea of a legitimate world ruler can be seen, after all, as the hegemonic complex *par excellence*.

If Duncan Kennedy's remarks on Gramsci's theory of hegemony point in the right direction, then a model of understanding legitimacy in terms of the political sublime is grounded. As a consequence, the aesthetics of seduction may lie at the root of both hegemony and of political theology, as the two extreme opposite standpoints in the analysis of secularisation, power, and politics.

Our model points toward a reappraisal of an *imagery of the ineffable* which transcends time and geographical location and that can be captured only through a

[45] FA Hayek, *Law, Legislation and Liberty: A New Statement of the Liberal Principles of Justice and Political Economy*, vol 1 (Chicago, The University of Chicago Press, 1976) 10, 76.

[46] We use 'residue' as meaning that which is left over when we try to define something. In other words, that which supersedes our capacity to represent through language. See G Agamben, *The Time that Remains: A Commentary on the Letter to the Romans* (P Dailey trans, Stanford, Stanford University Press, 2005) 132.

[47] G Agamben, *The Signature of all Things: on Method* (L D'Isanto and K Attell trans, New York, Zone Books, 2010).

reconsideration of the sublime: an appreciation of that which is always beyond words, beyond the human capacity of expression; a paradigm that can be thought of as an ongoing element in Western culture, notwithstanding any rationalist effort to exorcise it. In a way, the 'sublime dimension' or, as we prefer to call it, the 'too-muchness' *device* operates in politics and the law as a remainder.

We could label this functioning as the logic of the ineffable, assumed at an explicit level by romantic aesthetics, but also operating implicitly at the level of philosophical investigations. In his approach to Gramsci's theory of legitimacy, Duncan Kennedy uses the concept of 'mystery' in order to describe its operation:

> And it is how it all works that is the great mystery. It's all very well to say 'It is not just the national guard that prevents a revolution … there is more to it than that'… But if you want to figure out what the more to it than that is … there is extraordinarily little sustained, serious discussion of what might be meant by an idea like ideological hegemony.[48]

The parallel between the concept of 'too-muchness' and Kennedy's grasping of the great mystery of hegemony can be considered in terms of the 'more to it than that'. The fact that hegemony remains a mystery and that there is little sustained or serious discussion on what might be meant by it appears to be consistent with the assumption of a *hidden* device at work in the notion of legitimacy.

D. Two Models of Law, Global Sovereignty and Exception

In this vein, if we analyse the concept of universal legitimacy, two rather different models are made apparent.

The first is a 'compact' model of the *Dominus Mundi*, where the whole globe is under a unitary and uniform legitimate political authority. This world is without an inside or an outside because its sovereignty is all-encompassing. Some portion of the globe can be out of the actual control of the imperial sovereign, but this does not entail that he does not have a legitimate title to it. The limits of his or her authority are *factual*, not *legal*.

A totally opposite model may be represented by the 'fracture' of the space into different political sovereign units without any legally possible lordship over the entire globe. Such a world would be based on a variety of *disjunctures* between land and sea and between spaces, dominated by the binary of inside and outside. It would be a world of political diversity[49] not only from a purely factual point of view, but also from a *legal* one. It would be absolutely legitimate for every sovereign entity to try to be socialist, tsarist, liberal or capitalist, and any interference of an entity in the internal affairs of another sovereign would be *illegal*.

This partition of the world implies a mutual recognition of equality among sovereign units in a way in which substance diverges from form. One unit can be

[48] Du Kennedy, 'Antonio Gramsci and the Legal System' 33.
[49] Kissinger, *World Order* 365.

small or large, capitalist or radical, but none of them can claim any superiority to the other: they would be formally connected and formally equal also in time of war. War would be a form of legal relationship and would be legitimate. As long as this model remains 'pure', there could be no such a thing as an international crime, for there could be no judge superior to the alleged criminals. The world would not be a unitary 'thing' but a complex of separate 'things' connected through form.

It is rather evident that the Roman Empire, if our reading of it is correct, would represent the first model, and that international law as developed by the European powers represents the second model. It becomes also evident that the European system did not derive from the Roman model. Rather, it evolved as a major departure from it, a real *break* or rupture in political history. The Roman model is substantive and standardised, in the sense that there is one command and only one political uniform legitimation. The European one is formal and plural, as every political entity has the *right* to be different as it has the *right* to fight for existence and affirmation.[50]

What we are experimenting with now, from the end of the Second World War onward, is a *mixture* of these two pure models. We still have differentiated political entities affirming sovereignty, and at the same time we develop the paradigm of a world substantive legitimacy based on liberal, or neoliberal, values and human rights. War is no longer a right, and there are rogue states. There is no longer a unique Master, but political diversity seems destined to disappear. A ghost of the *Dominus Mundi* is hanging over the complex spatial devices adopted to cope with a world having a mixed ontology: it is simultaneously one and many 'things' together. This evolution implies a strong clash which is no longer 'external' but 'internal' to the whole world. States could try to unite into *blocs* of continental dimensions to reach a state of equilibrium among great spaces. But this equilibrium would always be unstable as long as the goal of a global rule of law, or a global constitutionalism, and global values remain a world shared ideal. Though we are still experimenting with *blocs* of independent spaces, no space can really be independent if global jurisdictions or global instruments of management and policy are put into practice and their implementation is deemed legitimate and proper. In other words, we have entered a phase of revolutionary indeterminacy of *fact* and *law* on a world scale.

This is why *exception* has attracted so much interest in the last decade. As long as exception emerges in a *political liminality*, it becomes the main feature of a world still split into different spheres of sovereign control and at the same time made to provide a world governance and a world rule of law. Our beliefs—and our good intentions—can make us believe in the possible coexistence of the two models in a newer blend that we can invent in a proximate future. Although our hopes can be well founded, we actually live in a liminal space, which is the space created by the clashing nature of the two models. In our reading, then, independent

[50] Kissinger, *World Order* 11.

of particular facts—such as acts of terrorism, the use of torture or humanitarian crises—exception *is* our present form of political life, as long as we are captured in a liminality.

What we maintain is that this ontological exception is different from the previous form of exceptionality. In the pure *Dominus Mundi* model there is indeed no space for exception. If there is just one legitimate Master of the World how can there be exception to his rule? He is himself an exceptional and overwhelming presence. There can be factual crises internal to the *locus* of supreme and global legal authority, but they do not amount to a state of exception because there is no conceptual space for them within the lordship of the Lord. This space can only be created by a fracture of this lordship, as had happened in the West between the authority of the Church and that of the emperor.

Under the second model of political plurality, as we know from history, exception developed from the *état de siège*,[51] the state of peril that originated from a mortal threat to those mortal entities which are the states. They can rise and disappear, and so there can really be the space for a modern state of exception, when the normal rule can be broken by the ruler himself for his own preservation against external or internal enemies.

Ancient exception, so to speak, was embodied within the exceptional and extraordinary nature of the universal Lord. Modern exception derived from the fractures of lordships into different spaces and spheres. It represented a *suspension* of normality, to be confined into a given time span, and to be resolved by *extraordinary* means.

Today, in the 'hyper-modern' age, exception possesses different traits. It is at the same time exceptional and ordinary. With respect to ancient exception, it became disincarnated from the existence of a real Master of the World, and with respect to modern exception, it escaped the inner boundaries of a state of peril of one of the various political entities composing the global community. It is no longer embodied within the *Dominus Mundi*, and it is no longer a purely political matter of survival of the mortal god which was the modern state. Exception is no more a locus within the political sphere, but *the* locus of the political, and the ordinary takes place within the exception.

In a way, that we shall try to understand, the modern political has been the *locus* of the exception, operating within the legal order as a governmental device, whereas hyper-modern exception became the *locus* of the political, which may happen only in the liminality of exception.

Exception is no longer a *miracle*. It is the ontological status within which political action can take its course. This is what we shall call the 'demonological inversion'.

We had it before our eyes from the very birth of modernity, but we can only now completely grasp it as modernity comes to an end. Political theology is no

[51] Saint-Bonnet, *L'état d'exception* 23.

longer attainable. The figure of the sovereign changed into the terrific and inexplicable figure of the Old Serpent. The *Dominus* left the world to Leviathan, and can return only as a ghost, as a haunting political spectre.

II. The *Dominus* and Its Several Meanings

A. A Close Reading of the *Digest*

We start our argument with a close reading of the assertion found in Dig 14.2.9 that the Roman Emperor is the legitimate Master of the World, and its actual relevance for the origins of contemporary theories of the world order.

Empires, of course, existed long before Rome,[52] though the definition of what is an empire is rather controversial,[53] and certainly the Romans borrowed many of their political ideas from Egypt[54] or from the East, including previous conceptions of imperialism and its ideological justifications.[55] Anyway, our main interest here is *not* devoted to the general idea of empire, but to that *particular mention* of imperial domain—in connection with property and legitimate government—which occurred in the *Digest* with far-reaching consequences on Western political history.

The statement 'I am Master of the World' (*Dominus Mundi*) was presumably made by the Roman emperor Antoninus Pius (86–161 CE) in the middle of the second century CE in the context of a case of maritime law. It then became a cornerstone of the political theology of the Byzantine Empire in the East. This legal passage was also used in the West, to develop imperial ideology and jurisprudence of sovereignty during the twelfth and thirteenth centuries,[56] in the context of the struggle for supremacy between the pope, the emperor and the kings, assuming several incompatible political meanings. The main object of these concrete struggles has always revolved around a nest of conflicting sovereign prerogatives, with no precise bounds or defined limits. A second essential point concerned the sea. Does a Master of the World really have a paramount lordship over the entire globe,

[52] SE Alcock, TN D'Altroy, KD Morrison and CM Sinopoli (eds), *Empires. Perspectives from Archaeology and History* (Cambridge, Cambridge University Press 2001).

[53] H Muenckler, *Empires: The Logic of World Domination from Ancient Rome to the United States* (Cambridge, Polity Press, 2007).

[54] J Assmann, *Herrschaft und Heil. Politische Theologie in Altägypten, Israel und Europa* (Frankfurt, Fischer Taschenbuch Verlag, 2002).

[55] See J Richardson, *The Language of Empire. Rome and the Idea of Empire from the Third Century BC to the Second Century AD* (Cambridge, Cambridge University Press, 2008); M Liverani, 'The Ideology of the Assyrian Empire' in MT Larsen (ed), *Power and Propaganda. A Symposium on Ancient Empires* (Copenhagen, Akademisk Vorlag, 1979) 297.

[56] K Pennington, *The Prince and the Law, 1200–1600: Sovereignty and Rights in the Western Legal Tradition* (Berkeley, University of California Press, 1993) 8, 37.

including the sea? Or is the sea incapable of possession, free by its very nature, ontologically different from land?[57]

This passage achieved an overwhelming importance much later than its composition (second century), at the time of Frederick I (1122–1190) and Frederick II (1194–1250) in the attempt to define the imperial prerogatives, and still later at the time of Charles V (1500–1558) and the colonisation of the Americas to provide an ideological basis for European imperialism. It even surfaced recently, for example, in the work of Legendre to mean the new technical world governance by private actors.[58]

Though the story of its varying meanings is multifarious and complicated, we concentrate our attention here on a single point, upon which two main theories compete.

According to the first theory, the assertion of a *dominium mundi* was not to be taken at face value.[59] The Roman emperor could not possess all things on earth, and especially could not possess the sea. Therefore, his claim was limited to an exercise of jurisdiction amounting instead to an acknowledgement that even if he could have had an *eminent domain* on lands, the sea was indeed governed by the law. The emperor could have been the master of lands, but the law was the 'master' of sea. The opposite theory has it that the Roman emperor stated exactly the claim to a universal political lordship over the whole world, as would be consistent with his status as a 'manifest god' on earth. His assertion could have become the basis for similar recurring universal claims throughout the ages, up to the modern ideal of a unique global legitimacy.

Given the narrowed scope of our analysis, we report the passage in question in this paragraph. We shall then discuss the ambiguities that must be confronted to get a historical understanding of it, and we shall try to grasp the bulk of the case decided by the emperor Antoninus Pius—whose rescript has been inserted into the *Digest*—to understand the concrete context in which this assertion of global dominion was framed. Then we shall proceed to consider some extant epigraphs and other sources *confirming* the theory that the passage on the Master of the World must be taken at face value. We shall refine these conclusions with reference to the actual remnants of this conception in the age of global political action.

Given this framework, we start our philological argument by reproducing the Greek text of the *Digest*, which received a Latin translation much later (probably around the twelfth century by Burgundius Pisanus); it has since been deeply revised by German philologists, and Mommsen in particular. We also provide for the reader a provisional English version. Major points will be marked in bold characters. This is only an attempt to render the text of the *Digest*, since every word

[57] J Selden, *Mare Clausum; the Right and Dominion of the Sea* (London, Andrew Kembe and Edward Thomas, 1663) 160.

[58] See J Muldoon, *Empire and Order. The Concept of Empire 800–1800* (London, Palgrave Macmillan, 1999) 87–100; and P Legendre, *Dominium mundi: L'empire du management* (Paris, Éd Mille et une nuits, 2007).

[59] See Pennington, *The Prince and the Law* 183.

can be contested, and we need additions to make clear the very synthetic nature of the Latin. It cannot help but be tentative because of the inner ambiguities of both Latin and Greek terms.

Dig 14.2.9

A) Greek version:

Ἀξίωσις Εὐδαίμονος Νικομηδέως πρὸς Ἀντωνῖνον βασιλέα· Κύριε βασιλεῦ Ἀντωνῖνε, ναυφράγιον ποιήσαντες ἐν τῇ Ἰταλίᾳ [Ἰκαρίᾳ—Gothofredus], διηρπάγημεν ὑπὸ τῶν δημοσίων [δημοσιωνῶν?—Salmasius] τῶν τὰς Κυκλάδας νήσους οἰκούντων. Ἀντωνῖνος εἶπεν Εὐ- δαίμονι· **ἐγὼ μὲν τοῦ κόσμου κύριος, ὁ δὲ νόμος τῆς θαλάσσης**, τῷ νόμῳ τῶν Ῥοδίων κρινέσθω τῷ ναυτικῷ, ἐν οἷς μήτις τῶν ἡμετέρων αὐτῷ νόμος ἐναντιοῦται. τοῦτο δὲ αὐτὸ καὶ ὁ θειότατος Αὔγουστος ἔκρινεν.

B) Traditional Latin version:

Deprecatio Eudaemonis Nicomediensis ad Antoninum Imperatorem: Domine Imperator Antonine, naufragium in Italiae facientes, direpti sumus a publicanis Cyclades Insulas habitantibus. Respondit Antoninus Eudaemoni. **Ego quidem Mundi Dominus, lex autem maris**, lege id Rhodia, quae de rebus nauticis praescripta est, judicetur, quatenus nulla nostrarum legum adversatur. Hoc idem Divus quoque Augustus judicavit.

C) Latin version revised by Mommsen:[60]

Petitio Eudaemonis Nicomedensis ad imperatorem Antoninum. Domine imperator Antonine, cum naufragium fecissemus in Italia [immo in Icaria], direpti sumus a publicis [immo a publicanis], qui in Cycladibus insulis habitant. Antoninus dicit Eudaemoni. **Ego orbis terrarum Dominus sum, lex autem maris**, lege Rhodia de re nautica res iudicetur, quatenus nulla lex ex nostris ei contraria est. Idem etiam divus Augustus iudicavit.

D) Tentative English translation, with alternatives given in brackets:

Application made by Eudaemonis to the Emperor Antoninus. My Lord Emperor Antoninus, having suffered a shipwreck in Italy, we have been vexed by the tax officers of the Cyclades Islands. Antoninus' Reply to Eudemonis. **I am the Lord of the World [I am the owner of lands], and the law of the Sea [but the sea is governed by the law]**, and the Law of the Rhodians, which is the law applicable to maritime cases, must govern the case, insofar as it is not contrary to our laws. The same case had already been so judged by the Divine Augustus.

Anyone who has studied a bit of Latin can appreciate how perfectly correct and 'gymnasial' the Latin of Mommsen is. But what is more astonishing is the freedom exercised by Mommsen in daring to change completely the traditional formula of *Dominus Mundi*. If we read his edition we do not even find it—a formula, after all, so marvellously capturing, but transformed into the rather shallow '*orbis terrarum Dominus*'.

[60] T Mommsen and P Krueger (eds), *Digesta Iustiniani Augusti* (Berlin, Weidmann, 1870); English edition: T Mommsen and P Krueger (eds), *Corpus Juris Civilis. Institutiones and Digesta*, vol 1 (Cambridge, Cambridge University Press, 2014) sub-s de lege Rhodia de iactu D. 14.2.

This choice reinforces the contrast between the land and the sea. The reading of Mommsen suggests that the emperor is the 'Lord-Owner' of emerged lands, but that the law governs the sea. This reading certainly reduces the global and theological dimension of the other possible interpretation of the emperor as the Lord of the Universe, which is immediately evoked by the use of Greek word *kosmos*.

This is surely one of the major points to confront in trying to construct a consistent reading of the passage, but having presented the texts in this way, we shall examine their ambiguities in more detail in the following section. Our final remark will be that the basis of our current conceptions of a global legitimate order lies upon this Roman *substratum*, a political phantom still governing us more than we can govern it.

B. Three Types of Ambiguities: *Kurios*, *Kosmos* and *Nomos*

In considering Dig 14.2.9, apart from minor differences in the various versions, we can identify three main ambiguities.

The first is related to the translation of the Greek term κύριος (*kurios*) into the Latin term *Dominus*. The second is represented by the translation of the Greek κόσμος (*kosmos*) into the Latin *mundus*, but the most dangerous and difficult ambiguity lays in the grammar of the Greek phrase and its use of two small words '… μὲν … δὲ …' (… *men* … *dè* …) meant to mark two commas of the phrase, but whose meaning can range from a contraposition, a mere juxtaposition, or a possible consequence between the first and the second half of the proposition. That is why our modern translations of the original Greek passage can vary so greatly from 'I am the Lord of the world, and the law of the sea', to 'I am the owner of lands, but the sea is governed by the law'.

Let us, then, try to cope with the first of these difficulties, given by the difference between the term '*kurios*' and its Latin translation as '*Dominus*'.

The word used in the Latin version, '*Dominus*', implies both ownership in a strict sense, as well as a lordship in broader terms.[61] Indeed, medieval jurists derived from this semantic uncertainty important and contrasting implications.

The Greek word *kurios* is patently different from the Roman word *Dominus*. It has nothing to do with normal private property. *Kurios* is a term unequivocally implying a lordship. In the Latin version we can have the impression, as the glossators had, that the emperor is an owner whose property is the entire world. In the Greek text we clearly have the idea that the Emperor is a Paramount Lord, something that does not entail his actual possession of all things.

[61] See M Koskenniemi 'Sovereignty, Property and Empire: Early Modern English Contexts' (2017) 18 *Theoretical Inquiries in Law* 355.

Besides, it is apparent that the Greek term *kurios* has a simple translation in English, and it is 'Lord', whereas the Latin term *Dominus* clearly indicates an Owner, but it can be used also to denote a Master or a Lord, in the sense that a Lord is also an owner, and an owner can be a Lord, and both could be called Masters.

In this regard, the word *kosmos* is strikingly different from the Latin word *mundus*. The latter may make reference only to the earth, whereas the former is more making reference to the 'whole' world or, better, to the universe.

This contrast is of extreme relevance for interpreting the two small words appearing in the Greek text: '… *men* … *dé* …'. These two words are the crux of every student of ancient Greek. They are supposed to denote, or to underline, a contrast, something that we may express grammatically by the use of the word 'but'.

A first reading of the passage could, then, be given as: 'I am the Lord of the World, *but* the law [governs] the sea', in the sense that on earth the Emperor has an eminent domain, but that the sea is governed by the law.

The use of this form would then indicate that *whereas* the earth is susceptible to having a Master, the sea is not, and therefore the sea cannot be governed by a man, but only by the law itself.

This interpretation is certainly strengthened by the consideration that legally the sea was unsusceptible of possession under Roman law, and as such it should be impossible to conceive of it as a *res*, a thing or an object of property.[62] Since the sea cannot be possessed, there cannot be an owner of it, but what about a Lord who is not simply an owner of lands, but also a universal Lord exercising some form of sovereignty on the sea different from mere ownership? In this case we may derive our interpretation of the couplet … *men* … *dé* … from our interpretation of the terms *kurios* and *Dominus*, in a vicious circle.

Indeed, if it is true that in ancient Greek the use of the form '… *men* … *dé* …' normally means a counter-opposition, it did not *necessarily* imply it, and, as we said, it could be used to mark a simple *juxtaposition*. As a matter of fact, the Latin translation maintained this ambiguity without resolving it, because the Latin term '*autem*' may, at the same time, signify an 'and' and a 'but'. So even in Latin we may have here a contraposition or a simple juxtaposition.

This is not all, because in Greek language '… *dé* …' can also express an implication, a kind of a consequence, so that the assertion could become: 'I am the Lord of the World, and therefore the law of the sea'. Once again the Latin '*autem*' cannot aid us, since it suffers from the same ambiguity. It can mark a strong opposition or allow for the latter sentence to be a development of the former.

Now we presume that the safest starting point for an interpretation resides in the term *kosmos*, as the key term to understand both the use of *kurios-Dominus* and that of the couplet '… *men* … *dé* …'. Indeed, in this case it is the Latin term *mundus* that is more ambivalent than the Greek word. *Kosmos* indicates more

[62] See G Samuel, 'On the Beach: What Can Beaches Reveal About Legal Reasoning and Categorisation?' (2017) 12 *Journal of Comparative Law* 187.

clearly a universe or a whole world, whereas *mundus* can indicate the earth, the whole world, or even the whole universe.

The ambiguity nested in these concepts is such that, as we have seen, as celebrated a scholar as Mommsen changed the medieval translation in his modern critical edition of the text of the *Digest*, deepening the difference between land and sea. In his version, *mundus* is narrowed and becomes the earth in strong opposition to the sea, and it is rather different to state that someone is the Lord of the Universe, or that he is just the owner of lands. It is also strikingly different to affirm that the sea is governed by political authorities of any kind, or that it is politically free and governed just by maritime laws.

Since the Greek *kosmos* is certainly wider than the mere earth, and certainly wider than just emerged lands, we think it would be rather unusual to assert a universal lordship and then to exclude the waters from it. Besides, Mommsen's reading would imply a rather unclear, and we presume unbearably anachronistic, opposition between the legitimate standing of the Roman emperor and the 'rule of law'. In a way, the passage would imply that the earth is under the discretionary rule of the emperor, whereas the sea is governed by an independent law of its own; lands would be the property of the emperor, but the sea would represent the domain of the law. If we read in such a strong way the opposition between '… *ho men kurios … ho de nomos*' we must conclude that there is an opposition between the emperor and the law, and that the former commands the lands but cannot control the seas, ie something which necessitates the assertion that the sea is the proper *locus* of the law with respect to the nature of earth, which is subject to despotism and imperial domain.

On this basis, we think that if in Greek someone defines himself as a Lord of the Universe, it is rather contradictory to acknowledge that he has no power on the sea. Since the Latin translation can be read as coherent with this view, and since the Latin term *Dominus* may be rendered not only as an owner but also as a Lord, and *mundus* can be an equivalent of the universe and not only of the earth, maybe the real meaning of the passage could have always been as it was interpreted by the Imperial partisans in the Middle Ages. In other words, that there was, and there can be, a unique legitimate universal lordship, and a legitimate single global government.

This conclusion is, we think, reinforced by the practical considerations concerning the case decided by Antoninus Pius, as will be discussed in the next section.

III. The *Dominus* and Its Genealogy

A. Jettison and Emergency

In Dig 14.2.9 we face a typical case of maritime jurisdiction, when the issue at stake is not the merit of the question but the applicable law to decide it. The case gave the emperor an 'occasion' to assert his universal lordship. Is this, then, to be interpreted as a mere *obiter dictum*? Or was this affirmation of universal lordship essential to decide the case?

Facts are briefly reported in the *Digest* under the general rubric referring to the actions that can be brought against the owner of a ship, and specifically under the the rubric concerning the Rhodian law of jettison. As we have seen in previous paragraphs, a petition was addressed to the emperor by Eudaimon of Nicomedia. We are faced with a case of jettison of cargo, appropriation of the cargo by some farmers, and a consequential matter of taxation. It is important to note that Antoninus is rendering his advice on the basis of a precedent already established by the 'Divine Augustus', concerning the value of the *Lex Rhodia* in these maritime cases.

There is no extant copy of the great *Lex Rhodia*; yet Rhodian maritime law was used by the Romans as the *general law of the sea*. Whenever no other law was applicable, reference had to be made to the Law of the Rhodians. However, the mere existence of a general law of the *sea* does not imply that the emperor could never depart from its rules. We should then suppose that Antoninus rated the Rhodian law more that the Roman law itself as the general law of the *land*.

What we mean is that it is hard to hold onto the notion that a Roman emperor paid more respect to the Law of the Rhodians than to the Law of the Romans. The latter was not binding him, whereas his lordship would have met a limit in the existence of a law of the sea. This seems like the expression of a much more modern ideology than a philologically accurate description of Roman ideas.[63] The only maritime law legacy which can be credited to *Lex Rhodia* with reasonable certainty is the cargo jettison rules, what present-day English maritime law experts refer to as general average.

In *The Law of Obligations*, Zimmermann explained how this feature of the *Lex Rhodia* worked: '(A)ny voyage by ship was a somewhat hazardous venture, especially in the Mediterranean Sea. It was (and still is) notorious for its storms and shipwreck was no rare occurrence …'.[64]

What is rightly underlined in his account is that this passage of the Rhodian law pertains to *emergency* cases: wrecks, jettisons, death by water. What we mean is that this law, and the occasioned decision by the emperor, had to deal with a case of necessity, and that it is tantalising to discover that an assertion of global sovereignty was rendered in a structural combination with states of *exception*.

In a case of wreck, all the goods saved were valued as potentially part of the restitution owed to *locatores* (the owners of the cargo), including those goods that did not contribute to the actual weight of the shipment, such as gemstones or

[63] R Benedict, 'The Historical Position of the Rhodian Law' (1909) 18 *Yale Law Journal* 241.

[64] R Zimmermann, *The Law of Obligations: Roman Foundations of the Civilian Tradition* (Oxford, Oxford University Press, 1996) 407.

pearls (Dig 14.2.2.2). The context in which the Rhodian law was applied was that of a storm creating actual danger of shipwreck, which forced the taking of extraordinary measures to avoid the sinking of the ship and the consequent loss of cargo (Dig 14.2.2; Dig 14.2.6). For the Rhodian law to apply, the ship had to have been saved by the adoption of those *extraordinary measures*, which included jettison but also extended to the severing of the mast or the riggings (Dig 14.2.3). The regulation of this sharing of risk was extended to *cases of piracy*, when part of the cargo was used as ransom to pay off the pirates (Dig 14.2.2.3).[65]

It is then rather intriguing to note that the occasion for the emperor to proclaim his universal sovereignty was given with reference to cases of emergency and peril, and also with reference to piracy. As long as our modern ideas are connecting sovereign powers with a state of exception, it could not be underscored enough that the most blatant assertion of a universal sovereignty came along in the *Digest* with direct reference to states of emergency in that which is the perilous, fluid and ontologically strange domain of the sea.[66]

B. Emperors as Manifest Gods

We have introduced the text of the *Digest*, and discussed the intricacies of its Greek version, allowing for interpretations based on opposite views of the powers and limits of imperial prerogatives. We also showed how the actual decision of the Roman emperor, from which the passage originated, was rendered in a case of emergency, and especially concerned a matter of jurisdiction. All these elements are strikingly similar to those around which the current reflection on sovereign powers has been revitalised. What, then, do we know of this case?

The surest thing we apprehend is that the case was covered by the Rhodian Law as the applicable law to the facts, as exposed by Eudaimon. The emperor could have decided that he was the Lord of the World, but that the seas were governed by the law (of the Rhodians), or he could have decided that since he was the Lord of the world as a whole he had the power to decide which law was applicable in maritime cases, and that, in this case, the general law of the sea (that of the Rhodians) was to be applied. As you may note, Antoninus is basing his decision not on general principles, or on the nature of land and sea, or other ontological principles, but on a *precedent* decided by the 'Divine Augustus'. His authority is grounded upon imperial authority, and there was a precedent established by the first emperor that in such cases the applicable law was that of Rhodes. This assertion is of great importance. In other words, it is the emperor who has the

[65] See Zimmermann, *The Law of Obligations* 409.

[66] C Schmitt, *Land and Sea: a World-Historical Meditation* (SG Zeitlin trans, New York, Telos Press Publishing, 2015).

jurisdiction over jurisdictions; in Schmittian terms, a '*Kompetenz über Kompetenz*' as the sublime mark of supreme authority.[67] He has the power of last decision on *Quis Judicabit*, on who is to judge, and which law is to be applied.

This interpretation would be much more consistent than the alternative theory of two separate spheres suggested by Mommsen's translation: the land submitted to the mastership of the emperor, and the sea governed by the rule of law. To accept this alternative theory we would have to imagine that the '*kùrios toù kòsmou*' would accept a limit to his powers in the existence of an independent law of the seas, a '*nòmos tès thalàsses*'. This is contrary to the fact that it was an emperor, Augustus, who established the reception of the Rhodian law on this point. Besides, Mommsen's reading does not account for the proviso actually stated by Antoninus in rendering his decision: the law of the Rhodians is applicable 'provided no enactment of ours is opposed to it'.

This clause means plainly that *he has* the power to govern the sea, to enact rules concerning maritime cases, and that the *lex* of the Rhodians is only a residual law that cannot conflict with imperial legislation. The emperor *could* legislate on the sea; he has authority over the seas, even if he did not, for the moment, exercise it.

How, then, can we explain the opposition marked by the original Greek texts by the use of the grammatical construction '... *hò men* ... *ho dé* ...'? Maybe the opposition is not running between the couple Emperor-Land/*Nomos*-Sea, but *between the different capacities* of the emperor on the land and on the sea. On the land the emperor is both a lord and a master. He owns things physically, because they are things susceptible of possession. The sea cannot be physically apprehended. It can only be regulated but not possessed. Thus *on the sea the emperor is the law, not the master*.

We would then construct the Greek phrase in this way:

> [*egò men*] ... on the land I am the Lord and Master ... [*ho dé*] ... on the sea I am the law ... henceforth I decide that (in this case) the applicable law is the Rhodian law of the sea—provided that no enactment of ours is opposed to it—as it is in the authority of the emperors to decide, as the divine Augustus already stated.

The opposition at the level of grammar marks a conceptual opposition between the capacity of the emperor to really be a *Dominus*—an owner—on land, and his capacity to be the law on the sea. His lordship is universal: as *Dominus* on land 'and/but also' as law at sea.

We think that this is the most consistent solution, but for it to be completely plausible we will need some further evidence, which may be found in the text of extant epigraphs parallel to the assertion inserted into the *Digest*.

The clearest expression of the universal lordship of the emperor, at least as it was perceived in the Eastern part of the empire (the richest and politically most important part of it), is a decree of the city of Acraephiae passed after Nero (54–68 CE)

[67] C Schmitt, *Constitutional Theory* (J Seitzer trans, Durham, Duke University Press, 2008) 150.

had restored freedom to Greece. The decree was issued much earlier than the times of Antoninus.

The extant epigraph[68] addresses Nero as:

> ... ὁ τοῦ παντός κὸσμου κύριος ... αὐτοκράτωρ μέγιστος
>
> ... the Lord of the entire world ... supreme self-ruler ...

This is a clear statement that much earlier than the times of Antoninus the emperor was considered a *Dominus Mundi*, a Lord of all the *kosmos*, the greatest of sovereign authorities (*autokrator megistos*).

It is rather strange that legal scholars have not looked at this inscription to explain the *Digest* sooner. It can help to explain the *Digest* by showing to what extent the title of *Dominus Mundi* was not an invention of Antoninus or of Stoic emperors, but was instead a long-established title, especially in the East. Antoninus also made it explicit for the rest of the empire, having had the occasion to decide a case of emergency.

With regard to the distinction between land and sea, we can look at the text[69] of the oath of loyalty taken by the island of Cyprus at the accession of Tiberius:

> αὐτο[ί] τε καὶ οἱ ἔκγονοι ἡμῶν ὑπακούσεσθαι πειθαρχήσειν κατά τε γῆν καὶ κατὰ θάλαττ[αν] εὐνοήσειν σεβάσ<ε>σθαι Τιβέριον Καίσαρα Σεβαστοῦ ὑὸν Σεβαστόν σὺν τῶι ἅπαντι αὐτοῦ οἴκωι.
>
> We and our descendants will heed and obey by land and sea and will regard with loyalty and revere (sebasthai) Tiberius Caesar Sebastos son of Sebastos.

'Sebastos' is the Greek term used to translate the Latin 'Augustus', with a marked religious connotation. *Sebastophantes* was the standard Greek term to denote those who were charged with organising celebrations concerning the imperial cult. As a matter of fact, the *sebastosphantes* probably displayed an imperial statue in the imperial celebrations, something which can derive from the Hellenistic, long-established imperial cult of the sovereign as an *Epiphanes*, a 'god made manifest' in the world,[70] when not even a 'son of god'.[71]

Hellenistic kings, from Ptolemy V onwards, used *Epiphanes* as part of their official titles, and Antiochus IV of Syria combined it with *theos*. The emperor too was often described as '*theos epiphanes*', or in the superlative form as '*epiphanestos*

[68] 2 ILS 8794.

[69] SRF Price, 'Gods and Emperors: The Greek Language of the Roman Imperial Cult' (1984) 104 *The Journal of Hellenic Studies* 88.

[70] M Hano, 'A l'origine du culte impérial: les autels des Lares Augusti. Recherches sur les thèmes iconographiques et leur signification' in W Haase and H Temporini (eds), *Aufstieg und Niedergang der römischen* (Berlin, Walter de Gruyter, 1998) 2333; J Gagé, 'Les pratiques magiques d'épiphanie royale—basileia—et la mystique impériale aux IIe et IIIe siècles' in W Haase and H Temporini (eds), *Aufstieg und Niedergang der römischen Welt* 2382.

[71] 4 IGRR 1124; 2 Syll 810.

theoon', the *most manifest of all gods*. For example, we may find reference[72] to the emperor as:

> Τιβέριον Κλαύδιον Καίσαρα Σεβαστόν Γερμανικόν, θεόν ἐπιφανῆ, σωτῆρα καί το[ῦ] ἡμετέρου δήμου.
>
> Tiberius Claudius Caesar Sebastos Germanicus, manifest god, saviour of our people.

We cannot today easily dismiss these outstanding examples of the political theology surrounding the figure of the emperor and how clearly connected this was with his self-assertion of being the Lord of the World.

Curiouser and curiouser—to quote Alice in Wonderland—is the fact that legal scholars have underscored that in the same age of Antoninus, Marcus Aurelius and Commodus were honored similarly as follows:[73]

> αὐτοκράτορα Μᾶ(ρκον) Αὐρήλιο[ν] Ἀντωνεῖνον, θεῶν ἐνφανέστατον, γῆς καί θαλάσσης δεσπότην.
>
> Emperor Marcus Aurelius Antoninus, the most manifest of gods, Master of land and sea [tes ges kai thalassis despoten].
>
> αὐτοκράτορα Κόμοδον Καίσαρα, τῶν θεῶν ἐνφανέστατον, γῆς θαλάσσης δεσπότην.
>
> Emperor Commodus Caesar, the most manifest of gods, Master of land and sea.

Here it is patently clear that the two emperors are lords, even masters, of law *and* sea. There is no grammatical opposition but a pure and simple conjunction '… *kaì* …' the unambiguous Greek term for 'and'. They do possess the whole of the globe, land and sea. They are *Domini Mundi*. We think it is impossible to put aside such testimonies, given how important they are, and the one on Marcus Aurelius is the most intriguing of all.

Marcus Aurelius was emperor from 161 to 180 CE, as the last of the 'five good emperors', succeeding Antoninus Pius who was emperor from 138 to 161 CE. So he was one of the heirs that officered the apotheosis of Antoninus, his elevation *post mortem* to the rank of a god, and erected his honorific column in Rome that we shall examine in the following section. He was patently using, or rather accepting, the title of *despotes*, *dominus* in the sense of owner of land *and* sea, to denote himself.

Why was Marcus Aurelius referred to as *despotes*, or 'Master', rather than as *kurios*, 'Lord', which has more important theological implications, but less devastating legal consequences?

When Marcus Aurelius was honoured in the way we have just seen, this happened after the rescript of Antoninus on the shipwreck case had been rendered. Different solutions are possible. The first is a form of re-translation that we

[72] 2 TAM 760c.

[73] CHE Haspels, *The Highlands of Phrygia. Sites and Monuments* (Princeton, Princeton University Press, 1971) 333, fn 93.

cannot exclude. The Greek *kurios-Lord* could have become a Latin *Dominus*, and the Latin *Dominus* could have been literally re-translated as *despotes*, which is its closest equivalent in Greek. It is also possible that in that precise time the difference between lordship and ownership had softened down, especially in the provinces. Maybe Marcus Aurelius, notwithstanding his fame as a philosopher, had lesser reservations than Antoninus about being called Master rather than Lord. It is also very plausible that, even if official titles are to be taken very seriously, a term like *kurios* was more acceptable in the more rigid setting of a formal legal decision over the applicable law in a proper legal case.

All of this is possible, but what is undeniable is that immediately after the rule of Antoninus, as well as before him, as we have seen, there was no striking opposition between land and sea, and that Marcus Aurelius and Commodus were actually honoured as masters of the whole world, land and sea, a title of universal sovereignty already attributed to Nero.

Consequently, there is a clear textual trace that shows that the Greek epigraphs are referring to the whole world. Their text is not simply saying that the emperor is Lord of the *cosmos*, but of '... *pantos kosmou* ...', that is, of the '*whole*' *cosmos*. Such an emphasis, as far as it can help us clarify the text of the *Digest*, can never be reduced to the whole of emerged lands as in Mommsen's formulation. Given the foregoing arguments, along with the fact that the *Digest* uses the term *cosmos*, it appears that Mommsen unduly restricted the 'universe' to the emerged lands, contrary to the parallel passages that can be found in the epigraphic material. Thus, the claim expressed by Antoninus could truly amount to an assertion of global domain.

This is why we think that Mommsen's theory and amendment of the transmitted text is simply wrong, as are all the interpretations based on the idea that the lordship of the emperor encountered a limit in the very existence of a *nomos*, an independent law, of the sea. Emperors were the *Domini Mundi* in the strongest sense, centuries before Burgundius Pisanus—as we shall see—rendered his Latin translation of this Greek passage of the *Digest*[74] to the benefit of German imperial claims that had been previously advanced at the Diet of Roncaglia (1158).

After all, it is very unrealistic to believe that for the Romans the law of the Rhodians could have enjoyed a status higher than their own civil law. It is, of course, possible that technicalities of Roman law could have barred the adoption of the title of owner to such things as the sea which are incapable of possession, but what becomes evident is that the legal-political claim of the Roman emperor was really universal. The whole of the globe, land *and* sea, was under his legitimate dominion. Legitimate because it was conferred on him originally by the Roman people, according to the *Lex Regia* (Dig 1.4.1). It was a global-legitimate-government.

[74] See W Berschin, *Griechisch-lateinisches Mittelalter. Von Hieronymus zu Nicolaus von Kues* (Bern, A Francke, 1980) 291.

Besides, it was certainly a theological pretension. Whatever the theology of the first emperors or the Stoic emperors could have been, the figure of the sovereign, as we have seen, was that of a 'saviour', and of a 'manifest god' or 'son of a god' (*Divii Filius*). The horizontal extension of his power to the whole world was paralleled by his vertical ascension to a more than human status, something which has been visualised in the column erected in honour of Antoninus by his heirs, and that we shall examine in the next section.

It is this manifestation of a sublime power on earth on a global level that is the real subject of the story of Dig 14.2.9 in its own 'too-muchness', in its excess as a hegemonic power acting from, by and through the law.

C. The Antonine Column

In her thorough study, Lise Vogel[75] describes in full detail the column—displayed in Image 1—that the sons of Antoninus Pius dedicated to him as a funerary monument shortly after his death.

Antonine's Column, by Giovanni Battista Piranesi[76]

[75] L Vogel, *The Column of Antoninus Pius* (Cambridge, Harvard University Press, 1973).
[76] <commons.wikimedia.org/wiki/File:Piranesi-14043.jpg>, copyright free.

The base of this monument depicts a woman on the right, sitting on a throne, with swords and shields at her feet. On the left we find a male figure handling a long obelisk pointing toward the sky. Above we may see the imperial couple, Antoninus and his wife, brought to heaven between two eagles. The late emperor holds in hand a long sceptre with what seems to be a phoenix at its end. In between a huge winged *genius* is flying with a globe wrapped about by a serpent, as if he were transporting the imperial couple from earth to heaven.

The form of the column in general and the reliefs on the pedestal in particular raise problems central to the understanding of Roman art, and in her cited study, Lise Vogel restored the column to its rightful place as one of its major extant monuments. In addition, she re-evaluated the meaning of the column in the context of the development of second-century Roman imperial sculpture. But beyond its artistic importance, the reliefs of the pedestal need a specific legal and political understanding to be entirely deciphered. The reliefs work like an emblem, and one of tremendous impact on the theory of legitimacy and world order. The reliefs represent the emperor's apotheosis: his becoming a god, entitling his successor to be a son of god on earth.

The religious aspect cannot be overstated. As Gibbon reminds us, in his peculiarly impeccable style, Titus Antoninus Pius has been justly denominated a second Numa, a mythical king of Rome who first established Roman religion. Antoninus diffused order and tranquility over the greatest part of the earth, but his reign was marked by the rare advantage of furnishing very few materials for history, '… which is, indeed, little more than the register of the crimes, follies and misfortunes of mankind …'.[77]

We have been told that in private life he was amiable, and that the native simplicity of his virtue was a stranger to vanity or affection. The benevolence of his soul displayed itself in a cheerful serenity of temper.

Notwithstanding this stereotyped image of the good emperor as incarnated by Antoninus, he was certainly not a man without conviction. The meaning of his column is unequivocal, as it represents his exaltation toward a more than human condition, something which is indeed rather sublime: something which goes beyond words, as it cannot be entirely captured by words alone, it escapes language.

The figure on the right of the base should represent the dwelling city of Rome, depicted as usual sat with a helm, possibly mimicking Athena, and with a shield over which we can half see the famous she-wolf. The man on the left, because of the obelisk, would then be a figure of the *campus martium*, the field where the Roman people were summoned as an army for practice and exercises and to eventually celebrate victories. The two figures together become a representation of the whole of the Roman people, both in their civil and their martial capacity. Indeed,

[77] E Gibbon, *The History of the Decline and Fall of the Roman Empire*, vol 1 (Claxton, Remsen & Haffelfinger, 1875) 94.

at the time the *campus martium*, which in the Middle Ages became densely populated and built, was almost a void military field in which the emperor Augustus erected a huge *gnomon*, a solar clock whose hand was the still existing tall obelisk in *Piazza Montecitorio* taken from Egypt to signal the hours.

The first meaning of the pedestal is then to represent the people of Rome, as well as the city of Rome. The two figures display the inhabited city elevated on its hills and the flat military field with the outstanding obelisk in a rather perfect mimetic depiction of the large town. If this interpretation is correct, we can also try to give a meaning to the huge winged *genius* in the very centre of the pedestal. Though different interpretations are possible, the most coherent could identify it with the *genius populi romani*, the spirit and the destiny of the Roman people. This *genius* is flying from the city, sustaining with his wide wings the ascension to heaven of Antoninus and Faustina, holding a globe in his left hand. This globe is a patent representation of the universe and not only of the earth, as we may clearly see the stars portrayed in a band circling the globe. Moreover, it is embraced by a serpent which can be assimilated to the *ouroboros*, or the symbol of time and eternity.

Above the *genius*, and in between the self-evident symbol of the Roman eagles, we find the imperial couple with the sceptre and the phoenix, meant to be a representation of the ever-renovating power and glory of the imperial authority. Taken as whole, the pedestal would then mean the legitimate conferment by the people to the emperor of an eternal power over the whole universe. This power is legitimate, because it is conferred by the people, as may be signified by the gesture with her right hand of the city of Rome. It is perennial, because of the phoenix and the *ouroboros*, and it is universal, because of the globe. This universal legitimate power as conferred to the emperor by the Roman people has, so to speak, also a soul and a destiny, consolidated in the figure of the winged *genius*. Is it a representation of political theology?

We may notice that there are no gods in the scene. The only supernatural being depicted in the pedestal is indeed the *genius* of Rome. The more than natural status acquired by the emperor after his death is made evident by his elevation to heaven on the wings of the genius, dominating Rome from above. As such the emperor is a kind of heavenly Lord, not because he is representing on earth some god, or the assembly of gods, but because he is ascending to heaven thanks to the people of Rome and his *genius*. The practice was that some emperors could acquire a more than human condition through the apotheosis conceded to them by the people and the senate of Rome only after their death. The power to appoint a dead emperor as a divinity was in this way maintained by the people itself. The lack of any other god in the representation may well testify to the evolution of paganism at the time of the Antonines. We can also imagine that a conception of heaven could exist without the need for faith in a universal personal god. In a rather stoic way, the belief in personal or collective geniuses was more important than a personal and clearly identified god of nature, even if the universe was thought to be rationally ordered according to everlasting laws.

What is, then, most apparent is the insistence on the legitimacy and universality of a dominion of imperial authority not only over all Roman territories, but over the whole universe, to the point that the globe held in hand by the great winged genius includes the stars! In a way, the whole of the universe was thought to be under Roman rule.

We cannot think that there is a more comprehensive interpretation of the image than this: that the winged *genius* is bringing the universal globe to an emperor ascending to a heavenly authority with a more than human status. There are stars in that globe, and if the authority of the dead emperor is established also on the stars, the *kosmos*, it can hardly be confined to earth alone and not be extended also to the sea.

If this interpretation is correct, we are facing here, thanks to the iconography of the column, a clear emblem illuminating the legal passages included in the *Digest*. In fact, we have here the astonishing image of the Lord of the World, the *Dominus Mundi*, and of his sublime claim to global government. He is not representing a god on earth, but he has acquired a divine status because he has been *augmented*, as the title of *augustus* implies. In this sublime way, the iconography adopted for the pious Antoninus, the man of good manners and tempered attitude as described by Gibbon, is presenting us with the haunting ghost of our times: the very possibility of a unitary and legitimate global world order.

IV. Re-Thinking the Greek Rome

A. Three Models of Political Theology

Our investigation of the deep theological-political facets of law illustrated by the sublimity of the emperor brings us now to one of the major and most decisive events in the history of the West, that is, the encounter of classical political thought with Christian revelation.

Indeed, a standard appraisal of Christian political theologies maintains that it had achieved an intellectual compromise between the initial persecution of Christian ideas and the subsequent conversion of the Emperor. Various Fathers of the church undertook the difficult enterprise to reconcile previously hostile political and legal institutions with a Christian understanding of the world order.

The three major elements around which these theories were built can be identified with the two sequences: God, the Church and the 'political'—or, in other terms, God, Christ and the Empire.[78]

The highest element constitutes the plan of *transcendence* of the invisible realities lying above and beyond the visible and perceptible institutions. This 'sublime'

[78] M Scattola, *Teologia Politica* (Bologna, Il Mulino, 2007) 38.

element was 'contingently' captured within the scheme of theological discourse. 'Contingently' because theology as such is not an integral part of every religion.[79] There are religions that evolved *without* a theology. Technically and concretely we could narrowly define 'theology' in this context as the application of the Greek philosophical discourse to the content of the Christian revelation. In this narrow sense, Schmitt's theory becomes a kind of *solecism*: as long as Western institutions, and Western theology, derive from Roman or Greek concepts, there is obviously a structural parallel between the two. Since theology preceded the modern secularised reflections on politics, the latter apparently derived from the former, but indeed both derived from ancient Roman and Greek models.

The second element—the Church—represented for the Fathers the *real* entity constituted by the Eucharist. The Church is the *corporate body*, the living community of all the faithful united in a 'mystic body' where human and divine secretly meet together. It is the sacramental mediation of the church administering the *corpus Christi* that unifies all believers into a single ontological unit. As long as this community remains alive and operating in history it cannot be denied, and it must be taken into political consideration, no more and no less than other existing universal institutions capable of acting as single units.

The third side of the mentioned triangle was obviously representing the excess of meaning that can be found in earthly institutions such as the Empire. The problem of political theology was mainly that of defining the proper relation between transcendence, the sacramental mediation residing in the church, and the political order.

We try, then, to sketch here for the reader the three major classical solutions that we have also already encountered in the previous section, because they have been re-used—and to a large extent even reverted and twisted—in the age of discoveries at the birth of modernity.

The first political theological solution to problems raised by the interplay of mundane and spiritual elements could be that of a mere *formal* adhesion to the rules of this world by the true believer. This would be a solution fit for times of uncertainty, and that indeed seems purported by many passages in the gospels (Matthew 22:15–22; Mark 12:13–17; Luke 20:20–26). Nevertheless, the well-known chapter XIII of the *Letter to the Romans* clearly stated that there is no authority on earth but from God, introducing the theological necessity to explain, if not to justify, the political order.[80] As we all know, the prologue of the Gospel of John—mentioning the Word (*logos*), whatever the original meaning could have been—allowed the first Christian theologians to meditate between the revelation and Greek and Roman conceptions.[81] Therefore, a first version of political

[79] L Strauss, 'Reason and Revelation' in H Meier (ed), *Leo Strauss and the Theological-Political Problem* (Cambridge, Cambridge University Press, 2007) 141.

[80] J Taubes, *The Political Theology of Paul* (D Hollander trans, Stanford, Stanford University Press, 2003) 23.

[81] M Scattola, *Das Naturrecht vor dem Naturrecht* (Tubingen, Max Niemeyer Verlag, 1999) 22–28.

theology could, then, emerge as the idea that transcendence operates in the world purely as 'The Eternal Word' rendered visible by an idealisation of the Empire.

A second view emerged as the possibility to emphasise the *incarnated logos* in the person of Jesus, from whence St Augustine could imply the prevalence of the Church over political institutions, since it is the church that constitutes and administers the body of Jesus.[82]

A third possibility was to underline and to stress the *parallel* between the human and the divine rule in the universe,[83] a solution that will patently prevail, as, for instance, in Dante's *Monarchy*.

In the letter of pope Gelasius I to the emperor Anastasios, as it was edited in the ninth century,[84] we find indeed a unitary conception of both the Empire and the Church as two parallel manifestations of the *same* universal order. God gave the pastoral to the bishops to govern the souls and administer the sacraments of the salvation of mankind, and He gave to the emperor the sword to protect the Church and to enforce the law, maintaining law and order. In such a way, the clergy are subject to the laws of the emperor, who has the highest authority on earth, but the emperor is subject to the jurisdiction of the Church over his soul and for his sins, and he cannot make his will prevail in religious matters. Using an argument that would be revived in the sixteenth century, Gelasius presumed the clergy authority to be higher than civil authority, because if the emperor will be held accountable by the Lord only for his own government of the world, the pope will have to account not only for his government of the Church, but also for the conduct of the emperor. The emperor may well be the Master of the World, but the pope is the pastor of the emperor, being held liable for his sins and his injustices if he does not try to avoid them or give relief.

It is rather apparent to what extent this paradigm fixed the whole of the medieval discourse on the interaction of the two world authorities coexisting in the West. The order of the world is thought, then, to consist of three main elements: (1) God as the source of all authority; (2) the Church as that power *constituted* to govern the *souls* for their salvation; and (3) the empire as the *second constituted* power to administer justice for the preservation of the community and for the government of *bodies*.

For us, the major important point of this rearrangement of Roman and Greek political thought in its encounter with Christianity is represented by the fact that, operating within a distinction of body and soul, and within the difference between *absolute* and *constituted* powers,[85] it creates also a *last instance*, to be meant in real legal terms. In the last instance, indeed, the spiritual power will have to decide whether the secular power has been maintained within its proper limits, and correctly used.

[82] HX Arquillière, *L'augustinisme politique* (Paris, Vrin, 1955).
[83] W Ullmann, *Medieval Political Thought* (London, Penguin Books, 1965) 77.
[84] See Scattola, *Teologia politica* 48.
[85] Scattola, *Teologia politica* 50.

As we may easily grasp in modern terms, it is a system of 'checks and balances': the clergy cannot violate the laws of the empire, and the emperor cannot interfere in religious matters; the emperor has full executive power, but it is the poor shepherd of Rome—apparently *the least dangerous branch*—having the power to judge on the correctness and the limits of such a mighty authority over the world.

These models of political theological discourse received varied institutional interpretations in the history of the East and the West. Perhaps the purest form of an ideology of the *Dominus Mundi* as a living image of God on earth is the one that can be found in the Byzantine arrangement, as built upon its own Roman background, even if in a deeply transformed way.

B. Byzantium and the Liturgy of the Presence

If we now look at the Byzantine empire, as the historical evolution of the Eastern Roman Empire, we may easily perceive that it fully realised historically the ontological parallel between human and divine institutions.

A first point to be taken into account is the 'perennial' nature attributed to the imperial domain.[86] The empire is an everlasting institution as the emperor is the image of God, and as such it is not confined to mere historical time. It exceeds it; it goes beyond it, it lives in a time different from history. This complex of the *imperium aeternum* became a recurring theme in the imperial ritual. Of course, it is very likely that this eternal nature of imperial power—and the cult associated with the emperor—has been derived by Hellenistic models and that these models have roots both in the Egyptian theology and in the Persian political speculations. In Greek terms this everlasting and trans-historical temporal dimension of imperial power was filtered by the word '*Aion*' (αἰών), which was a term actually used in political-philosophical enquiries on the nature of the power of Septimium Severus (146–211 CE) rendered in Latin through the idea of a *constant dominion*, or '*constans imperium*'.[87] At the threshold of modernity we would again find a similar definition of sovereignty in Jean Bodin (1530–1596) as that absolute, *perpetual* and undivided power which exceeds temporary occasions.[88]

In this way, the two key points of legitimation of Roman rule over the world as a whole were fixed as 'victory' and '*aeternitas*', in the sense of being an everlasting and perennial power exceeding historical contingency.[89] In our appraisal of the 'too-muchness' attached to the ideal of a world legitimacy, speculations of

[86] A Carile, *Teologia politica bizantina* (Spoleto, Fondazione Centro italiano di studi sull'Alto Medioevo, 2008) 5.

[87] HU Instinsky, 'Offene Fragen zum Bischofsstuhl und Kaiserthron' (1971) 66 *Römische Quartalschrif* 79.

[88] J Bodin, *Les six livres de la Republique*, book 1, ch 8; J Bodin, *Six Books of The Commonwealth* (KD McRae ed, Cambridge, Harvard University Press, 1962) 84.

[89] F Heim, *Virtus. Idéologie politique et croyances religieuses au IV siècle* (Berne, Publications Universitaires Européennes, 1991).

this kind are, of course, of great importance, given that they transcend a rational theory of mundane power to establish a metaphysics of the political, embracing the same ontology of time.

The imperial notion of 'Aion' tried to represent a *temporal eternity* embracing the different *times* (*aiones*) including *Kronos* or historical time. As the latter is a *chronological* flux that can be measured, dated, and reduced to precise intervals, the former is an ontological and stable entity of a rather different and *achronological* nature.

As long as the kingship of the emperor was thought of as an anticipation of the final kingdom, it could not be anything other than atemporal and over-historical, as it was connected with the *salvific* mission of the empire. The Christian *Basileus* (king), then, became an *ikon*, an image of God (*imago Dei*), and the world itself—the *kosmos*—was imagined as a *Basileia*, an enormous Royal Palace: the physical space of a universal monarchy where the earthly king was the emblem (μῑμησις, or ὕπαρχος) of the Great Emperor who is God himself.[90]

This model of representation of political entities, this political theological complex, was at various times widely imitated in the West, and it is certainly at the root of the ideals expressed by Dante Alighieri in *De Monarchia* as studied by the young Kelsen.[91] This imitation was rendered necessary by the original usurpation of power of the Western emperor over his Eastern counterpart. After all, the political theology of the West always suffered from this original intent.

The particular arrangement attained by pope Leo III at the 800 CE coronation of Charlemagne,[92] eventually made the Church assume the role of a 'legitimising authority' and the emperor that of a 'legitimised subject'. The Church had received from Christ the mission to save the world: the Byzantine emperor was no longer strong enough to protect it, and so the Church could legitimately elect another protector to fulfil her divine mission. Such theory can now be seen as a prototype of the political pact, whose essence is the exchange between protection and loyalty, and protection and legitimation, as the basis of political institutions. The pope can offer a legitimation to the emperor, who should then be faithful to the Church, and the emperor could in return legitimately demand loyalty from the clergy. Since a pact is broken when the two terms of the bargain are not respected, a treacherous emperor could be declared an unlawful tyrant, and a disloyal pope could be deposed as an anti-pope.

The fundamental origin of this typical Western dualism, with all that derived from it, including a mystic theory of checks and balances at the level of government, has its ultimate root in an act of usurpation due to the weakness of the Eastern emperor, who did not react only because he could not. For centuries, the

90 Carile, *Teologia politica bizantina* 7.

91 H Kelsen, *Die Staatslehre des Dante* (Wien, F Deuticke, 1905).

92 W Ullmann, *The Carolingian Renaissance and the Idea of Kingship* (London, Methuen Publishing, 1969) 91; AA Latowsky, *Emperor of the World: Charlemagne and the Construction of Imperial Authority, 800–1229* (Ithaca, Cornell University Press, 2016) 22.

Eastern emperors accepted the insincere avowals of allegiance continuously made to them by Western authorities.[93] We can really see here an *original fracture*, a wound of the world kingship of the Byzantine emperor producing a new partition of the globe. Of course, this original fracture rendered the transplant of Eastern political theology in the West always a pale imitation of it and of its complex character, at the same time opening new unprecedented paths for political thought. Moreover, this 'original sin' of the West, concerning an usurpation of the world legitimate dominion, provoked also a wound that never healed between what is *de jure* and why is *de facto*, between the legal and the factual. If we notice it, the founding reasoning of the political pact between the pope and Charlemagne uses a factual argument, the weakness of the *Basileus*, to establish a *legal* consequence: someone else would be emperor in the West. The glue of this argument resides in the divine mission of the Church and her need for a secular lord protector whose role is that of a guardian. So the law in the West received its legitimation by a factual argument. Not by might, but by the transcendence associated with a divine mission. The need of the Church for protection transformed the power of the Western emperor into a legitimate authority establishing a double duality of 'pope/emperor' and 'fact/law' which was never properly resolved.

If we then come back to considering the great refinement of political theology due to Eusebius of Caesarea (265–340 CE),[94] we cannot help but give the strongest importance to the Greek word *kosmos* as it appears in the *Digest*. The *kosmos* is to be conceived as a great space protected by God, whose king is his own faithful image, living—as He does—in the eternity of his power and glory. In this sense, the *Dominus Mundi*—the *kurios tou pantos kosmou*—is really the Master of the Universe, and his dominion can scarcely be limited to questions of possession, or of land and sea, and maritime laws. The question of eternity, of the special time in which the emperor is living, marks the difference between him and all the other mortals, and the mention of him once again deeply influences the Justinian's compilation where the emperor (Cod 21.8.8) expressly mentions his own eternity and the eternity of his laws (*aeterinats nostra … aeterna lex*). This conception is certainly confirmed by the formulas of imperial acclamation when the ruler was hailed as *kosmosustatos* or *mundi constitutor*, and at the same time *kronokrator* or Lord of the Time.[95]

If we then think of the emperor as a Lord of the World living in an over-historical time, the theory that he is an image of God assumes a meaning never really capable of imitation in the West. Image here is to be understood in its proper

[93] RJH Jenkins and LG Westerink (eds), *Nicholas I, Patriarch of Constantinople. Letters* (Washington DC, Dumbarton Oaks Center for Byzantine Studies, 1973) 2; Carile, *Teologia politica bizantina* 23.

[94] See D Leshem, *The Origins of Neoliberalism: Modeling the Economy from Jesus to Foucault* (New York, Columbia University Press, 2016) 51–54.

[95] A Cameron, 'The Construction of Court Ritual: the Byzantine Book of Ceremonies' in D Cannadine and S Price (eds), *Rituals of Royalty. Power and Ceremonial in Traditional Societies* (Cambridge, Cambridge University Press, 1987) 136.

iconoclastic meaning. When Leo Isauricos (675–741) launched his war against the images,[96] to destroy all representations of divinity, his probable intention was to leave on the whole earth only one real image of the Lord: himself.

As such, as an *ikon* of God, a special role was also attributed to the Byzantine emperor and that was to *shock* the world by his amazing and mystifying presence. It was as '*Stupor Mundi*' that the emperor held the earth against the aggressions of the barbarians, and that all nations had to bow to him. It is literary his *majesty*, a terrifying and unbelievable appearance governing the world and resisting against the forces of chaos. The Latin *stupor*, meaning exactly that which is at the same time frightening and attracting, denotes something 'sublime'.

Such a mixture of mystifying and terrific aspects was well represented by the red purple of the emperor's mantle, signifying that he had the power to shed blood.[97] This power represents in turn the political violence that can demonise the unpolitical violence that must be kept under control to instill justice in the world.

This eminently violent nature of the sublimity of imperial power was thought of not only as a metaphor but in a stronger sense as something pertaining to the same nature of the imperial persona. Justinian self-defined himself as a *living law*, a *lex animata in terris* (Nov 105.2.4).[98] The law can take the form of human flesh, it can assume and inhabit a body. Justice itself can be incarnated into a body and can start walking on earth. This is a theory that echoed even in the West, for example by John of Paris (fourteenth century), where the sovereign was seen as a *iustum animatum*, an *incarnation* of justice.[99]

If we look attentively to this model we can immediately perceive to what extent a general and structural theory of political theology as expressed by Schmitt—or, now, by Agamben—in terms of a peculiar feature, and maybe of a destiny of the West, has to be traced back much more properly to its own Eastern origins. The true theo-political 'complex' had its inner genealogy in Byzantium.

The denial of these roots can be, then, perceived as a strategy of appropriation and de-exoticisation. But what is striking is, on the contrary, to what extent the West has been constructed in juxtaposition to Eastern patterns, rendering the patterns a recurring theme of Western political reflection.

In particular, what appears to be at the root of many Schmittian conceptions is this Byzantine ontological reunion of violence and justice in the concept of sovereign power and in the same body of the ruler. This conception requires a manifestation of violence against the enemies, the forces of chaos trying to jeopardise the *taxis* or the *eutaxia* (the good world order), making them all the enemies of God in their association against Him. That is the real reason why they must

[96] G Ostrogorsky, *History of the Byzantine State* (J Hussey trans, Oxford, Basil Blackwell, 1956) 142.

[97] Carile, *Teologia politica bizantina* 15.

[98] A Steinwenter, *Nomos empsuchos: Zur Geschichte einer politischen Theorie* (Wien, Anzeiger der Akademie der Wissenschaften, 1946) 59. See Kantorowicz, *The King's Two Bodies* 130.

[99] F Dvornik, *Early Christian and Byzantine Political Philosophy: Origins and Backgrounds* (Washington DC, Dumbarton Oaks Center for Byzantine Studies, 1966) 736.

finally be banned and excluded by the 'speaking law' (*lex loquens*) incarnated in the emperor.[100] In this way, the law and the emperor could form a unitary complex, and the law, as it was incarnated in the sovereign body, could be proclaimed to be the 'real' *basileus* because there was indeed no possible real physical distinction between the law and its *guardian*.

[100] Dvornik, *Early Christian and Byzantine Political Philosophy* 476; Carile, *Teologia politica bizantina* 20.

2

The Christian Empire as World Order

I. The Revival of the *Dominus*

A. The Constitution of the *Dominus*

In this second chapter, we shall analyse the revival that the Roman legal and political notion of *Dominus Mundi* had in the West, in comparison to the Eastern empire, and its impact on the concept of sovereignty. We shall concentrate our attention on the two figures of Frederick I (1122–1190) and Frederick II (1194–1250), and the way they tried to shape their own powers.

Through this analysis we could single out three different historical outcomes which have characterised the encounter of Roman legal and political thought with Christian theology. This encounter obviously developed during a long span of time but it can, and must, be scrutinised here in relation to particular moments which characterised the revival of the complex notion of *Dominus Mundi* to better understand the genealogy of our modern conceptions of sovereignty, the law and the political.

The three main and divergent outcomes that emerged from this encounter may be sketched in the following terms.

A first way to frame the political world can be identified with the political theology which prevailed in the Byzantine empire from its very beginning. The self-assertion of the Eastern emperor of his unquestionable continuity with the old Roman empire paved the way, in Christian orthodox terms, to conceptualise his person as the major representative of God on earth. In practical terms, this theory implies that his prerogatives are generally indefinite and that he can always intervene at his will as the lord paramount of the world—a concept that we can certainly trace back to the very essence of the *Dominus Mundi* as the '*kurios tou pantos kosmou*' (lord of the whole universe). In these terms, there is a real parallel between the God of the Universe and the Emperor of the World, and both are personal and purposive entities which possess all the powers, including those powers which are undefined and that can be used in unpredictable ways. In this scheme, the law remains overwhelmingly important but it is incarnated into the sovereign persona, so much so that Justinian defined himself as the 'living law', the *lex animata in terris* (Nov 105.2.4).

As we have seen in the previous chapter, from an ontological orthodox point of view, the emperor was an *ikon,* an *image* of God on earth. In this sense, the *ikon* is *not* a *mimesis*, or an imitation of the represented entity, but rather participates in the metaphysical reality of the represented. As a consequence, the dwelling of the emperor on earth also realised an ontological presence of God in human political affairs, so that the palace of the emperor, his daily life, and public appearances became shaped as a kind of liturgy, the liturgy of the presence. According to this theory, the advent of Christ established the possibility of a legitimate and orthodox kingdom in the world as an anticipation of the future kingdom in heaven. The Lord is already present and directing human affairs through the emperor. His subjects must, by definition, be the faithful flock of a church that cannot represent a counter power to the empire since the empire is by its very essence a Christian institution.

Of course, this is a model where sovereignty and exception are not separate but reveal to be two sides of the same coin, of a sovereign whose prerogatives are undefined as are those of the Lord. The rule of law is ensured by the orthodox nature of the empire and its holder, who cannot violate the law any more than he can violate his own nature, since the emperor is a 'real image' of God and cannot do anything that would go against justice. We would stress that, according to these conceptions, since the royal presence is always miraculous, there is not really any room for the exception. As long as miracles are a suspension of the established order, if the order is already miraculous it is immaterial to speak of its miraculous suspension. This is a form of pure political theology where, in contrast to Schmitt's theory, sovereignty does not need to be exceptionally connected with miracles, because its connection with the miracle is *normal.*

A second model can be represented by the jurists, or glossators, at the origin of modern Western legal culture. The main feature of this model can be described as a lay and technical approach to political problems which tries to neutralise political clashes through a formal legal framework. It represents a *formalisation of the political* and the theological through legal language, where transcendence becomes embodied within the framework of the law, where the need for political decision disappears in the form of a logical conclusion from accepted premises and distinctions. One of its inherent characteristics is, nevertheless, that of a *denial*, and in particular the denial of the fact that politics requires an ultimate decision at the level of sovereignty and at the level of geopolitical interactions. If the world is completely legally defined, and social relations are all legally framed, there is no longer any real room for political decision: a solution for any problem will be found in the reasoning and the subtle distinctions of the jurists. The nature of the papacy, that of imperial sovereignty, and even the essence of war and peace are transformed into legal concepts, denying their political nature but with the advantage that political conclusions must be binding because they derive from the law and do not rest simply on the acceptance of a pure political decision. From a practical viewpoint, it is a way to transform *essentially contested concepts*—concepts susceptible to rival and competing meanings,[1] such as the concepts of sovereignty, war, and peace—into a system of defined legal relationships. From a theological perspective, this arrangement of human relations in pure legal terms always tends toward a kind of *Spinozism* in the sense of equating God with His own order. Indeed, in this scheme there is no need for an omnipotent god, or ultimate authority, governing the universe by his will and his decrees. Instead, God can be identified with the rational order of the universe. In such a logical universe, the space of exception tends to evaporate and disappear, as it becomes neutralised within the formal scheme of the law. In this case, the *Dominus Mundi* has no real power, as it is more of an abstraction, an entity almost nullified in its personality through its own assimilation into the legal order.

A third model that we term 'imperial messianism' is realised when the emperor, the *Dominus Mundi*, becomes the active agent of salvation. In opposition to the first two models, this one is rather *destabilising* to the world order, and it has formed the subject matter of Kantorowicz's analysis of Frederick II, as will be discussed. In this case, the figure of the emperor becomes similar to that of one of the possible interpretations of Christ as he who must destabilise this world and bring it to an end to realise its salvation. Therefore, when the *Dominus Mundi* interprets his political role as that of a such Christ-like figure, he must assume upon himself the duty to perform the end of history. If the *Dominus* is a Christ, in this sense, then he must assume an eschatological stance politically, and exceptionalism starts to be embodied within the structure of a power which is at once sovereign *and* subversive.

Messianism as such is naturally a strong destabilising force as long as it is directed toward a concrete and *actual* political action. An indefinitely postponed messianism loses all of its political strength. If the Second Coming will happen in an indefinite future, its impact on human relations or political decisions is nullified by its deferment. On the contrary, if the Coming is expected to be imminent, it will have immediate effects on world affairs. One of the most everlasting consequences of the general assimilation of the figure of the sovereign into that of a similar Christ could lead, in the West, to the sovereign assuming an unexpected destabilising role within his own realm and legal order, if he tries to act politically for the end of the world in order to realise the salvation of his subjects.

We can denote this mixture of imperial domain and active Christ-like role, this 'imperial messianism', as a special political form of 'Occidental eschatology'.[2] If Christ came the first time to subvert political institutions and the law, and if He succeeded in his mission, the new law and legal institutions may be thought to serve and possibly to facilitate the Second Coming. In this way, the sovereign

[1] WB Gallie, 'Essentially Contested Concepts' (1955–1956) 56 *Proceedings of the Aristotelian Society New Series* 167.

[2] J Taubes, *Occidental Eschatology* (D Ratmoko trans, Stanford, Stanford University Press, 2009).

becomes a force of subversion, and miracles and conversions are signs of the coming of the end. Exception becomes a sign of the political success of a destabilising force.

Given this context, the first argument that we shall then confront is the re-birth of the formal title of *Dominus Mundi* in the West in the context of the Diet of Roncaglia (1154–1158), a great assembly summoned by the emperor to formally state his own prerogatives.

B. Political Glossators and the Contested *Dominus*

The political aspects of medieval jurists' teachings have been a recurrent subject of academic reflection,[3] though often confined to an abstruse 'legal archaeology'. The most vivid part of these studies has been directed toward their contribution to the idea of sovereignty. From the time of Charlemagne there existed a rather vague theory that all kings should be subject to one emperor, who was thought of as a kind of temporal head of Christendom. With the revival of the study of Roman law in the twelfth century, this theory acquired sharper outlines, casting the German emperor in the role of *Dominus Mundi*.

Story has it[4] that emperor Frederick Barbarossa, riding on horseback with Bulgarus and Martinus, the two most preeminent jurists of the time, asked them whether, according to law, he was the Lord of the World. Bulgarus replied that though he was the master of the world generally speaking, he was not lord over private property. Martinus said that Frederick was the true lord of the world. Frederick got off of his horse and presented it to Martinus but gave nothing to Bulgarus, who replied with a pun: 'I lost an equine because I upheld equity, which is not equitable'.[5]

As Pennington has noted, part of the story's appeal was its cleverness and ambiguity. Perhaps Martinus was simply asserting a proposition likely intended to legitimate the Emperor's power to levy taxes on the basis of his global eminent domain, whereas Bulgarus was interested in asserting that though Frederick was Lord of the World, his authority was subject to limitations due to the need to respect private property, so that his government could not be arbitrary. Sources on the point are extremely scarce: there are only a few chronicles'[6] fragments of the glossators, and some extant imperial documents. Besides, these sources have always been interpreted according to the political inclinations of modern scholars.

[3] M Ryan, 'Bartolus of Sassoferrato and Free Cities' (2000) 10 *Transactions of the Royal Historical Society* 65.

[4] See K Pennington, *The Prince and the Law, 1200–1600: Sovereignty and Rights in the Western Legal Tradition* (Berkeley, California University Press, 1993) 15–19.

[5] See Otto Morena, *Historia Frederici* in 7 MGH (F Gueterbock ed, 1930) 59 and in 18 MGH (P Jaffé ed, 1863) 607.

[6] Godfrey of Viterbo, *Gesta Friderici* in 30 MGH (G Waitz ed, 1870) 1–45.

It is within this project that the claim of Frederick I to be considered the *Dominus Mundi* must be appraised. The dialogue between the emperor and Bulgarus and Martinus (the two main disciples of Irnerius (1060–1130), probably written by Otto Morena, or added to his work in the thirteenth century,[7] represents a narrative that links the political project of grounding the imperial authority to ancient Roman law.

The Latin words '*ego quidem mundi dominus*' as such derive from a translation of the Greek passages of the *Digest* that was probably due to Burgundius Pisanus (1110–1193).[8] Those passages were omitted in previous manuscripts available at Bologna, and were simply marked with a double 'G', meaning *lex graeca*, to signal that the original was written in Greek. What is certain is that Burgundius Pisanus used the very old and venerated manuscript of the *Digest* preserved in the Pisa Cathedral for his translations, after it had been taken as booty from the City of Amalfi and solemnly brought into that church with a spectacular religious procession. We can then legitimately presume that the Greek passage in question was indeed in the old Greek copies of the *Digest*, even if it was not available to the doctors of the University of Bologna. Because the Latin translation came later, this renders uncertain the plausibility of the emperor having a discussion about *Dominus Mundi* with the two main jurists of the time.

All of this textual history has furnished good material for legal scholars to doubt the very possibility that an actual discussion of the expression *Dominus Mundi* could ever happen. Burgundius Pisanus had, indeed, a very long career as a translator. He was already active in 1136, and was almost surely active up to 1184–85. Since Roncaglia was summoned in 1158, nothing can exclude nor prove that his translation was effectively used as a basis for discussion. The fact that Burgundius Pisanus does not mention his work on the *Digest* in the translation of the commentaries on the gospel of 1171–73 is weak evidence, as is any argument *e silentio*.

Anyway, most legal historians have extensively quarrelled about this passage mainly from the standpoint of ownership and the property, or eminent domain, that the emperor could claim to have over all the goods and lands of his subjects. Even if this point is, of course, of great practical importance, the main problem posed at the Diet of Roncaglia was not that of the property of the emperor, but that of his overall standing, of his universal rule. The matter of imperial property was inserted into the statute called *Bene a Zenone* (Cod 7.37.3) by which Justinian meant to protect the purchasers of fiscal or imperial goods against the claims of third parties. The statute declared that *all* the goods *of the imperial house* could be presumed legitimate property of the emperor (*omnia principis esse intelligantur*).

[7] Pennington, *The Prince and the Law* 16.

[8] W Berschin, *Griechisch-lateinisches Mittelalter. Von Hieronymus zu Nicolaus von Kues* (Bern, A Francke, 1980) 290; E Conte, '"Ego quidem mundi dominus". Ancora su Federico Barbarossa e il diritto giustinianeo' in L Gatto and P Supino Martini (eds), *Studi sulle società e le culture del Medioevo per Girolamo Arnaldi* (Roma, All'Insegna del Giglio, 2002) 135.

Taken out of context, this phrasing could be used to claim that all the goods *of the world* belonged to the emperor. This actual ownership would have conferred upon the emperor not only a general jurisdiction over mankind, but also all of the economic power of the world. It also had an overwhelming political implication, as it was used by heterodox revolutionaries such as Arnaldo da Brescia (1090–1155) to claim that the Church could not have any possession but for the permission of the emperor as the lord paramount. His subjects could have titles to possession only by his allowance. Here the boundaries between what we moderns classify as economic or political, public power or private property, blur and disappear,[9] by the very fact that these distinctions are clearly of modern origin.

Nevertheless, what remains at stake in these discussions is the emperor's universal lordship in itself, as expressed by the Greek original '*kurios tou kosmou*'. On this point, we believe that, given the constant trades and diplomatic contacts between the West and Byzantium, it could well have been rather unnecessary for the imperial chancellery to rely on a translation by a Pisan doctor to confront the matter of legitimate imperial domain. The matter at stake was that of the imperial prerogatives, and it was this matter upon which later commentators focused their debates.

C. Bartolus, Baldus and the Corporal God

How, then, did the great medieval jurists cope with the notion of *Dominus Mundi*, and how did they eventually change it? Quite naturally, the first to be examined for his eminence and influence is Bartolus of Saxoferrato (1313/1314–1357) and of main importance here are his ideas developed on the matter of sovereignty[10] and *dominium*.[11]

Bartolus confronts the difficulties implied by the title of *Dominus Totius Mundi* (Lord of the whole World) by affirming a 'necessary distinction', as this was his characteristic method of legal analysis.[12] According to Bartolus, we must distinguish between pure sovereignty (*de jure*) and actual control (*de facto*), and this distinction between right and fact seems to be at the core of the political conceptions of Bartolus.

[9] See M Koskenniemi 'Sovereignty, Property and Empire: Early Modern English Contexts' (2017) 18 *Theoretical Inquiries in Law* 370.

[10] F Maiolo, *Medieval Sovereignty: Marcilius of Padua and Bartolous of Saxoferrato* (Delft, Eburon Academic Publishers, 2008) 231, 250 ff.

[11] L Dias Schirm, *Omnem e Iurisdictio: Comentários De Bartolus Da Sassoferrato (1314–1357) Sobre Dominium* (Belo Horizonte, Universidade Federal De Minas Gerais, Faculdade de Filosofia e Ciências Humanas, 2011).

[12] Bartolus [Cod 1.1.1.7]. See CNS Woolf, *Bartolus of Sassoferrato. His Position in the History of Medieval Political Thought* (Cambridge, Cambridge University Press, 2012) 108–109; JN Figgis 'Bartolus and the Development of European Political Ideas' (1905) 19 *Transactions of the Royal Historical Society* 160.

The argument is, then, the following. There are some who do not obey the emperor, nor does his domain embrace *de facto* the whole globe, but the *Digest* affirms his *right* to rule the whole world. The emperor's sovereignty is purely legal and does not imply, nor is it denied by the lack of, an actual control exercised over all the territories. As we may easily perceive, Bartolus does not restrict the matter of *dominion* to the idea of property or possession. The question is framed in terms of lordship, even over those territories which are not under the emperor's actual control, and over those people who do not obey him. The emperor has a legitimate *claim* to universal domain which does not depend on his actual power.

How can this all-pervasive domain of the emperor co-exist with private properties? According to Bartolus, the legitimate rightful lordship of the emperor over the whole world *does not imply* that all other possessions are illegal. The emperor is the true Lord of the World in general terms (*generaliter*), but others can be owners of particular things (*domini particulariter*). The world in its entirety can be considered a single *res*, one thing, and as such it belongs to the emperor, but the various things composing the world, the *singulae res*, may also belong to others. In more basic terms, the domain of the emperor does not contrast with the *private properties* of his subjects. We should note here the particular ontology upon which Bartolus's comment is built, that the world as a whole can be at the same time 'one thing' and 'many things', having different owners. Once again, the law used to establish an almost divine right of the emperor is also used to limit his power. Bartolus is giving us a legal ontology of the world which can tolerate the coexistence of a single overall *Dominus* and of many individual owners.

Of no less importance is the way in which Bartolus discusses the status of free cities within the larger spatiality of the empire. Bartolus begins his analysis by asking whether all peoples are subject to the empire.[13] According to him, as we have seen, the emperor rules all over the world *de jure*: he is *dominus unversalis*, by which Bartolus means something specific. According to Bartolus, the emperor is the Lord of the entire world in a true sense, and it does not conflict with this that others are lords in a particular sense, for the world is a sort of *universitas*. Hence someone can possess the said *universitas* without owning the particular things within it.[14]

Moreover, the emperor is *dominus universalis* because he has jurisdiction over everything: '*dominus quoad jurisdictionem*' as Bartolus puts it.[15] In summary, the emperor is the true *Dominus Mundi*, but his dominion consists in a general overall jurisdiction and does not conflict with the rights to self-government of the free-cities, nor with the privileges of the kings. This means that the spatiality of the world is not really subverted by the recognition of a general abstract imperial jurisdiction.

In his passages, Bartolus is elaborating the intricate civilian theory of *universalities*. He affirms that the emperor is truly the *Dominus Mundi* but that this does not

[13] Ryan, 'Bartolus of Sassoferrato and Free Cities' 71.
[14] Bartolus [Dig 6.1.1].
[15] Bartolus [Const *Omnem*].

conflict with the dominions of others (such as the properties or lordships of the princes and kings) because the world is a *universitas*, a thing made of other things, like a flock or a library. From this it plainly follows that single goods or lands forming this totality can belong to others even if the emperor is emphatically entitled to the whole:[16] a rather sly way to neutralise imperial claims.

In his work, Bartolus makes direct reference to the controversy between Martinus and Bulgarus. For him, the emperor is *Dominus* of the world because he is bound *to defend* the whole world, and anyone is called *Dominus* of that which he protects or administers. Of course, this passage is of some importance in considering the 'pastoral paradigm' of sovereignty, where the title to govern is linked to the duty to protect and the need to procure the salvation of the subjects.[17]

At the very end we have different but conflicting conclusions made by the civilians. It is impossible to deny that the emperor is the Master of the World, but he cannot govern arbitrarily, nor can he levy arbitrary taxation. He must respect private property, and cannot interfere with the rights of cities, princes, and kings except under extreme circumstances. While this sounds like universal lordship, it actually amounts to a rather limited form of sovereignty.

Indeed, according to Pennington, the issue of the emperor's universal power was not nearly as important or as difficult for the jurists.[18] He believes that the Roman lawyers had never seriously considered the emperor to be *Dominus Mundi*, in the sense that he could exercise a universal control over all people and their properties. Ironically, he observes, the emperor could only call upon *canonists*, not *romanists*,[19] to bolster his claims against the kings and the pope. Bartolus asserted that the emperor was *de jure Dominus Mundi*, but they hedged their claims with *de facto* exceptions of every sort. Thus, Pennington concludes that they only argued for a theoretical overlordship with few concrete consequences.

We think, nevertheless, that in these debates there is more than that. Independently of the operative legal consequences, we cannot underestimate the ideological and ontological aspects of empire, haunting our political thought for centuries to come.

First of all, in his *Ad Reprimendam* Bartolus acknowledges the power of the emperor in pure theological terms, and secondly, on this basis, he almost frames a theory of political *heresy*. Indeed, he states the narrative of the empire in theological terms:

> Ultimo adveniente Christo istud Romanum imperium incipit esse Christi imperium, et ideo apud Christi vicarium est uterque gladius, scilicet spiritualis et temporalis … Dic ergo quod ante Christum imperium romanum dependebat ab eo solo et empreator recte

[16] Bartolus [Dig 6.1.1]: 'Ego dico quod Imperator est dominus totius mundi vere [variant: recte]'. See Woolf, *Bartolus of Saxoferrato* 23.

[17] D Leshem, *The Origins of Neoliberalism: Modeling the Economy from Jesus to Foucault* (New York, Columbia University Press, 2016) 147–50.

[18] Pennington, *The Prince and the Law* 183.

[19] The former are commentators of papal legislation, the latter are commentators of imperial law.

> dicebatur quod dominus mundi esse, et omnia sua sunt. Post Christum verum enim imperium est apud Christum et eius vicarium, et per papam transfertur in principem secularem, ut extra de elect. Venerabilem.[20]

What this text is saying is that before the coming of Christ, the Emperor was the Master of the Whole World, actually possessing all things (*et omnia sua sunt*). After His coming, Christ assumed upon Himself such dominion and exercised it through His vicar, the pope, who in his own turn grants secular powers to mundane sovereigns. The old pagan *Dominus*, then Christ and the pope held *both swords* in their hands (*uterque gladius*) even if the pope could delegate the temporal power to princes. This is a patently theological-historical reconstruction, leading Bartolus to assert that:

> Et forte si quis diceret dominum imperatorem non esse dominum et monarcham totius orbis, esset hereticus, quia diceret contra determinationem ecclesiae, contra textum sancti evangeli, dum dicit 'Exivit edictum a Cesare Augusto ut describeretur totuts orbis universus', ut habet Luce ii, vel iii c.[21]

In this passage, Bartolus is stating that 'Whoever would say that the emperor is not lord and monarch of the *entire* world would become a heretic'. He derives his argument directly from the gospel of Luke referring to the census supposedly ordered by Caesar Augustus [Tiberius]. For Bartolus, since it is written that the emperor commanded a census of the whole word, then he who does not believe that the emperor is the lord of the world does not believe in the gospels. It follows that he is a heretic.

According to Pennington, this is just grandiose pro-imperial prose, as long as Bartolus also affirms that the emperor did not own all things and did not have jurisdiction over all kings.[22] But there is a deeper layer which perhaps counts more than jurisdiction and property, and that is legitimacy and hegemony. In Bartolus's statement he who *does not believe* that the emperor is *Dominus Mundi* is a heretic. It is a matter of *faith* and orthodoxy; a proposition from which we could derive that since all modern states do not believe the emperor to be *Dominus Mundi*, they are all equally heretic, maybe even demonic, entities. The world of modernity, in Bartolus's frame, would originate from the heterodoxy of having abandoned faith in the *Dominus Mundi*.

It is in this formulation of Bartolus that we may find one of the major arguments for our thesis. If the dominion of the emperor is not simply a matter of fact, or of law, but a matter of *faith*, then since we do not believe the emperor is the Lord of the World, we are all heretics. Thus, modernity originated from a fall. If it is so, as a consequence, no theory of political theology in a Schmittian sense could any longer be maintained. It is not that theological concepts became political, keeping their hidden theological connotations in a secularised world; rather, it is from

20 Bartolus [X 1.31.8 *Ad reprimendam*].
21 Bartolus [Dig 49.15.24]; see Pennington, *The Prince and the Law* 197.
22 Pennington, *The Prince and the Law* 183.

a heterodox inversion that political concepts evolved such that they acquired new meanings, giving birth to modernity.

If we, then, examine the cultural value of legal ontologies in framing the world of politics, we may subsequently find in Baldus de Ubaldis (1327–1400) another major and very relevant 'spiritual' shift. In his works, we see several passages where he is clearly asserting the role of the emperor as a Master of the World. First of all, in his *Consilia* he reports that '*verissimum est quod imperator est dominus mundi*' (it is absolutely true that the emperor is the Lord of the World) and that he has the authority over '*omnimodam iurisdictionem et potestatem supremam*' (every jurisdiction and supreme power).[23]

Here not only is the global power of the emperor stated as 'the soundest truth (*verissimum*)', but also the question of imperial dominion is explicitly put in terms of his overall jurisdiction and his *supreme* sovereignty. This sounds deeply modern, as it presupposes an elaborated theory of the existence of a *locus of supreme power*, which at the time resided in the imperial authority, at least notionally.

Many subsequent authors derived their opinions from those expressed by Baldus and Bartolus. For instance, Brunemann asserted in his *Commentaries* that '*Imperator est mundi Dominus*' and that he is *ratione protectionis* (the protector of his subjects), for the need to protect and defend his people. He affirms that the emperor's authority is universal, extending to all lands and to the sea:

> … quidem Imperator Orbis Christiani tum fuerit Dominus, cujus legibus non terra tantum, verum etiam mare parere debeat, sed in mari tamen non lege propria se iudicare velle.[24]

For Brunemann it is clear that the liberty of the sea depends on the will of the emperor as the supreme guardian of the whole globe.

But beyond these more technical points there is one in Baldus which deserves special attention. His assertion of imperial prerogatives made in the *Consilia* is strongly reinforced in his comment on the Peace of Constance (1183),[25] where an open parallel is maintained between the world sovereign and God as the prince of heavens, to the point that the emperor is called *vicarium suum*, a vicar of God himself. Here we find a typical imperial assertion against the pope that cannot be confined to the mere opposition between the two powers. The transcendent

[23] Baldus, *Consilia, sive Responsa* (Venetiis, Nicolinus, 1589) n 4436 with reference to Dig 14.2.9; Cod 7.37.3; Cod 1.14.12. On the various clashes concerning the different editions of Baldus see K Pennington, 'The Consilia of Baldus the Ubaldis' (1988) 56 *Tijdschrift voor Rechtsgeschiedenis* 85.

[24] J Brunnemann, *Commentarius in quinquaginta libros Pandectarum* (Coloniae, Fratrum Cramer, 1762) 571 (misprint in the original for p 471). A possible transation could be: '… the emperor was the Lord of the whole Christian world, whose laws extended not only to the land but also to the sea, but he did not have the intention to judge maritime cases according to his own laws'.

[25] Baldus, *De pace constantie tractatus subtilissimus* (Mediolanum, Johannes, Jacomo & Fratelli De Legnano, 1502); Baldus, *Commentaire sur la paix de Constance (1183)* (D Gorlier trans, Limoges, Pulim, 2016) v *Imperialis clementie*. See J Canning, *The Political Thought of Baldus de Ubaldis* (Cambridge, Cambridge University Press, 2003) 104–113.

dimension of the emperor as *Dominus Mundi* implies for Baldus that '*omnis anima subdita sit principi*'. Namely, that all the *souls* of the inhabitants of the world must be subjected to the imperial power. In this way, any oath taken in the name of God is also an oath delivered in the name of the emperor, since he is the 'Prince of the World' (*quia princeps mundi est*). Not only the bodies but also the souls of men are governed by the emperor as the prince of *this* world.

Baldus's conception of the legal value of oath—an argument deeply confronted by Agamben[26]—deserves close reading:[27]

> Ab omni juramento fidelitatis excipitur imperator quia princeps mundi est, et, ut ita dixerim, corporalis mundo deus ...

> The emperor is free from any oath of loyalty because he is Prince of the World and, I already said, a corporal god of the world ...

We can hardly deny that here Baldus displays a certain mystical conception of the body sovereign. This metaphor of the 'corporal god' is to be found also in the *Consilia*[28] in an advice given to Gian Galeazzo Visconti of Milan[29]—attempting to assert feudal rights over his vassals—and used by Matthaeus de Afflictis to the benefit of the King of France in a passage emphasised by Kantorowicz:[30]

> Rex quoad suos subditos in regno suo est tanquam [*sic*] quidam corporalis deus

Moreover, in this context, Baldus[31] reaches the point of adopting a biblical metaphor[32] to exalt the emperor, equating his glory to the brightness of the morning star:

> tamquam stella matutina in medio nebulae

> like the morning star among the clouds.

These images used by Baldus are dramatically *romantic* as they are relevant for the birth of modern sovereignty. In these passages the sovereign is analogised to the morning star among the clouds—a sublime view of a cloudy dawn—and the *Dominus Mundi*, described as *the prince of the world*, starts to become a *corporal god.*

[26] G Agamben, *The Sacrament of Language: An Archaeology of the Oath* (A Kotsko trans, Stanford, Stanford University Press, 2011).
[27] Baldus [Feud 2.55]; Baldus, *In Usus Feudorum* (Augustae Taurinorum, Nicolai Beuilaquae, 1578) 80 sub-s *De prohibita feudi alienatione per Federicum, Praeterea si inter duos*, n 23–24.
[28] Baldus, *Consilia* 1141, n 4. See K Pennington, *Pope and Bishops. The Papal Monarchy in the Twelfth and Thirteenth Centuries* (Philadelphia, University of Pennsylvania Press, 1984) 30.
[29] F Cengarle, 'Il Sole ducale (1430): a proposito di una divisa viscontea', in F Cengarle and MN Covini (eds), *Il ducato di Filippo Maria Visconti, 1412–1447. Economia, politica, cultura* (Firenze, Firenze University Press, 2015) 240.
[30] Mattheus de Afflictis [Lib Aug 1.6 n 32]; see E Kantorowicz, *The King's Two Bodies* 143.
[31] Baldus, *In Usus Feudorum* 80.
[32] Sirach [Ecclesiasticus] 50:6.

There is certainly here not only grandiose prose but also a romanticisation of power and authority, and something like an occult conception of it. What, then, could such a 'morning star' and 'corporal god' mean for Baldus? What does it mean for us to find such poetic imagery in law books? And how did these mystifying conceptions of authority enter the technical discourse on imperial prerogatives and possessions?

In reading Baldus, we are quite certainly leaving the quiet gallery of legal archeology to enter the inner rooms of what we can call the political sublime.

II. Imperial Messianism

A. The Corporate Eagle

In the West, the theory of the parallel between God and the emperor reached its ideological and poetic peak in the works of Dante, and in particular, in his *Comedy* (1308–1321).

Dante, as a political thinker, received renewed attention by Agamben,[33] but his theory of the universal monarchy also formed the object of the first book by the young Kelsen,[34] a champion of legal formalism and orthodoxy. As we know, Kelsen conceived his *pure theory of law* to depict the legal order as a mere *nexus* of valid norms whose content is substantially indifferent; a world of pure validity indifferent to any meaning. In this sense, Schmitt became his major opponent. For Kelsen, the *Grundnorm*—the fundamental norm from which all other norms derive their validity—is a pure logical postulate. Schmitt, however, maintained the conception of the constitution as a concrete order based on a material apprehension and division of spaces and resources. While Kelsen was indifferent to any actual location of the legal order, and to any possible transcendent background of it, Schmitt emphasised spatial considerations and political theology. It is, then, of particular interest that the young Kelsen devoted his research to Dante, whose book *On Monarchy* (around 1310) contemplates an ideal universal world government based on the exquisite theological parallel with the cosmic rule of the Lord.

Kelsen's appraisal is as simple as it is anachronistic, but it can give us an insight into the way in which the most orthodox of twentieth-century jurists could reformulate Dante's conceptions. For him, Dante represented the last voice of the dying breed of believers in a world empire, destined to be superseded in the Renaissance by Machiavelli and Bodin as the modern thinkers on sovereignty and the state. Dante imagines God's own monarchy as encompassing the whole universe,[35]

[33] G Agamben, *Pilate and Jesus* (A Kotsko trans, Stanford, Stanford University Press, 2015) 39.
[34] H Kelsen, *Die Staatslehre des Dante* (Wien, F Deuticke, 1905).
[35] Dante Alighieri, *Monarchy* (P Shaw ed, Cambridge, Cambridge University Press, 1996) I, chs 6–7.

of which the earthly empire is just a copy or an imitation.[36] It is certainly not difficult to trace this model back to the imperial ideology that could be based on the *Digest* and the imitation of Byzantine models. Dante's universe, as we know, is strongly rooted in a sort of theological geography, as it is based on the depiction of a void earth at whose centre is located Satan, the prince of evil *and of gravity*, sitting at the end of an immense cone constituting his proper kingdom, hell. Above this huge void, in the midst of the ocean, is the Mount of Redemption—almost a mound on Satan's grave—which is pointing towards the skies. At its peak we find the Purgatory which souls must ascend to eventually reach heaven. At the opposite side of the earth, we find Jerusalem laying at the very centre of the emerged lands.[37]

The notion of *Dominus Mundi* and its associated ideology is easily illustrated by Dante's cosmography. The Master of the World is an earthly copy of God, reigning on a block of land. The conquest of Jerusalem is geopolitically relevant as the conquest of the very centre of this land. The proper habitat of human society is, then, a thin slice between the heavens above and the hell below attracting bodies as gravity does.

In these terms, there is no doubt that Dante believed in a universal legitimate lordship as the best possible government:

> The whole of mankind in its ideal state depends on the unity which is men's wills. But this cannot be unless there is one will which controls and directs all the others towards one goal, since the wills of mortals require guidance on the account of the seductive pleaser of youth, as Aristotle teaches at the end of the Ethics. Nor can such a single will exist, unless there is one ruler who rules over everybody, whose will can control and guide all the other wills.[38]

In the second part of *Monarchy*, Dante offers a historical demonstration of how in the past it was Rome that ruled the world rightfully for this purpose so that a 'perfect monarchy' was set up 'under the immortal Augustus',[39] with the German emperor representing Rome's legacy.[40]

Nevertheless, what we are mainly interested in is the peculiar theological role assigned by Dante to the emperor Justinian, both as *Dominus Mundi* and as the great codifier of Roman law. Notwithstanding his dubious moral character, Dante depicts him in *Paradise* as one inspired by God to undertake the 'high task', since it was through God's inspiration that Justinian created the *Codex*.[41]

[36] Dante Alighieri, *Monarchy*, III, ch 16.

[37] Dante Alighieri, *The Divine Comedy* (EH Wilkins and T Goddard Bergin eds, Cambridge, Harvard University Press, 1965) Hell, XXXIV, vv 106–126.

[38] Dante Alighieri, *Monarchy*, I, ch 25, sub-s 27.

[39] Dante Alighieri, *Monarchy*, I, ch 26, sub-s 28. See also M Koskenniemi, 'International Community from Dante to Vattel' in V Chetail and P Haggenmacher (eds), *Vattel's International Law from a XXIst Century Perspective* (Leiden, Nijhoff, 2011) 49.

[40] Dante Alighieri, *Monarchy*, IV, ch 9, sub-ss 69–80.

[41] Dante Alighieri, *The Divine Comedy*, Paradise, VI, vv 23–24.

The most intriguing visual image Dante used in relation to Justinian is an intricate description of the imperial eagle. Justinian's speech occupies the entire 6th *Canto* of *Paradise,* starting from showing the eagle, the sacred emblem of the empire ('*sacratissimo segno*', or the most sacred of signs), as it races through the ages.[42]

Dante introduces this *segno* as a personified subject with the effect of making it an actor, by means of conceits and intricate scholastic discussions on the relationship between the signifier and the signified, as well as long theological inquiries on the meaning of Christ's death at the peak of Roman imperial strength. We encounter this eagle again in the 18th *Canto*, when we learn that its body is composed of souls represented by bundles of lights:

> With each light settled quietly into place,
> I saw that the array of fire had shaped
> the image of an eagle's head and neck.
> He who paints there has no one as His guide: He guides Himself; in Him we recognize
> the shaping force the flows from nest to nest.[43]

And in the 20th *Canto* the eagle introduces the six souls that make up its eye, probably intended as the all-seeing eye of the law.[44]

The image of the eagle is highly complex, but one thing is certain and it is that the empire of the *Dominus* is represented as a corporate body of souls. This main feature has been marvellously illustrated in an illumination—as displayed in Image 2—created during the first half of the fifteenth century and attributed to Giovanni di Paolo di Grazia.

Dante's Eagle, By Giovanni di Paolo di Grazia[45]

[42] Dante Alighieri, *The Divine Comedy*, Paradise, VI, v 32.

[43] Dante Alighieri, *The Divine Comedy*, Paradise, XVIII, vv 106–111.

[44] Dante Alighieri, *The Divine Comedy*, Paradise, XX.

[45] www.bl.uk/catalogues/illuminatedmanuscripts/ILLUMIN.ASP?Size=mid&IllID=56969; Yates Thompson 36 f 162, The eagle of Justice, British Library Catalogue of Illuminated Manuscripts.

The 'corporate' body of the empire is perfectly portrayed here as a composite body assuming the shape of the imperial eagle. The eagle in turn became identified with Justinian himself as 'the' emperor *par excellence*, in the sense that he gave the world its rational law, as derived from the providential Roman historical evolution. The Roman people acted as God's instrument in establishing the imperial office, which existed by God's authority and the people's ministry. The image of the eagle conveys both the idea of a providential political salvation and that of the Roman people as a whole forming the body of the Empire reunited in the *persona* of the *Dominus Mundi*. The people of Rome, as a corporation, conferred all the powers to the emperor *through the Lex Regia* (Dig 1.2.1)—as we have seen already portrayed in the pedestal of Antoninus' column—to the point of forming its own composite body.

These are ideas that can easily be traced back in the literature to the civilians of the thirteenth and fourteenth centuries. For Baldus, the *Lex Regia* was the form of the event which gave meaning to the empire, the papacy, the rule of kings and city regimes,[46] and that, consequently, could be interpreted through the other concepts available in the *Corpus juris*. For him, the *Lex Regia* could stand as a model for the origins of monarchical and other political powers. But what is more important for us is the conception that Baldus had of the *populus* as a corporate legal person, as he applied the corporation theory to all citizen-bodies. In his works, terms such as *civitas*, *communitas*, *corpus*, and even *universitas* are often used interchangeably and can refer to the *populus* when it constitutes the unified body of the citizens.[47]

Dante's image, then, clearly represents the ontological and visual reality attributed to the sovereign as a *corporate body* constituted by the bodies of his subjects. This image must be kept in mind in relation to Baldus's depiction of the *Dominus Mundi* as a *corporal god*, and we can legitimately consider whether it was a source of the famous frontispiece of Hobbes. We know that Hobbes was indebted to Roman lawyers, especially in his theory on sovereignty.[48] Can this well-known frontispiece be an illustration of Baldus's and other civilians' passages? Can it be imagined as an unexpected and dramatic *inversion* of the imperial corporate eagle? For Dante, the corporate body of the *Dominus Mundi* is represented by the image of a dignified eagle wandering in the heavenly skies, but for Hobbes it will become a creeping serpent slithering over a mountain. Can this change in imagery mark a dramatic as well as a *demonological turn* of the concept of earthly sovereignty and its consequent apparatus? What were the hidden streams of political consciousness that led to this change?

Our task now is to carefully consider the imperial messianism which characterised the political actions of Frederick I and his grandson Frederick II, and which

[46] See Baldus [Feud 1.5]; Canning, *The Political Thought of Baldus de Ubaldis* 62, 185–87.

[47] See Baldus [Cod 7.53.5]; Canning, *The Political Thought of Baldus de Ubaldis* 141.

[48] See D Lee, 'Hobbes and the Civil Law. The Use of Roman Law in Hobbes's Civil Science' in D Dyzenhaus and T Poole (eds), *Hobbes and the Law* (Cambridge, Cambridge University Press, 2012) 227, 235.

led to the exceptional intervention of the pope in excommunicating and deposing the Lord of the World.

B. Barbarossa and the Peace of God Movement

Now that we have discussed the revival of the *Dominus Mundi* at Roncaglia and the consequences derived by jurists, as well as the puzzling mystic of the empire witnessed by Baldus and by Dante, we can investigate the framework of Frederick I's political action and its ideological bases.

In 1152, at 28 years old, Frederick was elected King of the Romans by an assembly of princes and bishops. At the time, Roger II (1112–1154) was still on the throne of Sicily, and Henry II (1154–1189) would soon become King of England and Duke of Normandy. Later on during Frederick's reign, Philip Augustus (1180–1223) would be crowned King of France.

Within months of his election, Frederick issued his first 'peace statute', asserting imperial jurisdiction over violent crimes and disputes over land property and possession. He was formally crowned emperor in 1155 in a ceremony in Rome which, notwithstanding its location, was carefully designed to symbolise his independence from papal power. It is during this journey to Rome that we are told he met with the professors of the law school in Bologna. A few years later, in 1158, Frederick relied on the civilian doctors to design the legislation concerning the essence of his royal prerogatives at the Diet of Roncaglia. For this reason, the decisions reached in that assembly amounted to a sort of constitution of the imperial status coping with the yet undefined prerogatives of sovereignty. In a way, Frederick provoked two opposite but parallel evolutions: on one hand, the never well-defined powers of the emperor were tentatively framed into words, granting them more legitimacy, and on the other hand, his powers became more limited just because they became less uncertain. The political theological apparatus of imperial prerogatives displayed all the intricacies of pre-modern sovereignty: an emperor elected by his subordinates, to be crowned by the pope, governing by the grace of God, but in need of an oath of fidelity from his subjects. At the same time, he was an overall universal lord *de jure*, but one who could hardly effectively control *de facto* most of his territories. He was both a political and a religious figure connected with the salvation of his people.

Nevertheless, the *climax* of the Roncaglia statutes can be found in the statement that all jurisdiction and all judicial powers belong to the prince, and all judges must accept office from the prince and must swear an oath as required by law[49]—a climax that was reached as a peak in the path of the 'peace of God

[49] Constitutio Habita in W Stelzer (ed), 'Zum Scholarenprivileg Friedrick Barbarossas (Authentica Habita)' (1978) *Deutsches Archiv fur Erforschung des Mittelalters* 123–165, upon which see also HJ Berman, *Law and Revolution, I: The Formation of the Western Legal Tradition* (Cambridge, Harvard University Press, 1983) 490.

movement' (*Gottesfrieden*).[50] From this perspective, Roncaglia was preceded by a series of proclamations of the 'advent of peace' in southern France, Normandy, and elsewhere, especially in Germany, though normally limited to certain times, places and groups of people. Princes and dukes issued statutes throughout the twelfth and thirteenth centuries framed through the Latin expressions of *constitutio pacis*, *pax terrae*, or *Landfriede* (the peace of the land) and exacted from their subjects an oath to observe the peace imposed through ecclesiastical sanctions, like excommunication, for violations. Of course, we see in this movement the evident meaninglessness of a lay/religious distinction as applied to that age. The first secular peace statute issued by an emperor appeared in 1103, followed by several additional imperial peace proclamations. These statutes were also accompanied by various similar provisions in Swabia, Bavaria, Saxony, Hennegau and Alsace, for instance. The scope and content of the peace statutes were gradually extended and they came to be concerned not only with the prevention of violence (blood feuds and duels), but also with the preservation of public order generally, including matters of an economic nature.

We may, as Berman and others did, fully appreciate this legislation by comparing the earlier proclamations of peace with the peace statutes issued by Frederick Barbarossa between 1152 and 1186 and with the one promulgated by his grandson Frederick II at Mainz in 1235.

In order to take effect, the Bavarian peace statute of 1094 needed to be sworn by the Bavarian agnates assembled at a diet. The statute contained seven very short articles. The first imperial peace statute, issued at Mainz in 1103, was rather similar in style and scope to the Bavarian one.[51] It also required the oaths of the agnates and the people, and was to last for four years. Frederick's first peace statute, issued in 1152, differed greatly from these earlier examples because it stated only that Frederick was emperor of the Romans by the grace of God and he was also august for all the bishops, the dukes, the counts, the margraves and the officials who received the document.[52]

In its text, the statute set no time limit for peace, and there was no mention of oaths. The emperor had acquired the power to unilaterally proclaim the peace of the kingdom to preserve the right (*jus*) of all persons. This transformation is all the more apparent in the already mentioned climax reached at the Diet of Roncaglia in 1158, when Frederick issued another peace statute as well as other related pieces of legislation. The statute was addressed to 'all the subjects of his

[50] HEJ Cowdrey, 'The Peace and the Truce of God in the Eleventh Century' (1970) 46 *Past and Present* 42; G Duby, *The Laity and the Peace of God. The Age of Chivalry* (C Postan trans, London, Edward Arnold, 1977); T Head and R Landes, *The Peace of God: Social Violence and Religious Response in France around 1000* (Ithaca, Cornell University Press, 1995).

[51] See Berman, *Law and Revolution* I 493–94. For all the original sources see L Weinrich (ed), *Quellen zu deutscher Verfassungs-Wirtschaft und Sozialgeschichte bis 1250. Ausgewallte Quellen zur deutschen Geschichte des Mittelalter* (Darmstadt, Wissenschaftliche Buchgesellschaft, 1977).

[52] Berman, *Law and Revolution* I 465.

empire', even if it required the oath as a necessary device for its validity, taking the form of a social non-aggression agreement.

Article 2 of the Roncaglia peace statute expressly provided that if anyone believed that he had a right against anyone in any cause or transaction, he should resort to the judicial power and through it he should pursue his appropriate right.[53] Heavy financial penalties were imposed on anyone who was presumed to violate the aforesaid peace. In this way, as may be easily understood, the proclamation of a general and perennial peace consisted in the enforcement of rights by the judicial power which fell under the control of the emperor since all jurisdictions and judicial power were vested in him. Thus, the concentration of all powers was pursued and attained not through a proclamation of a state of exception, but through the proclamation of universal peace as the normal state of the world. And, for our purposes, this ideological apparatus is much more important than the futility of Frederick's policy, since his empire was never really in a condition to become the strong, centralised territorial state that he presumably planned.

First of all, the Roncaglia statute was clearly intended to be legislation and not merely a restatement of customary or ancient law, for it concludes with the order that this law (*lex*) has to be inserted among the imperial decrees under the title '*Ne filius pro patre, etc*' (post Cod Liber IV, 13.5). Barbarossa's instruction was then duly followed and his decree was inserted in the *Novellae*, the collection of legislative acts integrating the *Codex* of Justinian, and so they became part of the very *corpus*, or body, of the Roman law. Secondly, the emperor acquired an unlimited dominion over all the jurisdictions of the empire, an achievement that was explicitly marked—in messianic terms—as a *reformatio totius orbis*, a reform of the whole world. The 'advent of peace', and related universal imperial jurisdiction, would mark the triumph of the 'last of emperors', after whom the Day of Judgment could arrive inaugurating the post-historical age of eternity. The point has been roundly established by Peter Munz: 'we cannot avoid the conclusion that Frederick … was confirmed in his belief that he was to be the last emperor'.[54]

We think that it was such a *sublime* vision which underlay Frederick's plans to undertake a new crusade to liberate Jerusalem and the Holy Sepulchre from the infidels; a liberation that—as we have seen when considering Dante's geography—was understood as an essential part of the apocalyptic drama, as long as Jerusalem represented the centre of the earth. If this is true, the consequence to be drawn is that we should reconsider in its full proper value the messianic character of Frederick's politics and his reassessment of the emperor as a *Dominus Mundi*. This assertion assumes a completely different feature if we take it at its face value as that of the Lord who has to fulfil the economy of salvation, bringing the world government to its ultimate end. In this way, the emperor becomes the one who must

[53] See H Koeppler, 'Frederick Barbarossa and the School of Bologna. Some remarks on the Authentica Habita' (1939) 54 *The English Historical Review* 577.

[54] P Munz, *Frederick Barbarossa: A Study in Mediaeval Politics* (Ithaca, Cornell University Press, 1969) 31.

provoke, not refrain, the advent of the Antichrist which must precede the Second Coming. Frederick did not represent a Schmittian *katechon*[55] resisting the forces of evil, but rather he who has the task to provoke their final appearance, fulfilling the end of government. It is in this way that we must appraise the strong commitment of Frederick toward the importance both of peace through law, and of justice through the law. The emperor's mission to secure peace and to do justice was the sign of his appointment by God to fulfil the divine plan of salvation, in the sense of an ultimately trans-political end of the universal empire, concerning not so much the bodies but the souls of his subjects. From this standpoint, Frederick I was an 'apocalyptic sovereign' in the most strict sense of the expression.

Frederick's imperial project received a peculiar artistic form in the work of the so-called 'Archpoet'. The Archpoet was an anonymous poet, probably born in 1130 and died in 1165, who was from 1161 at the service of Rheinald von Dassel, the chancellor of Frederick I.[56] Author of *Confessio Goliae*, the Archpoet was represented as a character in Eco's novel *Baudolino*, and one of the identified poets whose texts have been collected in the *Carmina Burana*. He also composed in the 1160s a poem entitled '*Salve mundi domine, Caesar noster ave*'.

This 'Hail Caesar, Lord of the World'—as we can easily translate it—proves that the title of *Dominus Mundi* could be used in a political ideological context even before any actual technical translation of legal texts from the jurists. It is immaterial to consider whether this hymn to Frederick I was written as a joke or seriously, if it was great or mediocre poetry. What does matter is the simple *use* of the title in question, mocking the long discussions of sceptical scholars on the possibility that Frederick could have attempted to interpret his own prerogatives as those pertaining to a Master of the World.

Salve mundi domine, Cesar noster ave!
cuius bonis omnibus iugum est suave;
quisquis contra calcitrat putans illud grave,
obstinati cordis est et cervicis prave.
Princeps terre principum, Cesar Friderice,
cuius tuba titubant arces inimice,
tibi colla subdimus, tygres et formice
et cum cedris Libani vepres et mirice.
...
Imperator nobilis, age sicut agis!
sicut exaltatus es, exaltare magis!

[55] A Greek term meaning 'restrainer' adopted by St Paul (2 Thessalonians 2:6–12) to denote that power which must resist chaos in the interval between the First and the Second Coming. Schmitt used this same term to frame the role of the Christian Emperor: see C Schmitt, *The Nomos of the Earth in the International Law of the Jus Publicum Europaeum* (GL Ulmen trans, New York, Telos Press Publishing, 2006) 59–60.

[56] J Eberle, *Die Gedichte des Archipoeta: Lateinisch und deutsch* (Frankfurt am Main, Insel Verlag, 1966) 80; W Stach, *Salve, mundi domine! Kommentierende Betrachtungen zum Kaiserhymnus des Archipoeta* (Leipzig, Sächsische Akademie der Wissenschaften. Berichte. Philologisch-historische Klasse, 1939) 33–49.

fove tuos subditos, hostes cede plagis
super eos irruens ultione stragis!

In this poem Frederick is expressly nominated as Lord of the World and king of kings, as well as *exalted* to a more than human status. Without plunging into further considerations, we face here an exaltation of the role of the *Dominus* in the context of an imperial ideology that is perfectly reflected, for instance in the later *Gloss* of Johannes Teutonicus, which appeared between 1215 and 1219:

> Est autem imperator iste super omnes reges ... et omnes nationes sub eo sunt ... Ipse enim est dominus mundi ... etiam Judei sub eo sunt ... et omnes provinciae sub eo sunt.[57]

We can translate this passage as the assertion that the emperor stands above all other kings, and that all nations and provinces are subject to him, even the Jews. This is a significant point. He is the lord of the whole world, so much so that *even* the Jews are under his jurisdiction, which means that his dominion is larger than that of the pope, as it is truly universal. Nevertheless, with the passing of time, witnessing the continuation of this imperial ideology, the title of Master of the World entered into the ordinary lexicon as '*Ipse enim est princeps mundi et dominus*'.[58]

Such a poetic use of the Latin formula of the *Dominus Mundi* during the same approximate time as the Diet increases the plausibility of the story of a dialogue between Frederick, Bulgarus and Martinus, and in particular, the plausibility that Frederick really advanced his universal claim to legitimate world government. And what is even more relevant here is the messianic project of a complete reform of the whole world (*reformatio totius orbis*), which deeply transformed the emperor-*Dominus* into the revolutionary figure destined to realise the end of history, a *sublime* project which immediately casts a trembling light upon the romanticisation of the life of his grandson, Frederick II, that was portrayed by Ernst Kantorowicz.

III. The Lord of the Flies

A. Kantorowicz and the Romanticisation of the *Dominus*

Now that we have laid the premises for an analysis of world dominion claims in the West, we should consider the impact of recurring theories of power on our current political and legal thought, especially those raised in the 1920s and 1930s by such eminent scholars as Bloch and Kantorowicz.

[57] Johannes Teutonicus, *Apparatus Glossarum in Compilationem Tertiam*, 1 MIC (1981) gloss to 3 Comp 1.6.19 v *in Germanos* 84–85.

[58] Accursius, *Glossa in Digestum vetum* in *Corpus Glossatorum Iuris Civilis*, vol 7 (M Viora ed, Torino, Officina Erasmiana, 1969) gloss to X 1.6.34 v *Transtulit in Germanos*: 'Ipse enim est princeps mundi et dominus'. On the complex history of the text of Accursius see now HH Jakobs, *Hugolinusglossen im accursischen Apparat zum Digestum vetus. Studien zur europäischen Rechtsgeschichte* (Frankfurt am Main, Klostermann, 2017).

What we shall do in this section is first to analyse the romanticisation of the subject of *Dominus Mundi*, which lays at the heart of the work of Kantorowicz on Frederick II. Then, we shall emphasise the magic elements of kingship as appraised by Bloch to reformulate the genealogy of modern sovereignty. In so doing, we shall try to reinforce the distinction, and the opposition, between a theology of sovereignty and a demonology of power that can be perceived in the folkloric element of the magic royalty. Finally, we will plunge into the details of the deposition of Frederick II by the pope through the studies of Saint-Bonnet,[59] since they uncover the roots of the 'modern' theory of the state of exception. As we will show, this theory derived from a disjuncture between the spiritual and the temporal, between the government of the souls and the government of the bodies.

If we then re-analyse Kantorowicz's work on Frederick II[60] (1220–50)—a very influential book at the time, especially in right wing circles[61]—we can easily grasp that the eighth chapter is entitled and entirely devoted to '*Dominus Mundi*', and the final chapter is dedicated to the '*Antichrist*'. What is, then, the boundary between the former and the latter? How can the representative of the Lord as an established legitimate monarch become the Enemy, and the adversary of God Himself?

The chapter on the *Dominus Mundi* starts with a phrase of Frederick II as a clear statement of his legitimate world lordship. Independently from any lawyer's advice or rescript, this still sounds like the most prominent assertion of a claim to global dominion: 'Tho' we cannot everywhere be present *in the flesh*, yet our restraining hand is felt even to remotest frontiers on earth'.[62] This phrase, according to Kantorowicz, would be 'characteristic of Frederick and his *sacrum imperium*', he who '*with mysterious power* sucked the *whole globe* into the vortex of his strife with Rome'. A project destined to fail, because eventually '… his dash for the City of Cities, whose possession would *magically* have assured his world dominion, has *unfortunately* failed'. We can hardly say that on this point the tone of Kantorowicz is objective. In a way, Kantorowicz is perpetrating a narrative about Frederick which has nevertheless been based on his myth. This myth of Frederick, as a powerful political remnant capable of lasting for centuries, was nurtured by Kantorowicz's portrayal of him that caused him to become an Antichrist for the Church and a Saviour and a Messiah for his enthusiastic followers:

> The world held its breath to catch the wing-beat of those birds of fate which in the starry heavens should hover round the Prince of the Last Days… I am Frederick, the Hammer, the Doom of the world. Rome … shall shiver to atoms and never again be the Lord of the World.

[59] F Saint-Bonnet, *L'état d'exception* (Paris, Presses Universitaires de France, 2001).

[60] E Kantorowicz, *Frederick the Second: 1194–1250* (EO Lorimer trans, New York, Frederick Ungar Publishing Co, 1957) 603.

[61] RE Lerner, *Ernst Kantorowicz: a Life* (Princeton, Princeton University Press, 2017) 115 with special reference to Hitler who is said to have read the book twice and gifted a copy to Mussolini. We should remember that Kantorowicz was a Jew and deeply regretted his book's influence.

[62] This passage and those that follow are to be found in Kantorowicz, *Frederick the Second* 519, emphasis added.

In this dramatic presentation of the emperor a crucial point is certainly played by the title of *Dominus Mundi* and its strong ambiguity '… for Satan also was the Lord of the World'.[63] Thus Frederick could be simultaneously the Bringer of Absolute Good or of Absolute Evil. In either case, he was the 'Expected One'. Kantorowicz reports Frederick as saying: 'The earth obeyth us *and the sea doeth homage* and all that we desire cometh forthwith to pass'.[64]

In these passages we fully witness, as we said, the threshold between a theological and demonological dimension of sovereignty. What seemed to the Church so satanic, so acutely dangerous, was the particular pregnancy that the title of *Dominus Mundi* could acquire if used by a messianic emperor. This is especially the case because Frederick's followers gave him new titles to honour him and his mission, and they certainly hinted of heterodox cult. He became the one 'versed in the divine plans', and the one 'ceaselessly illuminated by the eye of God', as Kantorowicz reports.

From a purely historical perspective, it is important to remember that the grandson of Frederick Barbarossa and of Roger II, the Norman King of Sicily, Frederick II, dominated a considerable geopolitical space to the point of being not only the real master of the continental Europe but also the effective ruler of the Mediterranean Sea. His approach followed mostly that of Frederick I, reaching a high point in the Mainz peace statute promulgated in 1235. The statute of Mainz[65] was a deliberate use of legal reform as a means of reviving imperial unity, which was nevertheless destined to become seriously weakened at the end of his reign in 1250.[66]

From our own perspective, the most relevant disposition is contained in article 5, stating that no one shall avenge himself before bringing his complaint before a judge, except that he may immediately repel force by force if necessary for the protection of his body or goods, that is, in case of 'necessary defence'. Here, we are facing a decree defining in explicit terms the 'state of exception' and the legitimate use of force within it, a case in which the peace of the empire could be lawfully suspended and self-help allowed.

Article 28 provides a justiciar to be appointed to chair the daily working of the imperial court, whenever the emperor could not be 'personally present', reserving the most important cases to the emperor's 'personal investigation and judgment'. This means that in exceptional cases all subjects could be captured in the liminal zone of imperial discretion. An interplay of norms created in the context of mystic conceptions of the emperor's *presence*, but with the more than superficial transition from an orthodox theology toward a rather heterodox conception of his sovereignty.

[63] Kantorowicz, *Frederick the Second* 520.
[64] Kantorowicz, *Frederick the Second* 520–21.
[65] 2 MGH (L Weiland ed, 1896) IV, 2.
[66] See Berman, *Law and Revolution* I 499–500.

As a matter of fact, it was Pier delle Vigne (1190–1249)—whom Dante put in hell amongst those who committed suicide in Canto XIII of *Inferno*—and his circle of jurists and *literati* who had the largest part in creating the stunning figure of his master as a saviour emperor, to the point of seeing the pope as the false one, and Frederick as the *true* Vicar of Christ. For this reason, Pier delle Vigne was compared to Saint Peter, Prince of the Apostles of this new imperial cult, and Kantorowicz advances, with some credibility, the development of an 'imperial church' composed by the 'jurist hierarchy', something which would transform the association of lawyers into a heterodox body led by an anti-pope.

All of this, of course, may represent a rather important turning point: the definition of the empire as a church, an *imperialis ecclesia*, celebrating the *Dominus Mundi* through a *sacratissimum ministerium*, the solemn exotic ritual of the High Court where the 'incarnated law' (*lex animata in terris*) could be revealed in the emperor's persona. In this ritual of the imperial presence, we may obviously find an element of imitation of the Eastern empire, as Frederick assumed his counterpart's title of 'Wonder of the World' (*Stupor Mundi*). There is also something alchemic, or proximate to witchcraft, as he was also called the 'Great Transformer'. What we want to suggest is that in this context, elaborated by lay *literati* such as Pier delle Vigne, the theological models of worship of the emperor as *Dominus* may have been mixed with some qualities of magic, starting a particular evolution toward a royal occultism.

A clear sign of the magic surrounding Frederick may be seen in the association that spread all over Europe between him and the esoteric figure of Prester John, a fabulous king of the 'order of Melchizedek'—a mysterious title mentioned in the Letter to the Hebrews (7:1) with reference to Christ as the perennial High Priest of the Church. This fabulous king had to come from the East to obliterate the teachings of Mohammed and to unite Jerusalem with the King of the West, the Roman emperor, fulfilling the prophecies on the end of time. The air was so full with eschatology that many Jewish communities believed that this King, appearing under the rule of Frederick, was King David returning as Messiah to redeem them. The messianic turmoil was strengthened by the consideration that the year 1240 corresponded to the biblical year 5,000, the first year of the crucial sixth millennium, in some esoteric speculations. A typical messianic act was indeed fulfilled by Frederick II when he married Isabella II of Jerusalem in 1225 and immediately seized the kingdom of Jerusalem from her father, John of Brienne, in a coup.[67] The role of pope Honorius III (1216–1227), who acted as an intermediary between the two kings of Jerusalem, remained ambivalent, despite the traditional interpretation that he was appalled by the coup and tried to recover John's throne. In this case, the pope was a strong supporter of Frederick, with whom he was working

[67] TW Smith, 'Between Two Kings: Pope Honorius III and the Seizure of the Kingdom of Jerusalem by Frederick II in 1225' (2015) 41 *Journal of Medieval History* 42.

closely to achieve the long awaited imperial crusade to the Holy Land, yet he also appeared to champion the claim of John as the rightful king of Jerusalem.

Kantorowicz's chapter on the *Dominus Mundi* ends with the death of Gregory IX (1227–1241), who excommunicated Frederick in 1225 for his claims to a global spiritual overlordship, a claim that would have actually rendered Frederick the sole Lord in matters temporal as well as spiritual, a real *Dominus Mundi*.[68] Eventually Frederick was not only excommunicated, but was also *deposed* by Gregory's successor, pope Innocent IV (1243–1254)—for perjury and breach of the peace—at the Council of Lyons, where Frederick was defined as a 'Proteus', incapable of being caught because he constantly changed his form through *metamorphosis*, which is also one of the main magical features of the Devil.

In the words of Kantorowicz, Frederick received the blow with 'pain and wrath and scorn' while he was in Turin, in the north of Italy, and reacted by placing one of his many crowns on his head. Now that he had become an 'Antichrist' and was defined as the 'Scourge of the World', he turned to his followers with a new saying: 'I have been anvil long enough … Now I shall play the hammer!'.[69] This rather dramatic and romantic cry much later led Nietzsche, who also eventually found himself in Turin, to hail the *Dominus* Frederick as one of his nearest kin.[70] It was an outstanding reference, which brings us one step further towards the understanding of the possible heterodox role of the *Dominus*. Our main point resides precisely in this *dark romantic* ambiguity—revealed in the text of Kantorowicz—of the existence of a threshold between the theological and the demoniac. This is left open by the very literal formulation of the expression of *Dominus Mundi* as the Lord of *this* World[71] and therefore in the magic 'sublime-kitsch' element that can surround the political sovereign, and thus the political as such.

This sublime *and* kitsch element is reinforced in the final chapter of the book on Frederick. Kantorowicz appends to this last chapter a grandiose epigraph that was originally attributed to Goethe,[72] but also used by Schmitt and Moltmann:

> Nemo contra Deum nisi Deus Ipse.
> Nobody can stand against God but God Himself

A strange mixture of an occult flavour pervades the whole of Kantorowicz's scholarly studies, and yet few commentators on Kantorowicz's work have sufficiently highlighted the tremendous heterodox importance of this epigraph.

[68] Kantorowicz, *Frederick the Second* 561.

[69] Kantorowicz, *Frederick the Second* 599.

[70] "[…] einem meiner Nāchstverwandten": F Nietzsche, *Ecce homo*, § 4, *EH-ZA-4 (02/01/1889)* in F Nietzsche, *Werke, Complete Critical Edition* (G Colli and M Montinari eds, Berlin, Walter de Gruyter, 1967).

[71] Luke 2:1. On the possible connections between Luke and the text of the *Digest* in medieval interpretations see C Fasolt *The Limits of History* (Chicago, The University of Chicago Press, 2004) 156–58, also with reference to Grotius.

[72] JW Goethe, *Goethes Werke: illustrierte Auswahl mit Einl. und erklär. Anmerkungen im Verein mit mehreren Goethefreunden*, vol 6 (H Steuding ed, Leipzig, Albrecht Seemann Verlag, 1905) 588.

As we said, the same citation was used by Moltmann right in the middle of his masterpiece on *The Crucified God*, one of the seminal texts of twentieth-century theology,[73] without any reference to Kantorowicz but with a direct reference to Carl Schmitt's *Politische Theologie*.[74] Since Moltmann is a famous anti-Nazi theologian it is rather paradoxical that we may find a key role assigned to Schmitt at the centre of his conception of the Cross. According to Moltmann, Schmitt rightly remarks: 'If a unity is a duality and consequently the possibility of an uproar, a stasis, is immanent, then theology seems to become "stasiology"': something which would inscribe the very essence of political crisis (*stasis*) at the centre of trinitarianism.

Moltmann attributes this rather occult and *dualist* saying to Goethe's *Dichtung und Wahrheit* 'at the beginning of book IV'. But, as a matter of fact, the quotation appears in the fourth part of book 20 and it concerns the 'daemonic element' and its manifestations.

When Schmitt used this phrase, he referred to it as coming—through Goethe—from JM Lenz (1751–1792) and his drama *Catharina von Siena*.[75]

Kantorowicz does not offer any source for this quotation.

For Schmitt, this saying expresses the content of the *stasis* as the 'height of the legal suspension provoked in a state of exception', and as such it is then perhaps at the heart of his rather occult emphasis of it as *the void centre* of the legal order: *normality is nothing, the exception explains everything*.[76] On the other hand, Moltmann, a famous anti-Nazi theologian, acknowledges that the theory of Schmitt—as hideous as it can be—casts an important light upon the crucifixion and its mysteries, to be interpreted as a kind of cosmic state of exception, but in the sense of the final disappearance of every scheme of friend or foe: 'If the conflict in God is overcome by God himself, the external conclusion is: 'All feuds now have an end'.[77]

What could this saying mean for Kantorowicz in relation to Frederick II, who was at the same time the *Dominus* and the *Antichrist*?

In the words of Kantorowicz,[78] Frederick—after the excommunication—became the demon in whom all the evil of the world was incarnate but he *remained* 'him who ruleth over earth *and* sea', the *formula* of the *Digest*. He was no longer associated with the jurists, poets and artists, but rather in conspiracy with witches, wizards and astrologists.

[73] J Moltmann, *The Crucified God: The Cross of Christ as the Foundation and Criticism of Christian Theology* (RA Wilson and J Bowden trans, Minneapolis, Fortress Press, 1993) 158, fn 74.

[74] C Schmitt, *Political Theology. II. The Myth of the Closure of any Political Theology* (M Hoelzl and G Ward trans, Cambridge, Polity Press, 2008) 126.

[75] See JMR Lenz, *Catharina von Siena* [1777?] in *Dramtischer Nachlass von J M.R. Lenz* (K Weinhold ed, Frankfurt, Ruten and Loening, 1884).

[76] G Frankenberg, *Political Technology and the Erosion of the Rule of Law: Normalizing the State of Exception* (H Bauer and G Frankenberg trans, Cheltenham, Edward Elgar, 2015) 107.

[77] Moltmann, *The Crucified God* 159, fn 74.

[78] Kantorowicz, *Frederick the Second* 605–608.

> Ceasar, Messiah, Antichrist … these are the three fundamental identical manifestations of Frederick II … since the beginning of his World Rule.

Maybe the striking point underlined by Kantorowicz is that the whole life of Frederick, and his own *persona*, could be explained *both* in a messianic *as well as* in a demonic sense. Frederick could be satanic or divine, because, perhaps there is a *political* threshold between the Christ and the Antichrist, something which would certainly constitute the heart of a heterodox hegemony. We denote it here as the 'Sovereign Ambiguity'. So much so that Frederick, the master of this world, became assimilated to the fallen angel whose countenance had once been like God's. After all, was Pier delle Vigne not celebrating his master as 'like unto God'? Once again we may find in Kantorowicz a grandiose prose aimed at underlining the sublime nature of his hero-sovereign, but also revealing a sublime heterodox side of the genealogy of the modern political.

In Kantorowicz's account, the Antichrist Frederick II set up his throne in the Temple and called himself the Son of God, even if he did so with a cohort of wizards and magicians reintroducing demon worship. Frederick II shall perform wonders, and when men shall see his deeds then even the perfect and the chosen of God *shall be in doubt*, whether he be Christ, who shall come again at the end of the World, or whether he be Antichrist:

> For both must be like and equal.
>
> …
>
> For nearly three hundred years—the era of the Renaissance—the strife of the one yet dual God was the spur of mankind.[79]

This passage is striking because of its clear reference to some sort of ditheism, and also because of its possible esoteric allusion to a dark side of God. Kantorowicz may have thought Goethe's passage was the emblem of this inescapable *sovereign ambiguity*: the figure of the sovereign who can simultaneously be holy and doomed, a Christ and a Devil, the Lord of the World and the Lord of the Flies. The same ambiguity affecting the *signs*: are they miracles or wonders? Do they derive from God, or from Beelzebub?[80]

What we may presume is that in these final chapters of the romanticisation of Frederick II, Kantorowicz reflected on the inner ambiguity of monarchy. This may be contingently ascribed to the presence of the counter-power of the church, possessing the privilege to bind and to release, and thus to dispose of legitimacy and depose the emperors. But perhaps there is also something more deeply *inscribed* within the *structure* of sovereignty, a structural ambiguity which could allow a demonological inversion of political theology.

[79] Kantorowicz, *Frederick the Second* 609, 611.
[80] Mark 3:21–31.

All of this is reinforced in Kantorowicz's text by the almost gothic representation of the figure of Frederick as the *Dominus Mundi*, to the point of reconstructing the threatening legends of a pagan Christ of the German *Heiland*. This romanticisation of Frederick, as influential as it has been, leads to a kind of gothic sublime. Not only did Frederick's cry 'Now I shall be hammer!' pass into a supernatural world, but—taking the guise of the 'Great Transformer'—as a powerful wizard he could polish his iron chains until they shone like gold, and voluntarily adorn himself with them.[81]

In this fantastic exaltation of Frederick II we witness a climax in the representation of the *Dominus Mundi*, as well as the emergence of the dark side of the political in the midst of the last century as a terrific ghostly remnant of imperial messianism.

B. Bloch and the Dark Side of Kingship

In his book on the structure and practice of National Socialism, Franz Neumann[82] connected Kantorowicz's *Frederick II* to the work of Bloch on the thaumaturgic kings,[83] and investigated the political role of the charismatic leader. From his perspective, the dark side of political authority may also be found in the magical powers of the kings to ward off demons.

In his penetrating analysis, Neumann shows the way in which the church administered 'charisma', making the ointment of Carolingian Kings a sacrament, and transplanted the ritual of bowing and devotion to the emperor (*proskunesis*) from Byzantium into the West.[84] But, he suggests, the political theological struggle between the emperor and the pope could have had a third side: that of the *magic powers* claimed by the kings.

This was a matter of great importance for John of Salisbury, and upon which Marc Bloch wrote diffusely in his masterpiece on kingship.[85] To a large extent, we presume that Gregory VII's (1073–1085) attacks on secular authorities, an important part of Berman's theory of the papal revolution,[86] were indeed also an assault on the king's 'magic' prerogatives. Bloch's enquiry was especially devoted to the royal touch, whereby French and English monarchs touched their subjects to heal them of their disease: the *tuberculous cervical lymphadenitis*, better known as *scrofula* or, by metonymy, the King's Evil.

[81] Kantorowicz, *Frederick the Second* 603.

[82] F Neumann, *Behemoth: The Structure and Practice of National Socialism, 1933–1944* (Oxford, Oxford University Press, 1944) 92.

[83] M Bloch, *Les rois thaumaturges. Étude sur le caractère surnaturel attribué à la puissance royale, particulièrement en France et en Angleterre* (Paris, Colin, 1961).

[84] Neumann, *Behemoth* 94.

[85] John of Salisbury, *Policraticus* III, X (CCI Webb ed, Oxford, The Clarendon Press, 1909) 203, edition used by Bloch, *Les rois thaumaturges* 353.

[86] Berman, *Law and Revolution* I 99.

We would now stress, in relation to Bloch, the importance of this dazzling element of magic in our appraisal of the role and legitimacy of the *Dominus Mundi*. As far as the spatial partition of the world is concerned, the various Kings of Europe have been reduced, as expected for Barbarossa, to '… *reges provinciarum*', or local authorities, almost to the rank of 'governors'.[87] They became representatives of the only world legitimate and supreme authority of the *Dominus* and the related cult due to a messianic emperor, which for John of Salisbury almost amounted to a regression towards paganism.

Neumann, in still another romanticisation of this subject, invokes the theory of Rudolf Otto to depict the sublime awe of a thaumaturgic king in his capacity to handle and administer, in brief to govern, the *mysterium tremendum* which lies at the basis of all that is sacred. This is something which, once again, evokes the aesthetic of the sublime as that which being always beyond words simultaneously provokes attraction and fear. It is rather apparent here how easy it is to shift from religion to magic and demonology. Neumann also observed that the claim to possess magic powers coincided with a royal claim to independence from the empire and the church.

Magic escapes precise definitions, and is essentially a cultural artifact changing through the ages, susceptible to different and clashing interpretations.[88] But what is particularly relevant here is that *structurally*, magic is almost atheological. It does not depend on exact concepts about divinity, but on the perceived efficacy of powers, names and forms. Of course, pure conceptions change if we consider sovereignty connected with miracles, or if it is linked to wonders. After all, to speak of *coups d'état* or exceptions, such as the coup of 18 Brumaire of Napoleon Bonaparte, or the burning of the *Reichstag*, as miracles is a way to ennoble them. What if *coups d'état* or exceptions were wonders and not at all 'miracles' in a Schmittian sense?

This ambiguous nature of magic implies that a wonder could be interpreted either as a divine sign or as evidence of a commerce with spirits or the Devil. This same dual nature of magic parallels the dual nature of the emperor as the Lord of *this* World or the Antichrist, the Lord of Flies, but a genealogy of modern sovereignty based on the magic arts would necessarily be very different from one based on theology.

As we know from Bloch's historical enquiry, French and English monarchs asserted to have the healing power to cure the *scrofula* by their touch, tracing the origin of this gift to St Edward the Confessor (1042–1066) or alternatively to Philip I (1059–1108) or even Robert II (987–1031). Bloch reports an impressive list of all records confirming the widespread popularity of the belief in the efficacy

[87] J Muldoon, *Empire and Order. The Concept of Empire 800–1800* (London, Palgrave Macmillan, 1999) 37; D Lee, 'Sources of Sovereignty: Roman Imperium and Dominium in Civilian Theories of Sovereignty' (2012) 1 *Politica Antica* 79.

[88] C Ginzburg, *Myths, Emblems, Clues* (J Tedeschi and AC Tedeschi trans, London, Hutchinson Radius, 1990).

of the royal touch, and its persistence, so much so that in the sixteenth century it was still believed that the healing power was retained by Saint Louis IX's arm, preserved in the Poblet Monastery in Catalonia.[89]

The kings of Castile developed an even more intriguing talent. They were thought to possess the ability to *exorcise demons* through the sign of the cross and an invocation to God, a rather giant leap in the magic arts. The power of exorcism is a power to command the demons. Thus the claims of the kings of Castile were even stronger than those advanced by the kings of France and England. The matter of exorcism is not to be underestimated, as we can derive from the following passage cited by Bloch.[90]

In the letter written by Gregory VII to the Bishop Hermann of Metz,[91] in the midst of the war of investitures, excommunicating for the second time emperor Henry IV, the pope stated rather clearly why he believed the Lord of the World to be absolutely inferior to any member of the clergy. The point is that an emperor, as powerful as he can be on earth, *does not* possess the priestly power to transform bread into wine by a 'mere utterance of words'. Nor does he possess the *powers of an exorcist* appointed by the church. Emperors and kings can only command men, an exorcist, and the pope himself is one of them, has the power to command and expel the spirits.

This is, of course, a point of great significance, as we have seen Frederick II pretending to have power over the *souls* of his subjects, and such a reference being made also by Baldus in relation to the *Dominus Mundi*. We shall see then in the next chapter how witchcraft was construed to be a political felony both by James I and Bodin in order to affirm a *royal* jurisdiction on it. The problem of the government of spirits and magic forces appears thus to be of acute importance in the definition of supreme powers and royal prerogatives.

In pope Gregory's letter, the power to hunt and expel the spirits is especially connected to the subject of miracles:

> Namque, ut de apostolis et martyribus taceamus, quis imperatorum vel regum aeque ut beatus Martinus, Antonius et Benedictus miraculis claruit? Quis enim imperator aut rex mortuos suscitavit, leprosos mundavit, cecos illuminavit?

Here,[92] Gregory VII expressly denies emperors and kings the power of operating *miracles*, a power possessed only by the real supreme sovereign authority: that of God. Of course, the entire question revolves around the ambiguity and continuity-through-disjuncture between a miracle and a wonder. This is peculiar because the link between sovereignty and miracles is explicitly confronted by the pope much

[89] S Clark, *Thinking with Demons: the Idea of Witchcraft in Early Modern Europe* (Oxford, Oxford University Press, 1999) 660.

[90] Bloch, *Les rois thaumaturges* 193.

[91] 148 PL (1853) clm 594; English translation in EF Henderson (ed), *Select Historical Documents of the Middle Ages* (London, George Bell & Sons, 1905) 394.

[92] 148 PL clm 599.

earlier than by Schmitt. But we also meet a definition of what is temporal and what is spiritual rather different, and much more thrilling, than the usual. The *spiritual* power is not only the possibility to have contact with the high and good spiritual forces, but it is more to be taken at its face value: *spiritual*, in the sense of having the power to command the spirits. This formulation can certainly be enlightened by one of the popular titles which, according to Kantorowicz, was attributed to Frederick, the Lord of the Souls.[93]

Certainly, the doctrine of miracles has always been rather slippery. The Church of Rome maintained that miracles by themselves are not sure evidence of holiness, and that God can use, at His complete discretion, any instruments that he chooses to operate. A delicate point is raised by William of Malmesbury (1080–1143), at the beginning of the history of the royal touch, and consists in the denial that the king, in this case Edward the Saint (1042–1066), could possess such virtues, not because of his holiness but as a hereditary privilege.[94] The king operates not because he is orthodox or saint, but because he inherits these magic powers. They are in his blood.

As Bloch stresses, for the Church it was important to eradicate the popular belief in the magic of the kings, an enterprise which proved to be very difficult, especially in relation to royal rings thought to possess special virtues.[95] This folk belief protracted up to the age of Mary Tudor, and the rites associated with the royal cramp-rings seem to have been reconstructed also at the time of James II.[96] The connection of a likely widespread belief in the magic of the royal touch or the rings with miracles remains uncertain; but the most important point is the *structural* question concerning the control and command of spirits and magical forces. Gregory's letter, while asserting that kings and emperors cannot practise an exorcism, confirms that they were trying to capture this *dark* spiritual sphere within their own prerogatives. This effective dark *spiritual* power of the clergy, bishops and popes, has been used as a major argument to claim the superiority of the church over all other political institutions. This is a surprising view, bypassing the paradigm of political theology. After all, Schmittian and Byzantine theological interpretations connect the power of the sovereign to a miraculous power, in parallel with God. This is in itself less dazzling and mystifying than the possibility of a foundation of power based on the capacity to command the spirits, and to exorcise men from the Devil's presence.

Here we meet, of course, a structural ambiguity in the encounter of political reflections with Christian sources, which precisely concerns the blurring distinction between miracles, typically attributed to saints, and wonders, typically

[93] Kantorowicz, *Frederick the Second* 687.

[94] W Malmesbury, *Historia regum*, II, I, § 222 (W Stubbs ed, London, Her Majesty's Stationery Office, 1889) I, 273.

[95] Bloch, *Les rois thaumaturges* 133.

[96] CJS Thompson, *Royal Cramp and Other Medycinable Rings* (London, Wellcome Historical Medical Museum, 1921) 9–10.

thought to be performed by wizards. Many of Jesus' miracles could indeed be defined exorcism in a strict sense.[97] Others were performed by the use of a given formula so peculiar to be maintained in its original form even in Greek.[98] Still others were performed not by words alone, but by the actual use of something material, as in the case of the healing of the man who was born blind. In John 9:1–7, Jesus affirmed to be 'the Light of the World' and then 'after saying this, *he spat on the ground, and made clay of the spittle,* and he anointed the eyes of the blind man with the clay … and [the man] came seeing' [KJV].

It is evident how popular interpretations could be confounded about the distinction between miracles and wonders, as the distinction is not ontologically based. Highly sophisticated and more modern distinctions—between miracles, magic, and other kind of spiritual interventions—are hardly seen in ancient folk tales and beliefs. At the folk level, the kings could have been sacred beings and wizards at the same time. The church tried to establish some order in their consecration. What the church certainly claimed was the unique *legitimate* power to command the spirits and control witchcraft, a point which was later contrasted by English legislation and Bodin's theory of sovereignty.

C. The Pope and the Abyss of Exception

We should consider now to what extent the matter of exceptional powers in case of emergency grew because of papal intervention, within the context of the theory of the global powers of the emperor in his fight against the kings. If we consider not only the duality of church and empire but also the triangle they form with the rising royal powers, the genealogy of sovereignty and exception can become a little clearer.

The imperial power was simultaneously attacked from two sides during the late eleventh and twelfth century. The doctrine embodied in the *Dictatus Papae*[99] (1075), where the pope had the power to depose the emperor, had been applied by Gregory VII in his judgments against Henry IV in 1076 and 1080 importing his deposition. This last decision ended with the vow that every Christian would understand that the fall of the emperor does not happen by chance but rather by the power of God, so that the emperor could repent and be saved on the day of the last judgment.

As we have seen, the Christian Commonwealth (*Respublica christiana*) was thought to be ruled by two coordinated authorities. Their different missions are for one to govern the bodies and the other to govern the souls. The former

[97] J Ashton, *The Religion of Paul the Apostle* (New Haven, Yale University Press, 2000) 94, with reference to Mark 1: 21–27; Mark 4: 35–41; Luke 10: 17–20.

[98] As in the case (Mark 5: 41) of the formula *talitha kum* (ταλιθὰ κούμι, tlīthā qūm) by which Jesus raised a young maid from her unconscious state.

[99] Berman, *Law and Revolution* I 104; Pennington, *The Prince and the Law* 135–36.

belonged to the sole discretion of the prince according to divine law, while the latter belonged to the church. No supreme authority is envisaged here, one that can reunite in the same *locus* the government of the souls *and* the bodies. Rather, this latter form of government is subordinated to the former. In deposing Henry IV, the pope was deposing a bad servant of the divine law. Imperial government of the bodies is an 'office' and as such can be judged by whomever holds the superior office to govern the souls. The emperor was deposed for the salvation of *his* soul.

As some author has done,[100] it is possible to see here the beginning of the modern disjuncture between a constituting power and a constituted power, in other words, the disjuncture between a spiritual power and a temporal one. God is the constituting power of the Christian Commonwealth, the pope is the constituted authority having the power to direct and govern the souls in relation to the other constituted powers having to govern the bodies. In this way, the capacity to explain the divine law is permanent and normal, whereas the necessity of papal intervention upon the secular authority's use of its prerogatives on bodies is rare. Normally, the emperor acts for the good of the people, so the normal rule depends on his independence from the Holy See. The intervention of the pope is then at the same time normal, if unusual.

The doctrine upon which the pope acted against Frederick II is of a different nature. In the case of Frederick II, who sought to re-establish the fullness of the spatial Roman rule reuniting the South and the geopolitically fundamental isle of Sicily, governing the Mediterranean to the northlands of Germany, he was trying to occupy the same territorial space as the Papacy. If the Northern and Southern regions of the empire reunited, they would have clinched the regions in between them belonging to the Church. This is something that pope Gregory IX (1227–1241) tried to avoid, to preserve the 'political' freedom of the Church, not only as a global institution but also as a delimited land power.

It is amidst this geopolitical conflict, where the land possessed by the Church represented *the* fracture splitting the domains of the empire into a North and a South, that *legal* arguments were refined to support the claims of the two opposing parties. Gregory IX underlined the notion of his full power as guardian of Christianity (*Plenitudo Potestatis*). This full power is his by nature, but it becomes manifest only occasionally or *exceptionally*: so that the sovereignty over temporal matters belongs to the emperor, as *Dominus Mundi*, but returns to the pontiff *in cases of exception*. Gregory IX wrote to Frederick II[101] that he was the Vicar of the Prince of the Apostles on the whole earth, to whom belongs the global *imperium* (sovereignty) of souls. As supreme governor of souls, he is also entitled to the same degree as the princes with respect to all material things and bodies in the whole world.

[100] See diffusely Saint Bonnet, *L'état d'exception* 91 ff.

[101] GH Perz and C Rodenberg (eds), *Epistolae saeculi XIII e Regestis Pontificum Romanorum Selectae* in MGH (1883) I, 703, 599–605 at 604.

The doctrine which led to the excommunication and deposition of Frederick II was probably manufactured by a Bolognese canonist, Huguccio of Pisa,[102] and supported by the theories of Innocent III (1161–1216). This doctrine was anticipated by Rufin's distinctions (1157–1159) between the *authority* of the pope and the *administratio*, or 'governance' pertaining to the emperor: all terms that are of particular relevance for today's debates over legitimacy and economic government. Indeed, Rufin traced a very hazardous metaphor between the Bishop and his *oeconomus*, his secretary appointed to administer the bishopric, and the 'world order'. In brief, the territory of an episcopate was deemed to be a representation of the universe as a whole, and thus the pope, who is the head of bishops and a bishop himself, had a right to world legitimate dominance; in contrast, the various princes, including the emperor, have the right to administer its different regions, *except* in the case of a papal intervention.

Huguccio, who wrote his *Summa* around 1188, went a step further. Acknowledging that the emperor had a superior authority in temporal matters, he stated that the pope could interfere only in accord with the wills of the princes. While the pope could not depose the emperor by his own intention, he could *proclaim* it at least formally if not in substance because he possessed the 'bare power', the *nuda potestas*.

Huguccio's main contribution to the theory of the state of exception may be found in canon 10 of the XCVI distinction of his *Summa*.[103] When the princes are unable or barred from judging the emperor's conduct, *exceptionally* the pope can judge on the merit and opportunity of his deposition, because he is *the last instance* on the earth who can take such decision. The authority of the pope over the political is *exceptional* and can be triggered only in case of necessity, where all other instances have failed.

Here we find the terms of the modern theories of the state of exception clearly stated. First of all, the exception is loosely defined, for its very nature is unpredictable and undefinable. Second, we meet the idea of a supreme instance of last resort, which would become very important after Bodin for the definition of modern sovereignty, and it is the sovereign who possesses this last *bare power* to decide over the occurrence of the exception, precisely as in Schmitt's theory. The only limits to papal *nuda potestas* are self-limitations.

Lothaire de Segni, a pupil of Huguccio who was elected pope as Innocent III in 1198, went still further than his mentor, proclaiming his own absolute authority on all spiritual matters as *plenitudo potestatis*, the reunion in the same locus of all possible, defined and undefined prerogatives. In one of his deliberations dated 1199, issued to confirm the election of Otto IV as emperor,[104] he stated that it is the duty of the papacy to guard the Roman empire because the emperor receives

[102] Saint Bonnet, *L'état d'exception* 93 for all references.
[103] Huguccio Pisanus, *Summa Decretorum* 6 MIC (U Přerovský ed, 2006) dist XCVI, clm 10.
[104] Saint Bonnet, *L'état d'exception* 94.

from him his investiture, so that it is within the papal prerogatives to measure and administer the *gap*, the *gulf*, the *divide* (the *Kluft*)[105] between the ideal ends of the imperial institution and the actual capacity of the emperor-elect to accomplish these ends.

We want to highlight this notion of government of the divide between the ideal and the actual world of political institutions, because it is such authority that allows the pope to refute the election of a lunatic, a pagan, a heretic, a tyrant, or a heterodox or excommunicated person. In this way, the pope can intervene '*causa urgente*'—as a matter of *urgency*—when the election appears to be the work of the Devil and not of the Lord.

It is, then, through this *governance of the divide* that the authority of the pope *widens* from the abyss between potency and actuality, becoming strength and effectiveness in the exceptional. It is through the exception that the abyss and its government can operate, transforming the symbolic into a real power. Princes *normally* act as inspired by God, but *exceptionally* they may be seduced by the Devil, and in this extreme and serious case it is up to the pope to intervene as the guardian of all Christianity.

All Schmittian conceptions are met in this context, but with a strong variance of something which is never explicitly named in his writings, nor explicitly confronted in those of Agamben: the Devil. This is an element which we shall try to increasingly emphasise from now on to appraise the rise of modern sovereignty. It is because of the Devil that the pope can interfere with political authorities and it is the *Devil's intervention which makes that case a case of exception.*

This doctrine, adopted against Frederick II, is rather different from that of Gregory VII in the *Dictatus Papae* (Dictates of the Pope) in 1075, which forms the cornerstone of Berman's analysis of the birth of the Western legal tradition.[106] In a way Gregory spiritualised the whole realm of politics, whereas Innocent spiritualised the exception. The pope, as the possessor of a *bare* power of last instance, that is, the capacity to intervene in a case of emergency, acts when, because of a demonic intervention, the very existence of the Christian world could be put at risk.

Innocent does not violate a standard partition of powers between temporal and spiritual authorities: he creates a sphere for its exceptional derogation. The global legitimacy of the emperor as a Master of the World can be checked and suspended, and even reversed, by a further superior instance: that of his guardian, the pope, who really possesses the authority of last resort over the world. This bare power has nothing superior to it but the power of God, whom the pope is representing on earth.

It is then in Innocent III that we may find a refined theory of exceptional powers. It is in his capacity as *guardian* of the Christendom that the pope can act.

[105] The German word *Kluft* can range from 'gap' to 'abyss'.
[106] Berman, *Law and Revolution* I 94 ff.

His intervention is *exceptional* because it is dictated by the necessity of saving the Church from the spread of sin.

Whereas Gregory VII considered his power of intervention normal, if *unusual*, and eventually limited to the adjudication of the human conduct of the emperor, Innocent III envisaged his capacity of intervention as an exceptional but necessary interference within the independent domain of the lay political authorities. The necessity of this interference was implied by the mission of eradicating sin, a superior mission of the papacy touching the very existence of a Christian Commonwealth threatened by the demons. It is his function as guardian over the evil spirits which ensures the power of the pope to intervene in a case of exception, when the Devil is proximate to reaching the centre of the political powers, the emperor himself.

Forms like *causa urgente*, *ratione peccati*, and *causaliter* (emergency cases) became the forms of legal acts of intervention in the state of exception, as justifications for the pope's power to derogate from the normal rules by virtue of the hierarchy placing the souls and the spirits above the bodies. It is a *spiritual* emergency creating the exception that allows and calls for the guardian of the spirits and souls to interfere with the government of the bodies. The whole field of exception had then become that of a spiritual government of the abyss.

3

Political Theology from Satan to Legitimacy

I. Spatiality, Sovereignty and the Geopolitics of Discovery

A. Westphalia and Political Diversity: A Demonological Origin?

In the second chapter, we analysed the revival of the Roman legal and political notion of *Dominus Mundi* in the context of Western medieval politics. In particular, we saw the two major examples of what we have called 'imperial messianism' as epitomised by the figures of Frederick I and Frederick II.

Another, though very different, considerable renewal of the ideology of the *Dominus* characterised the times of Charles V (1500–1558).[1] This was a period when the world experienced the last materialisation of the possibility of a universal empire before the world itself was split among warring states fighting for supremacy. From this angle, the recovery of imperialism under Charles V was a frantic but phantasmatic resurgence, occurring almost at the same time as the spatial fragmentation of the earth.

When the new Europe was taking shape, another manifestation of the Lord of the World occurred just as the Reformation destroyed the religious unity of the imperial space. A new model of statecraft came into being, characterised by the thrilling and mesmerising icon of the Sovereign-Leviathan perspicuously depicted in Hobbes's frontispiece. The eventual resurrection of the *Dominus* materialised on the brink of its dissolution. This is a rather intriguing fact to be analysed in discerning the genealogy of our modern conceptions of law, power and hegemony in the West. How then did the world become populated by Leviathans? How did the mysticism and occult metaphors of the inventors of modern political imagery succeed as much as they did?

[1] F Bosbach, *Monarchia Universalis. Ein politischer Leitbegriff der fruehen Neuzeit* (Goettingen, Vandenhoeck & Ruprecht, 1988) 43; J Muldoon, *Empire and Order. The Concept of Empire 800–1800* (London, Palgrave Macmillan, 1999) 87–100.

From our perspective, it is hard not to see the constitution of modern political bodies as a specifically European revolution,[2] originated by the dissolution of the body of the Holy Roman Empire and the collapse of its universal Catholic space. It is from this *ontological* dissolution that the *new political* feature of the modern legal order emerged, and it is from this *historical* fact that previously theological concepts evolved into the major conceptions underlying the general theory of the state.

This political aspect of law is often referred to in legal literature as *positive* or *positivistic*, not with reference to the antonym positive-negative but to the distinction natural-positive. 'Positive'—in this sense—is a word that may have many different meanings in a legal and political context.[3] It may mean something that is good, but also, especially after Kelsen,[4] something which is *positum*, or which has been established and enacted by authority. In this context, we use it in reference to 'decision' as the key feature of the modern political, pointing at the very core of Schmittian analysis. The key feature of what is *positive* in this context is then its opposition to what is ontological. Something ontological is based on the nature of things, such as Dante's parallel between the Lord and the sovereign. That which is ontological, in this sense, can only be 'revealed' or 'discovered', *not* decided. The *positive* aspect of the modern order is, then, based on the assumption that it derives from a decision, that it is not ontologically given, but rather it is the offspring of contingent political choices. In other words, it is an order that has been politically decided.

French history provides a very good example. King Henry IV (1367–1413) deliberately exterminated most of his Protestant subjects in one night in the St Bartholomew's Day Massacre (1572), not because they had wrong opinions on the nature of divine things, but purely for *political reasons* determined by the need to restore the peace of the kingdom. In this respect, almost all political decisions are contingent. They depend on the contingencies of available means and their effects, and the concurrent actions and plans of friends and enemies. There was nothing necessary about Henry IV's decision, except the 'political necessity' of concretising rulership.

From this standpoint, Schmitt's conception of the political as the decision between friends and foes seems more like a memory than a theory. Before its fragmentation, the imperial space, that of the *Dominus Mundi*, was ontologically perceived and construed. It was the same universal space of the *corpus juris* as the *ratio scripta* of its inner law. The empire was holy, sacred, and its space was global. This metaphor of the *corpus*, of the body of the law, represented a real ontological experience of the consistency of the law and its institutions in the consciousness

[2] H Kissinger, *World Order* (New York, Penguin Books, 2014) 31.

[3] GC Christie, *Jurisprudence. Text and Readings on the Philosophy of Law* (St Paul, West Publishing, 1973) 292.

[4] H Kelsen, *Pure Theory of Law* (M Knight trans, Berkeley, University of California Press, 1967) 7, 106.

of the time. The empire, as a single *real* body constituted by the universally practiced Holy Communion, was ruled not by discretion but by the body of rational prescriptions forming the Justinian compilation (the *corpus juris*) as a peculiar revelation of the law.[5] The new order that was realised in the aftermath of the conflict between the Protestant Reformers and the Catholics revealed that the old ontology of the world order had collapsed, and the political decision over the state of exception was placed at the centre of the new global order. The sovereign's decision over the state of exception became the core device of the new purely political order.

This character of *revelation* of the *corpus juris* and the belief in the unity of the *corpus christianum*, the mystic unitary body of Christendom, represented the ontological unity of a world which continued to be substantially the same as that of the Romans. The *corpus juris* was a physical object, thought to be the written revelation of Reason as applied to the legal and political domain, just as the Empire was a physical body united by Holy Communion.

This conception was, of course, political theology at its height. The body of the Empire was essentially a legal body whose value derived from the fact that it was *truly* a single body, ontological and mystical as it was, by virtue of the Eucharist. Since all of the subjects were Christian and Catholic, they were eating the same bread, and so they were of the same flesh, the same body (1 Corinthians 11:26). This body of the Empire had a *ratio* (reason) concretised in the words of the law. We must understand that living in a revealed world with a revealed law is completely different than living in a contingent, historical world whose laws and rules are contingently decided.

It is from this ontological collapse that the modern conception of the political, which saw decision as the foundation of order, arose; thus, we must conclude that we are living in a completely different way politically than our pre-modern ancestors. We do not share the same notion and experience of the political. Nor do we share the same notion of the law.

From this point of view, the *corpus juris* could hardly be reduced to a mere collection of legal rules. Rather, it was almost a universal constitution of a world unaffected by a distinction between national and international, as this distinction was rather a consequence of the dissolution of the universal order of the *Dominus*. Thus, the modern world order could be seen as a consequence of the disruption of the *Dominus Mundi*'s power by Westphalian Leviathans.

B. The Collapse of the Catholic Space

In his *Nomos der Erde*, Schmitt insisted on the way in which the discovery of the Americas in the late fifteenth century broke the ancient spatiality to produce

[5] F Wieacker, *A History of Private Law in Europe* (T Weir trans, Oxford, Oxford University Press, 1996) 25, 47.

a new concrete world order.[6] Attempts to rationalise this new concrete spatial order produced new ideologies of empire that aimed to characterise the division of the globe under the contrasting claims, to use the words of Pagden, of various 'would be' Lords of the world.[7] At the same time, it gave different Catholic thinkers the opportunity to reconcretise the pope's pretension to be the only universal *Dominus Mundi*, having the authority to legitimise the conquests and colonisation of the discovered continent.[8]

The period from the late fifteenth century to the middle of the seventeenth century shaped the known part of the world into a great battlefield among the heirs of the *Dominus*, leading to an interminable *religious* endo-Christian conflict in Europe known as the Thirty Years' War (1618–1648). The conflict was so tremendous and bloody that we could label it as an enormous state of exception at a continental level. The impossibility of reaching a theological ending of the conflict was managed through a pure political compromise between Protestant and Catholic powers in the Treaty of Westphalia, where the concept of national interest and *raison d'état* superseded religious or ideological differences.

As Kissinger recounts the story, with the Treaty of Westphalia:

> the papacy had been confined to ecclesiastical functions, and the doctrine of sovereign equality reigned. What political theory could then explain the origin and justify the functions of secular political order? In his Leviathan, published in 1651, three years after the Peace of Westphalia, Thomas Hobbes provided such a theory.[9]

Kissinger's *résumé* is deeply intriguing for its capture of power politics and its ideological and theological justifications. This is especially true if we consider the Treaty of Westphalia as a compromise rather than the conscious design of a new order. The war was interminable; nobody had the power to reach the status of master of the world. Consequently, the resolution of the stalemate resulted in the mutual recognition of States, while acknowledging and accepting their political diversity.

The Peace of Westphalia created a double crisis: first, a fracture of the Christian space into separate religious beliefs and the consequent death of the ontological body of the universal empire; second, a compromise between the new international actors allotting each of them a sovereign portion of the European space, and the possibility of enlargement by conquest in the extra-European spaces.[10]

It is in this context that we must notice a passage of Grotius[11]—connecting the Lex Rhodia (Dig 14.2.9) to Bartolus (comment to Dig 49.15.24) and Luke on the

[6] C Schmitt, *The Nomos of the Earth in the International Law of the Jus Publicum Europaeum* (GL Ulmen trans, New York, Telos Press Publishing, 2006) 101.

[7] A Pagden, *Lords of All the World: Ideologies of Empire in Spain, Britain and France c. 1500–c. 1800* (New Haven, Yale University Press, 1995).

[8] F de Vitoria, 'De Indis noviter inventis' in JB Scott (ed), *The Spanish Origin of International Law: Francisco de Vitoria and His Law of Nations* (Oxford, Oxford University Press, 1934) xxi, 122.

[9] Kissinger, *World Order* 11.

[10] Pagden, *Lords of All the World* 78.

[11] C Fasolt *The Limits of History* (Chicago, The University of Chicago Press, 2004) 157, 268.

census (2:1)—where we may find a full consideration of the *coming absence* of the *Dominus*.

As Blom has rightly argued[12] Grotius sharply distinguished God's rule from that of man. As Creator of the World, and *Dominus Mundi*, God has absolute rule, but among men *this dominium* is *absent* and rule can only be based on *fides*, namely on contract or international treaties. Here the Byzantine 'liturgy of the presence' comes to a definitive end and the world becomes the locus of the political absence of God. So much so that Grotius reaches the point of labelling as 'foolish' (*stultum esse*) the opinion of some, who have ascribed to the Roman emperors dominion over the most and uknown nations.[13] It would scarce have been necessary to refute this foolish opinion if Bartolus (*princeps iuriconsultorum*) had not pronounced it *heresy* to deny those pretensions. For Grotius, of course, similar claims advanced by the Roman pointiff are equally unsound. Such claims over the sea are contrary to the law of nature and the law of nations;[14] the sea is not susceptible to a servitude (... *mari quod servire non potest*).[15]

Nowhere else than in these passages of Grotius can the rise of international law be better appreciated in its connection with the freedom the seas[16] and with the fading away of the presence of the *Dominus* in its connection with property and empire.[17]

It is not our task here to dive into the details of this turbulent era of the world. Rather, it is to investigate the dark side of the ideologies of world dominance that emerged from the death of the *Dominus* and its astounding revival as an ideological device used to sustain both the claims of the Spanish, French, and English empires and the universal authority of the pope.

From one point of view, it is surprising that the fragmentation of the European space happened just when the concrete possibility to reach world dominance occurred. From another, it is also intriguing that the birth of national empires came after the collapse of 'the' empire. Our aim in this chapter will then be to engage in an enquiry into the *occult* side of the geopolitical order, out of which rose the modern notion of the political as a peculiar and exotic concept, in contrast to Schmitt's general and universal conception of what is *the* political.

We shall do this first by analysing the mystic nature of the *Dominus* as it was reincarnated into the ideal of a *real* world empire. Then we shall consider the

[12] HW Blom, 'Grotius and Socinianism' in M Muslow and J Rohls (eds), *Sociananism and Arminianism. Antitrinitarians, Calvinists and Cultural Exchange in Seventeenth Century Europe* (Leiden, Brill, 2005) 121, at 143.

[13] H Grotius, *De Jure Belli ac Pacis* [1646] book 2, ch 22, sect 13–14 (JB Scott ed, Washington, Carnegie Institute, 1913) I, 387.

[14] H Grotius, *Mare Liberum* [1608] caput V, *The Freedom of the Seas* (JB Scott ed, R van Deman Magoffin trans, New York, Oxford University Press, 1916) 66.

[15] Grotius, *Mare Liberum* 36.

[16] For the relation of Grotius to Selden see SLB Coccej, *Grotius Illustratus* (Wratislaviae, Johannes Jacobi Korn, 1752) 175.

[17] See M Barducci, *Hugo Grotius and the Century of Revolutions 1613–1718* (Oxford, Oxford University Press, 2017) 139 ff.

fragmentation of Christianity provoked by the Augustinian version of political theology that can be traced back to the radical writings of Martin Luther, given their extreme importance for a reappraisal of the roots of the Western legal tradition.[18] Finally, we must face the striking compact of mixed theological, occult and magical models that featured a particular Jacobean conception of royal prerogatives. We maintain that it was especially within this framework that major shifts occurred to shape the modern, apparently rational conceptions of political sovereignty. Our task here is consequently to reappraise the encounter between classical political thought and Christianity within the context of theological rethinking of the sixteenth century, with special attention to the heterodox nature of Jacobean political theology.

C. Charles V, Astraea and a Gelasian Papacy

As noted by Yates, the ideal of a universal world empire came close to realisation under Charles V of Spain. In her account, the Holy Roman Empire, which had seemed to be increasingly dwindling into a local German concern at the time, suddenly took on once more something of its old significance in the middle of the sixteenth century.[19] We want to highlight the contradiction underlying the late manifestation of the Lord of the World in the person of the emperor occurring in the century in which a new Europe was in progress, with its great states built up on principles of realistic statecraft and infused with national patriotism. As Yates recounts, this revival of imperialism was, indeed, a 'phantom revival', because of its anachronistic nature. It was already superseded by political developments at the time. Notwithstanding its anachronism, this imperial ideology revamped old myths and images in an attempt to revitalise the mystic of the *Dominus*:

> According to these notions, the first Just World Ruler was Adam before the Fall; it is therefore the function of the Just Emperor to establish such a rule upon earth as will lead men back to the state of Adam before the Fall, that is to say, to the Earthly Paradise. This implies a Christ-like redemptive role for the Emperor, though limited to the temporal sphere, and it is related to that interpretation of the golden age as being identical with the Earthly Paradise.[20]

Of course, in this interpretation, the imperial *Dominus Mundi* is seen as a kind of temporal Christ, redeeming man back to the Earthly Paradise with his justice, bringing in a full golden age with his world order.

These ideologies of the empire pervaded also Renaissance literature, and, as Yates reports,[21] one of the most important pieces of this ideological renewal can be

[18] HJ Berman, *Law and Revolution, II: The Impact of the Protestant Reformations on the Western Legal Tradition* (Cambridge, Harvard University Press, 2009) 71, 100 ff.

[19] FA Yates, *Astraea: The Imperial Theme in the Sixteenth Century* (London, Pimlico, 1993) 1.

[20] Yates, *Astraea* 8.

[21] Yates, *Astraea* 22.

found in the poem *Orlando furioso* by Ludovico Ariosto. First published in 1516, the poem includes a glorification of Charles V as the new Charlemagne and the new Augustus. In the fifteenth canto of the poem, Astolfo hears a prophecy about the future of the empire: the prophetess foretells that the world will be placed, once again, under a universal monarchy by one who will succeed to the diadem of Augustus, Trajan, Marcus Aurelius, and Severus. This ruler, Charles V, would spring from the union of the houses of Austria and Aragon, and he would bring *Astraea*, the personification of Justice, along with all the banished virtues back to earth.

As a complement to this grandiose representation, the discovery of the Americas, which dominated the thinking of the time, had a particular impact on world politics. Ariosto spoke of those new worlds that were unknown to the Romans, repeating the widely held belief that these discoveries were themselves a portent, or a *miracle*, from which a new world monarchy could spring. According to the prophetess in Ariosto's poem, God wanted to keep these undiscovered lands unknown until He would give rise to a new emperor. The prophetess then foresees the time when these discoveries would be made, and when the World Ruler would appear in the person of Charles V.[22]

These passages, according to Yates, give us a fuller meaning of Charles's famous emblem with the two columns and the motto *Plus Oultre*. Its obvious meaning is that the empire of Charles V extended further than that of the Romans, which had been bounded by the columns of Hercules. The device also carried with it the prophetic implication that the discovery of the new worlds was providentially timed to coincide with the coming of the one who should be the *Dominus Mundi* in a broader sense than was known to the Romans.[23] Thus, the old argument from Providence was brought up to date in order to cover the new geopolitical situation. As Yates clearly states: 'It raised again the phantom of empire which had haunted the Middle Ages, but in a modernised form'.[24] Now our point is precisely the one highlighted in *Astraea*: why and how in Charles V, and in the image of his magnificence, could the *phantom* of empire be revived? How could a new sublime apparition of the empire come back from past times?

This notion of a political phantom, or political *refoulé*, must be analysed for its outstanding importance in rethinking the too-muchness of hegemony and its sublime nature. The revival of the ghost of the *Dominus* is, as Yates points out, in itself a historical fact deserving careful study. In this vein, why did it find a wide acceptance in people's imagination?

One theory is that the *memory* of the idea of imperial universality which Charles V seemed to evoke may have been psychologically comforting.

[22] L Ariosto, *Orlando Furioso* (E Bigi and C Zampese eds, Milano, Rizzoli, 2012) canto XV, stanzas xxi–xxv.

[23] See also E Rosenthal, 'Plus Ultra, Non plus Ultra, and the Columnar Device of Emperor Charles V' (1971) 34 *Journal of the Warburg and Courtauld Institutes* 204.

[24] Yates, *Astraea* 23.

This explanation suggests an idea of cultural models which govern us more than we can govern them. Thus, this historical and political paradigm of imperial universality would confirm the permanence of a political sublime layer, that is, a cultural model that bypasses and supersedes our own words and political rationality, and lies at the heart of a global hegemony. As we will discuss in a later chapter, this sublime character could have been construed in the latter half of the sixteenth century in terms of a 'theological menace'. The reappearance of the *Dominus* could have been a reaction to cope with this menace, revealing the dark side from which European modernity eventually emerged.

The work of Yates showed that the reappearance of the *Dominus* was also the key to understanding how the Tudor monarchy, including its most famous representative Queen Elizabeth I, was presented to the world. The glorification of the Tudor monarchy as a religious imperial institution derives from the Tudor reform which dispensed with the pope and made the monarch supreme in both church and state.[25] This glorification could well have been a political reply to the reemergence of the Lord of the World. In this sense, the symbolic use of a pastoral in one hand and a sword in the other—the image that would characterise the frontispiece of Hobbes' Leviathan as the emblem of political modernity—could have been an appropriate icon for the Tudors to the extent they initially conceived of the idea of England as a sea power, more so than for the Stuarts.

Nevertheless, this emblematic shift in the conception of sovereignty has to be understood in the context of the political theology that was pursued by the papacy at the time. Indeed, on the opposite side of imperialism and its ideologies, we may find the active use of Gelasius (a Father of the Church of the fifth century) by the papacy[26] to affirm its monopoly of the world order legitimacy. According to this interpretation the pope had to be ultimately deemed the proper heir of the ancient *Dominus Mundi*, and this affirmation could be elaborated following the schemes of Gelasian political theology.

In this framework, the two streams of temporal and spiritual government are kept at separate levels, each independent from the other. Gelasius's followers normally adhered to the natural law theory that God described in the heart of Adam the principles of justice as a sort of innate idea, later summarised in the Ten Commandments and repeated in the Christian revelation. Knowledge of good and evil were deemed to be accessible to all, even if only the very few, and the most learned, could derive all the consequences of these basic principles and solve the hardest cases. Consequently, all human beings are able to distinguish the good prince from the evil one, and therefore, in contrast to Luther, a right of resistance is allowed against the prevalence of the latter.

In this line of thought, political authority is a natural institution and its relationship with the spiritual can assume three different forms. In the first model,

[25] Yates, *Astraea* 99.

[26] M Scattola, *Teologia politica* (Bologna, Il Mulino, 2007) 85–87.

the world government is seen as an extension of the parental prevalence established by the Fourth Commandment. Political authority does not differ from parental authority and is just as natural. It generates the hierarchical order demanded by the laws of nature, which is at the same time religious and secular. In a second sense, secular authority is generated by a divine command but in an *indirect* way, differentiating political from family authority. When kings are instituted by the people, this happens not simply as an extension of the natural institution of the family, but rather invents a new and more complex scheme of relationships. As we may see here, public authority evolves bottom up but also needs recognition from above. The covenant among the subjects must also be approved by the Almighty through a series of signs or other manifestations of His consent to the political pact. A third form, as developed by Àlvaro Pelayo (1280–1352) and Niccolò Tedeschi (1386–1445),[27] was a solution which underlines even more this aspect of designating a sphere for natural law and justice independent from the spiritual, *but* subject to the *indirect* authority of the pope. Indeed in Tedeschi's term also all the infidels are subject to papal jurisdiction because all humankind is bound by natural law. In this way the pope could claim to have an indirect power over the all world through sophisticated speculations about his office.

D. Lutheran Augustinism and Political Eschatology

The greatest representative of fifteenth century radical revision of political theology was undoubtedly Martin Luther (1483–1586) with his reprisal of St Augustine's theory of the two kingdoms.[28] Harold J Berman has tried at length to show the importance of the Reformation for a comprehensive understanding of the evolution of the Western legal tradition.[29] Berman's work is a study of the impact of Western Protestantism in both its Lutheran and Calvinist forms upon the development of Western law and constitutionalism. In his view, this impact was revolutionary, and his focus is Weber's thesis in *The Protestant Ethic and the Spirit of Capitalism*, though we can agree with Tim Murphy that such a thesis, if there is one, remains enigmatic.[30] For Berman, there was an extended revolution in England between 1640 and 1689 driven by Calvinism. Since Berman's book tries to cope with the inner core of the Western legal tradition, and we believe that a major trait of this tradition is the 'haunt of the *Dominus*', it is rather important

[27] A Pelayo, *De Planctu Ecclesie Libri Duo* (Venetiis, Sansovinus, 1560) I, 37, fol 9rb-vb; N Tedeschi, *Lectura super Tertio* (Venetiis, Iohannes de Colonia, 1475) III, 34, 8 fol bb6; see Scattola, *Teologia Politica* 87.

[28] WDJ Cargill Thompson, *The Political Thought of Martin Luther* (P Broadhead ed, Brighton, Harvester Press, 1984) 42.

[29] Berman, *Law and Revolution* II 100.

[30] T Murphy, 'Law and Revolution, II: The Impact of the Protestant Reformations on the Western Legal Tradition. Book Review' (2006) 69 *The Modern Law Review* 480.

to reappraise the impact of Lutheranism on it, the reaction of the Stuarts, and the pivotal role played by Calvinism.

In fact, Luther adopted a radical version of political Augustinism only in the first 20 years of the sixteenth century. In the 1530s, he elaborated a variant of this approach, which amounted to a very different theory of power, that can be labelled as his *Politica Christiana*. From the standpoint of God's government of the world, Luther reenacted the split at the heart of Augustine's theory of the two cities, one in heaven and one on earth.[31] This stresses the dual situation of the true Christian as both an autonomous and independent 'Lord of all things' (1 Corinthians 9:19; Romans 13:8) and simultaneously the servant of all (Galatians 4:1–15). The two propositions can conflict if we consider the dual nature of the faithful, composed of a soul and a body of flesh and bones. Her soul is regenerated as an internal and spiritual aspect of her being; his or her body remains the old body, corporeal, external and subject to all the heritage of the flesh. To be reborn, she does not need any corporeality, but rather must only possess faith (John 6:28). Since man is incapable of self-salvation, God sent Jesus to earth, and it is *only* the faith in His mission that can save us, without any consideration given to our deeds. As we know, this position can be radicalised to the point of believing in the absolute freedom of the Christian. Since deeds are immaterial to salvation, the true Christian is freed from the law. He is above the law and beyond its commandments, and there cannot be a separate clergy possessing a higher degree of election, for all people are ministers of God.

These well-known premises, which led toward a revolution within the church, also had a tremendous impact on political institutions and their conception. If all true Christians belong to the Kingdom of God, whose Lord is Jesus, they all form a separate and widespread spiritual community of free men obeying only the Holy Spirit, to the point that if they all believed 'that Jesus is the Lord', there would be no need for kings or laws on earth. Nevertheless, since only few are truly faithful, God created the earthly kingdom in order to restrain people from committing sins out of fear of the secular power and its sword. Thus, even if political authority has been instituted by God (John 9:6; Matthew 26:52; Luke 3:14; Romans 13:1–7) to participate in the divine order of the *kósmos*, it is fear that acts.[32]

The two governments appointed by God are the spiritual and the *temporal*. Jesus and the Holy Spirit (*not* the church) rule the former, which forms a perfect society, a *societas perfecta*. The latter, made necessary because of the evils, keeps the peace of the realm *against* the enemies of the Kingdom, because the Christians, being saved and reborn, already operate freely for the good. The two governments are so intimately separated: one inner and spiritual, instituted for the free elected Christians, and the other external and *temporal*.

[31] V Mantey, *Zwei Schwerter—Zwei Reiche. Martin Luthers Zwei-Reiche-Lehre vor ihrem spätmittelalterlichen Hintergrund* (Tübingen, Mohr Siebeck, 2005).

[32] Scattola, *Teologia politica* 79.

This theoretical device, based as it is on a clear distinction between an 'in' and an 'out', leaves no room for public or political action of the church, which must operate only at the inner level of souls. The rest of its activity, in the outer space of the external world, must be submitted to the guardianship of civil authorities instituted by the Lord.

These authorities, in their own turn, cannot interfere with the freedom of the souls. If they try to compress the souls they would usurp God's own government, contributing to the damnation rather than the salvation of the world. No command can impel someone to follow this or that faith, because an act of faith is an intrinsically free and incoercible one.[33]

Just as temporal laws cannot have any validity in the spiritual order, so too evangelical norms cannot be invoked against the prince's laws. Civil authorities have been instituted to preserve peace by the sword, not by the gospel.

Here Luther's argument becomes much more legal than expected: whoever disobeys political authority is guilty of *sedition* and cannot invoke a right of resistance, because *there is not* a higher temporal jurisdiction over the political power. We would underline just how modern and justifying this notion is. The civil authority, whether an emperor, a king, a prince or a parliament, is supreme for the very legal and technical reason that no action can be filed against it by a superior authority. If the real legal problem is always *quis judicabit*,[34] Luther's answer is that there is no judge to hear a case against the king. A political case is *not* justiciable. Everything that is temporal is political, and therefore, there cannot be a judgment over the political.

A Christian must always obey the rules. If these rules are heretic and directed to reinstate paganism, the faithful subject can and must disobey them to save his soul, but *must* subject himself to the prescribed sanctions, being ready to lose his property and even his own life. The only admissible form of resistance is passive; God had reserved vengeance to Himself (Romans 12:19; Deuteronomy 32:35; Matthew 7:1). God will punish the tyrants with disgraces, provoking invasions from enemies, and making them suffer with an eternal pain in Hell.

It is easy to stress the deep abyss separating Luther's conceptions from those prevailing in the Middle Ages. In Luther's depiction, Roman law, as the law of the Empire, loses its status as *ratio scripta*, or Reason as applied to the law, to become an instrument directed against the enemies of the Christian religion. These enemies are not simply the unorthodox or the heretics, they are most of humankind, since many are called to faith but few are chosen. In this sense, the law is against evil people, which means that the law is against the majority. The law is not an instrument of reason but of 'justified' repression. Any necessary measure taken to maintain peace is justified as it is within the scope of political power.

[33] M Luther, 'On Secular Authority: How Far does the Obedience Owed to It Extend?' in H Höpfl (ed), *Luther and Calvin on Secular Authority* (Cambridge, Cambridge University Press, 2005) 3.

[34] C Schmitt, *Constitutional Theory* (J Seitzer trans, Durham, Duke University Press, 2008) 120.

There is no superior court that can judge the appropriateness of these *Maßnahmen*, or security measures. Being constantly at risk of danger, the world is always in a state of exception. Once more, the exception becomes normalised to the point of being at the heart of the daily government of the temporal dimension. Not even Luther or the most pious Christian can escape these measures or possess rights against them. Everyone must comply with them, or be ready to die with faith in God's vengeance. God Almighty is the only instance above political power and He will act by His supreme will. The Lord of this World is instituted as a whip against evil people, he is indeed the Scourge of the World. He is certainly supreme on the earth as there is no one, except for God, that can judge his actions, which implies that the political world is absolutely free from a temporal viewpoint. If we take this model seriously, not only is there no room for temporal action by the church, but there is also no room for any rule of law. The temporal, historical dimension of the world is purely political, which means that it is always exceptional. There is no rule of law because the only task of the ruler is to maintain peace through fear, but even against an inept or evil ruler there can be no legal or political remedy, because active resistance is forbidden. A right to resistance is indeed the possibility to resist and combat against the power claiming the legitimacy of the revolt, and, notoriously, Luther denied this claim even to the poorest farmers who revolted against the tyrannical actions of secular princes.

Locating the state of emergency at the heart of power itself entailed placing the apocalyptic element in the daily life of the political order, and only our unquestioned faith could sustain us in the active intervention of the Lord:

> Our God is an unfaltering fortress, a good defense and weapon. He freely helps us out of every adversity that has now affected us. The ancient evil enemy is now deadly serious; his armour is great power and much guile. *There is none on earth who can equal him* (....) And even if the world were full of devils who wanted to wolf us down completely, we wouldn't tremble so badly—we'll manage it. However acidly the prince of this world portrays himself, he can do nothing to us. One tiny word can fell him.
>
> [The devils] have no thanks for the word and have to let it stand. [The word] is fully on our side with his spirit and gifts, according to his plan. If [the devils] were to take the body, goodness, honour, child, and wife, let them go, for they profit us nothing. The kingdom certainly must remain ours.[35]

We hope that in these words of Luther the reader will notice both the reference to the 'prince of this world' and the reference to the Leviathan—'*There is none on earth who can equal him*' (Job 41:24)—the same words we shall find in the frontispiece of Hobbes '*cuis ei comparetur*'. This is not a matter of philological transplant, but rather, we think, one of structural interdependence within the new political eschatology introduced by the Reformation: the Lord is already fighting against

[35] M Luther, 'Der XLVI Psalm' in M Luther, *D Martin Luthers Werke: Kritische Gesamtausgabe*, vol 35 (Weimar, Hermann Böhlaus Nachfolger, 1883–1980) 455–457. The English translation is taken from K Sundet Jones, 'Apocalyptic Luther' (2005) 25 *Word & World* 309.

the *prince of this world*, and it is only our faith that can sustain us in this rather apocalyptic political landscape.

II. From Justinian in Paradise to Royal Occultism

A. James and the Path towards Heterodoxy

A very different synthesis of ancient political theology, with direct reference to Eusebius of Caesarea (265–340), can be found in the works of the intellectual King James I (1566–1625), who composed *The True Law of Free Monarchies*, and circulated it as an anonymous work in 1598.[36] Identifying the two targets of James as King of Scotland is rather simple. On one side, he would hit John Knox (1505–1572) and the Presbyterians for their theory that the king was bound in his actions by an original covenant with the people. On the other side, he would combat the Catholics submitting the sovereign to the direct or indirect control of the Roman pontiff.[37]

As King of England, he endeavoured to fight against the Puritans and the *common lawyers*. This last point must be strictly scrutinised, since the common lawyers, in contrast to the Catholics, the Presbyterians and the Puritans, were *not* a sect or a religious group, but their tenets were, rather obviously, the most dangerous of all for a monarch of his kind. Indeed, the definition of English law as the 'law of the land', which today goes practically unnoticed, implies that it is not the king's law.

In his cited book as well as in his speech in Parliament of 21 March 1609, James I designed a sketch of a royal sovereignty of supernatural origin, otherwise known as the divine right of kings. He described it as a form of perfect government because it was the closest to the divine archetype that could not be limited by any other earthly power.[38] Three are the pillars of this royal authority: divine revelation, the laws of nature, and the laws of the *realm*.

The first pillar is based on Psalms 82:6 '*ego dixi dii estis*' (I say that you are gods), where according to His Majesty's interpretation, God is affirming that the kings are divine, and that, as in Luther, they can respond only to Him for their actions. The king's duty is that of administering justice (Psalms 101) and to give just laws to the people (2 Kings 18 and 22–23; 2 Corinthians 29 and 34–35), to keep the peace (Psalms 72) and to be a good shepherd procuring abundance to his realm

[36] King James I was the author of works such as *Daemonologie* (1597), *The True Law of Free Monarchies* (1598) and *Basilikon Doron* (1599). See CH McIlwain (ed), *The Political Works of James I* (Cambridge, Harvard University Press, 1918).

[37] F Oakley, *The Watershed of Modern Politics. Law, Virtue, Kingship and Consent (1300–1650)* (New Haven, Yale University Press, 2015) 254.

[38] James I, 'Basilikon Doron' in CH McIlwain (ed), *The Political Works of James I* 1.

(1 Samuel 8; Jeremiah 29). As a minister, he is a servant of God for the good of all the righteous (Romans 13:1–7).

The second pillar is legal and historical and pertains particularly to the origins of the Scottish monarchy. In theory, we could imagine that the flock of the feeble convened to entrust their protection to the strongest under certain specified conditions. Until then the law would have preceded the institution of the monarchy. But story has it that King Fergus left Ireland to conquer a Scotland inhabited by barbarians to whom, after their defeat and submission, he gave his laws. It follows that it is the king who precedes the law and not vice versa, and that is why he has precedence over all other classes, the parliament and its laws. As a necessary consequence, the kings make the laws, and it is not the laws that make the kings.[39] A sovereign will always try to remain faithful to his laws, but in no way is he bound by them. He can act as he wishes without being questioned by any jurisdiction.

A third argument advanced in the name of the law of nature is as follows: a king is like a father to his people, or like a head to the body; in both cases he is leading the subordinate parts of the whole. Just as a father can punish a son for the sake of the family, so can the head cut an arm off for the salvation of the whole body. It is understood that the body could not reciprocally cut the head off, even if sick, for it would immediately perish.[40]

His conclusion is almost apparent. Obedience is always due to a sovereign king, as he has been enthroned by God. He is also owed guardianship of the faith in accord with the Act of Supremacy of Henry VIII (1534). He is the rightful and legitimate head of the Church of England, and has full power to reprise, punish, reform, rule, correct and amend all the mistakes, heresies and abuses for the glory of the Christian religion and for the keeping of the union and peace of the realm.

As has been noted, the political theology of James I seems to be based on two apparently inconsistent premises.[41] On one hand, the king is clearly bound to realise the good of the kingdom, and he is responsible for it. Then there would be a divine order establishing what is right or wrong on earth and would sanction every deviation, even those of a king. Right and wrong, good and evil have been laid down by God, *before* the institution of civil governments and the elevation of monarchs so that justice does not depend on the king's will. An arbitrary monarch becomes a tyrant and an enemy of God's justice. We could well say that for James a monarch is free because 'he does not recognise any other power on earth above himself' (Job 41:25). No one on earth has jurisdiction over him. This contradiction leads to an inescapable conclusion: the sovereign must obey God's laws, but on earth, his laws are God's laws. There is no *residue* left from the heavenly order to the worldly political one. The latter is perfectly mirroring the former, and the

[39] James I, 'The True Law of Free Monarchies' in CH McIlwain (ed), *The Political Works of James I* 53.
[40] James I, 'The True Law of Free Monarchies' 64–66.
[41] Scattola, *Teologia politica* 82.

former is completely transfused in the latter. The world order is a hierarchy of jurisdictions and obedience designed by God. There is no disjuncture, nor discontinuity between the temporal and the spiritual. Only the king knows what is good and evil and when and how to act. The only duty of the subjects is to obey.

At this point, we can certainly trace an important parallel with the work of Jean Bodin (1530–1596), and especially his reception in Germany, even if we may find in these matters an obviously much more complex and baroque evolution toward the metaphysics of metaphors applied to political theory.[42] The world political order described by these authors becomes indeed a *representation* of the divine order of the universe. This point is rather important from an ontological perspective. The Roman Emperor *was* the Lord of the World. The Byzantine Emperor was the *ikon*, the true image of God on earth, participating in His essence. German emperors became *figures* of the Christ or the Anti-Christ. Now the world could start to be seen as a theatre, the physical space of a representation of invisible characters and forces. The king re-presents God, making Him present again.

As Walter Benjamin has noted, there is an ontological side in a metaphor as a metaphor *is* an experience.[43] We can read the original passage on the *Dominus Mundi* in the *Digest* either in the sense that the Roman emperor *is* the master of the world or in the sense that he is like the Lord of it. But what does it really mean that he is a *representation* of the Lord?

Here we touch upon the existence of invisible entities that become visible even if they are not *incarnated* by someone. A king is not an incarnation of some invisible entity; rather, he is a representation, no less than parliaments are representations of the people. We turn toward a world theatre that is essentially an aesthetic world, where aesthetics is to be thought of as the dimension in which something invisible becomes visible. The matter is then, as we think James likely understood, that of the *residue* that can separate that which is represented and that which is representing. For his theory of sovereignty, it was essential that no residue could be left in the king's performance of God's role on earth. Any possible residue would operate politically and legally in the very possibility of a jurisdiction over the king's acts, if not finally in the possibility of his execution for high treason.

James's theological reflections can be seen in the context of strongly alternative and competing political and constitutional theories. This is especially so against the background of those murky discussions which have characterised the definition of emergency powers and of the king's different *personae*. This debate bypasses the problem of the Stuarts' presumed despotism,[44] and must be fully

[42] M Stolleis, 'La reception de Bodin en Allemagne' (1995) 24 *Quaderni fiorentini* 141.

[43] W Benjamin, *The Origin of German Tragic Drama* (J Osborne trans, London, Verso, 2009). See also B Cowan, 'Benjamin's Theory of Allegory' (1981) 22 *New German Critique* 109.

[44] GR Elton, *England under the Tudors* (London, Routledge, 1960) 403; F Oakley 'Jacobean Political Theology: The Absolute and Ordinary Powers of the King' (1968) 29 *Journal of the History of Ideas* 323, 346.

appreciated in relation to the revival of the imperial mysticism grounded upon the notion of *dominium mundi*.

From our perspective, the judgment delivered in 1606 by Chief Baron Fleming in the *Bate's Case* is of critical importance.[45] At its heart lies the crucial remark that Fleming made about the 'absolute' and 'ordinary' powers of the king, and we will give this remark the close scrutiny it deserves.

From this case, it emerges that the king's power is double, both ordinary and absolute, and that these two powers have several and different laws and ends. Ordinary powers are possessed for the *particular* profit of the *subjects*, the execution of civil justice in ordinary courts, and are nominated by the civilians under the rubric of the *jus privatum*. In England, these powers belong to the realm of the common law.[46] These laws cannot be changed without a parliamentary vote, yet they can never really be changed in substance, as they seem to express rather universal and immutable principles of justice.

On the contrary, the *absolute* power of the King is that which is applied for the *general* benefit of the *people*, for the *salus populi*: as the people are the body, and the king is the head.[47] It follows that this power is most properly named 'Policy and Government'. As the constitution of the body of the people varies with time, so too does this 'absolute law' vary according to the wisdom of the king and for the common good.

There is then an absolute and a common law, as there are ordinary and absolute powers, a distinction that already appeared in the Year Book for 1469 under the Latin names of *potentia ordinata* and *absoluta*.[48]

Of course, here we face a distinction destined to have great impact. It was Dr James Cowell, Professor of Civil Law at Cambridge, who in 1607 described the king as *supra legem* because of his absolute powers, reigning beyond the ordinary course of the common law.[49]

In the words of Davies, Attorney-General for Ireland, the king exercises a double power, namely, an absolute power, or *merum Imperium*, when he 'doth use Prerogatives only, which is not bound by positive law',[50] and an ordinary power of jurisdiction. Moreover, as we know, following James, Blackstone paralleled these prerogatives with the *mysteries* of the *bona dea*, ranking them among the

[45] *Bate's Case or Case of Impositions* [1606] 2 State Trial 371; see also JW Allen, *English Political Thought, 1603–1660* (London, Methuen & Co, 1938) 8.

[46] F Oakley 'Jacobean Political Theology: the Absolute and Ordinary Powers of the King' 327.

[47] *Money Case* [1637] in TB Howell (ed), *A Complete Collection of State Trials and Proceedings for High Treason and Other Crimes and Misdemeanors from the Earliest Period to the Year 1783, with Notes and Other Illustrations*, vol 2 (London, Longman, Hurst, Rees, Orme and Brown, 1816) 389.

[48] Year Book 9, Edward IV, Trinity 9; F Oakley, 'Jacobean Political Theology: the Absolute and Ordinary Powers of the King' 324.

[49] F Oakley, *Kingship: the Politics of Enchantment* (Malden, Blackwell Publishing, 2006) 129.

[50] J Davies, *The Question Concerning Impositions, Tonnage, Poundage … Fully Stated and Argued from Reason, Law and Policy* (London, H Twyford, 1656) 30–31; see Oakley, *Jacobean Political Theology* 325.

arcana imperii. In particular, Blackstone reaches the point of speaking of a necessary 'initiation' into the mysteries of the royal prerogatives.[51]

Through this distinction between *potestas ordinata* and *potestas absoluta*, we can conceive of the king as *having a large and indefinite reserve of power*, which he could *on occasion* use for the benefit of the state.[52] Significantly, the existence of that reserve of power goes beyond definition, constitution and words, as awe and charisma, as a *sublime* political power to deal with matters of state. As hidden powers, they are *mysteries*. This hidden and unspeakable *residue* constitutes the essence of the political sublime. This is the most important point.

The shift toward an *occultism* of royal prerogatives was widespread. It goes far beyond the neutralising concept of *absolutism* by which we normally try to capture this form of monarchy. Absolutism is, rather, a royal occultism. As we know, Baldus[53] spoke of the prince as being capable of derogating from the ordinary right by his absolute power, *though* not from the laws of 'God and of nature', in this sense using the same words as Spinoza and his devastating formula of *Deus sive Natura*, whose implications are still to be fully apprehended. It is not just a matter of emphasis on Roman law, or the revival of forms used by Cynus of Pistoia or Bartolus.[54] As Oakley reports, Baldus also had introduced the terms absolute and ordinary in his gloss on the *Lex Digna* (Cod 1.14.4) in an attempt to clarify that the prince was bound to live according to the laws out of his benevolence, not out of necessity. The point—for us—is rather the sovereign possessing an occult dimension that supersedes orthodox political theologies.

All of this is lost in the standard accounts of Romanists for the good reason that, to a large extent, it was the *canon* law that deeply influenced conceptions of modern sovereignty. The insertion of canonist principles into the body of Roman law led to a kind of *double modality* in the exercise of sovereign powers: a modality—to use the words of Oakley—running in accordance with the common law, or the common course of nature; and an exercise of the *plenitudo potestatis*, or of the *special* providence of the Lord. We could say that, according to these speculations, in God and in the pope resides a plenitude of power, a residue of an undefinable power to act.

This residue is the one that Schmitt tried to capture in his analogies between the state of exception and miracles. God can act outside the laws of nature and perform a miracle, just as when He did when He enabled Shadrach, Meshach, and Abednego to emerge unscathed from the flames of Nebuchadnezzar's

[51] W Blackstone, *Commentaries on the Laws of England, Volume 1: A Facsimile of the First Edition of 1765–1769* (Chicago, The University of Chicago Press, 1979) book 1, ch 7, 231.

[52] CH McIlwain, *Constitutionalism Ancient and Modern* (London, The Lawbook Exchange, 2005) 94.

[53] Baldus [Cod 1.14.4].

[54] Bartolus, *Commentaria in primam Codicis partem* (Venetiis, Baptista de Tortis, 1493) fol 36; Cynus of Pistoia, *Lectura super aurea volumine Codicis* (Venetiis, Andrea de Thoresanis de Asula, 1493) fol b 8 v; see Oakley, *Jacobean Political Theology* 330.

fiery furnace.[55] In the same way, the pope can perform a papal miracle[56] by an exercise of his absolute power. But can a king perform miracles? It is hard not to see here a strong heterodox normative inversion where that which is unorthodox becomes political.

Of course, we may find several references[57] to the omnipotence of God in St Jerome (347–420), through Gratian (359–383) and St Peter Damian (1007–1073), in Hugo of Saint Victor (1096–1141), Peter Abelard (1079–1142), Peter Lombard (1096–1160) and in William of Ockham (1280–1349). Albert the Great (1200–1280) was, perhaps, the first scholastic to have used the precise distinction between *potentia absoluta* and *potentia ordinate*.[58] Given this theoretical background and the revival of theological concepts in the twentieth century, what distinguishes Schmitt's conception of political theology from the medieval discourse is his neutralisation of the pure political dimension of modern sovereignty. For us, his theory is a conscious *cover up* of the change in values that occurred after the Reformation. Its real purpose is to reactivate Roman Catholicism and its philosophical-historical tradition against the heterodox political forces that prevailed in modernity.

If we place the sovereign as the *locus* of exception, his position lies on the threshold where the *Dominus*, the guardian of order, merges with Belial, the angel of anomie (2 Cortinthians 6:15). We could say that the angel of anomie operates in a state of exception, in an extraordinary state of affairs. In his *Speech of the Star Chamber* in 1616 on his prerogatives, James placed a particular emphasis on the 'extraordinary'.[59]

There are multiple examples from this age. In 1528, Henry VIII asked for a dispensation to proceed with a second marriage, something that the pope could not do using his ordinary power, but that, the king claimed, he could dispense out of his *mere* and *absolute* power above the law.[60] But, we insist, it is one thing to ask the pope to act in a miraculous way; it is another to take possession of the extraordinary and locate it at the centre of political sovereignty as the power to act *praeter legem vel contra eam* (beyond and against law).[61]

As we have already seen, Bartolus elaborated on this dichotomy in his representation of the figure of the *Dominus Mundi*. Nevertheless, as long as we speak of the exceptional powers of the pope, we remain in the realm of orthodoxy.

[55] Daniel 3:20 ff.

[56] See Oakley, 'Jacobean Political Theology' 333 with reference to Aegidius Romanus, *De ecclesiastica potestate* (Richard Scholz ed, Weimar, Hermann Bohlaus Nachfolger, 1929) 158 and 192.

[57] For all references see Oakley, 'Jacobean Political Theology' 334.

[58] F Oakley, *Politics and Eternity: Studies in the History of Medieval and Early Modern Political Thought* (Leiden, Brill, 1999) 261.

[59] James I, 'Speech of the Star Chamber' (1616) in CH McIlwain (ed), *The Political Works of James I* 333; and see Blackstone, *Commentaries on the Law of England*, book 1, ch 7, 231.

[60] Henry VIII, 'Instructions to Sir Francis Bryan and Peter Vannes, Rome' in JS Brewer (ed), *Letters and Papers, Foreign and Domestic of the Reign of Henry VIII*, vol 4 (London, Royal Commission for State Papers, 1870) part 2, n 4977, 2158.

[61] Oakley, 'Jacobean Political Theology' 334.

When we start to speak of the circumstances by which the king can do things *de facto* which he cannot do *de jure*, and especially when we clearly speak of a reserve of power possessed by the king for extraordinary cases[62] (or as Charleton put it in 1652, a royal 'reserved power'),[63] we get out of the pure economy of salvation. We face an explicit normative inversion, either in relation to the pope, or in relation to the emperor. It is in this perspective that we can really appreciate the work of Bloch as an antithesis to Schmitt's efforts to bridge the disjuncture between prior theological concepts and those of the modern theory of law and the state.

Certainly, royal prerogatives derive from the consideration that God Himself has created a general law of nature, but he has made no law for miracles. There is no logically necessary connection between this premise and the conclusion that the prerogatives of the king, like those of God, clearly transcend the ordinary. Indeed, there is a gap, a *Kluft*, between the two propositions, which is bridged over by an usurpation, legitimated by the fact that the sovereign must act *pro bono publico*. This is something that could be justified long before Christianity ever entered the stage of history. A political *refoulé* reemerges in the heterodoxy of modernity, not in orthodoxy. This heterodoxy was denied by political theology and the parallel created between earthly institutions and divine power. It was Schmitt who established a link between miracles and exception so stringent as to appear logical. The kings never had a government of exorcism or the miraculous. They had *magic* powers in Bloch's reconstruction, and this magic of the royals was transmuted into a theory of their power backed by theological prerogatives. The path from magic to theology is not a logical necessity, as magic is independent from theology. The disconnection between magic and theology could be bridged by the large and indefinite reserve of power that could be triggered by the exception, *ratione status*. This term, here, is not meant in the derived sense of *State reason*, but in the original sense of the necessary measures to be taken *in reason of the state of things*.

In this way, the exception is then located within the mysterious residue of indefinite power residing in the prerogatives of the Sovereign; that sublime and terrific reserve of power that can end up reversing the legal order.

B. James and Royal Occultism

From our standpoint, there is a still more occult side in James's thought that must be apprehended here. It has to do with the general framework of James's idea of order and the argument by correspondence between kings and God on

[62] James I, 'A Speach to the Lords and Commons of the Parliament at White-Hall' (1609), in CH McIlwain (ed), *The Political Works of James I* 309–10.

[63] W Charleton, *The Darkness of Atheism Dispelled by the Light of Nature: a Physico-Theological Treatise* (1652) (Bristol, Thoemmes, 2002) 329.

which James leaned so heavily in his political writings,[64] and that can ultimately be deemed if not 'blasphemy' certainly 'heterodox'.

This theory of the parallel, or theory of correspondence, between God as *Dominus* in heaven and the monarch as *Dominus* on earth reached its ideological peak in the works of Dante where it was mingled with the imagery of the Roman people as the 'flesh' of the composite corporate body of the empire. According to us, this parallel took a rather heterodox turn starting with James, especially concerning the abyss of tacit powers.

The matter of royal prerogatives is echoed in both James's Star Chamber Speech in 1616 and earlier in 1609 in his important address to Parliament, which is central to understanding his particular political theory.[65] In the Star Chamber Speech, James clearly developed a mystical view of his powers:

> The mysteries of the Kings power is not lawfully to be disputed …
>
> It would amount to take away to mystical reverence that belongs unto them that sit in the Throne of God.[66]

This is a peculiarly heterodox position. Not even Frederick I could admit to sitting on the Throne of God, even if he proclaimed himself to be the Lord of the World and conceived his mission in messianic terms. Only the Son of Man (Mark 14:62; Daniel 7:13; Psalms 110:1) could have been elevated to the point of sitting in heaven with God on his *left*.

Once he established this heterodox correspondence, James considerably elaborated his ideas by the introduction of a further analogy between on the one hand, the absolute and ordinary powers of God, and, on the other, the absolute and ordinary, or regulated, powers of the king.

> I desire you to give much more right in my private Prerogative, that you give to any Subject; and therein will I be acquiescent: As to the absolute Prerogative of the Crowne, that is no Subject for the tongue of a lawyer, nor is lawful to be disputed.
>
> As it is Atheisme and blasphemy to dispute what God can doe: good Christians content themselves with his will revealed in his word. So, it is presumption and high contempt in a Subject to dispute what a King can doe; but rest in that which is the Kings revealed will in his Law.[67]

Here the distinction between the private prerogatives of the person of the monarch and the absolute prerogatives of the Crown is strikingly clear. James's argument relies on a metonymy where the king is represented by the *objective* nature of kingship, which is the crown, and not the person of the king. In this

[64] WH Greenleaf, 'James I and the Divine Right of Kings' (1957) 5 *Political Studies* 36.

[65] F Oakley, 'Jacobean Political Theology' 337; WH Greenleaf, *Order, Empiricism and Politics: Two Traditions of English Political Thought: 1500–1700* (Oxford, Oxford University Press, 1964) 58 ff.

[66] James I, 'Speech of the Star Chamber' (1616) in CH McIlwain (ed), *The Political Works of James I* 333.

[67] James I, 'Speech of the Star Chamber' (1616) 333–34.

sense, kingship is elevated beyond the holder. We can also stress the value of the term '*absolute*' from its meaning of a power being beyond laws and regulations, to the very idea that this prerogative is *beyond words and language*.

In substance, for James it would have been blasphemy to try to ontologise royal mysteries through the use of language, even if done by a lawyer, because not even a lawyer, an oracle of the law, or a *sacerdos* (in this view a priest of royal cult) can articulate those mysteries. Such absolute powers are ineffable. We are certainly shifting toward the aesthetic of the political sublime of modern royal authority in a way that we think would have been completely alien to previous medieval conceptions of the prince.

We would also highlight the distinction between the terms absolute and ordinary, something that offers a different perspective to the term absolute monarchy: if absolute is contrary to ordinary, it is because it is exceptional. Just as in the case of Innocent IV against Frederick II, the mystic of absolute power lies in the fact that it is simultaneously beyond law, beyond language and beyond the ordinary. It is the terrific unspeakable power that can manifest itself in a state of exception, or, if you prefer, in the midst of the storm as in the Book of Job. This power is so unfathomable that, indeed, it does not belong, and cannot belong, to an ordinary man, and consequently it is rhetorically transferred to the crown.

It is in this light that James's address to Parliament in 1609 must be understood, with all its surrounding hints of paganism:

> Kings are justly called Gods, for that they exercise a manner or resemblance of Divine power upon earth.[68]

If kings are justly called gods, can they command the spirits? Can they perform an exorcism? Do they also have jurisdiction over the fairy world? Given James's attitude toward witchcraft revealed in his *Daemonologie*, these questions are not unfounded.

Oakley argued that the distinction between the absolute and ordinary powers of the king was in effect a piece of political theology, generated by the cognate distinction between absolute and ordinary powers of God that emerged in the scholastic theology of the twelfth century and subsequently survived as a commonplace.[69] Later he suggested considering that sixteenth and seventeenth century lawyers were thinking not in terms of two coordinate or parallel powers, each confined by law to its proper sphere, but rather of two powers. One power (the absolute) was in essence superior to the other (the ordinary) and 'in times of necessity' or for 'reason of state' the former could transcend the latter, and, by reaching 'above the ordinary course of the law', encroach upon its domain. This implied that there could have been the perception of a strong difference between the nature of one power and that of the other.

[68] James I, 'A Speech to the Lords and Commons' 307.

[69] F Oakley, 'The "Hidden" and "Revealed" Wills of James I: More Political Theology' (1972) 15 *Studia Gratiana* 367–68.

If we emphasise the distinction made by James, as we did, one power is mysterious, unlimited and 'not lawful to be disputed', whereas the other is clearly fit for discussion, for it is 'the Kings' revealed will in his law'. In sum, we confront a *revealed* power and an *occult* power of the kings—the same distinction meaning, on one side, the 'hidden' will of God, and on the other side, God's 'revealed' will.

Here, we face a concealed, secret or hidden will of God and/or of the Sovereign, and a revealed will of God/Sovereign, that is revealed in the word of God contained in the Holy Scriptures, just as the will of the sovereign is revealed in his laws. This is along the same lines as an unorthodox Gnostic revelation of the existence of a hidden, or occult divine beyond the revealed truth of the scriptures. Even the laws have a visible revealed side but also a hidden occult side pertaining to the sublime of the legal. There is always occult excess, an unfathomable and unexhausted reserve of sense in political action and in the law. There is also something in the juridical-political domain which exceeds it, bypassing and superseding our capacities of verbalisation, and which redirects us toward the excessive nature of the title of the *Dominus Mundi*. The occultism of the political and of hegemony goes far beyond its tentative capture in irenic notions of soft-power.[70]

The distinction between the absolute and ordinary powers had enjoyed a long history, as well as the parallel distinction between the *potentia Dei absoluta* and *ordinata* with which it was linked. The intent of this distinction was to stress the retention in the hands of God or of the king of an absolute, unlimited power whereby the ordinary dispositions of the law could be transcended.[71]

What we want to stress here is the connection with occultism, emphasised by the insistence on the dark side of law and politics, which was reserved for those who were initiated in its mysteries. After all, this was also at the root of the counterargument used by Coke (1552–1634) to deny the king in court: he was not initiated into the mysteries of the temple.[72] The mysteries cannot be deduced by reason, even we cannot know if the occult god has any resemblance to the revealed one. We call this device of a political occultism the too-muchness device, as it is rooted both in Gramscian theory of hegemony as well as in other philosophical theories of the last century.

From certain passages of James's works we could derive Oakley's conclusion that:

> … the vital thing for man is to eschew futile speculation about the dispositions of God's hidden will, and to acquaint himself, instead, with that revealed will thereby God makes known to man the divine *modus operandi* in the moral sphere and in the economy of salvation […][73]

[70] JS Nye, *Soft Power: The Means to Succes in Foreign Politics* (New York, PublicAffairs, 2009).

[71] See W(illiam of) Ockham, *Quodlibeta Septem*, VI.1.1, nn 13–40, in G de Ockham, *Opera Theologica*, vol 9 (JC Wey ed, New York, The Franciscan Institute of St Bonaventure University, 1980) 585 f.

[72] W Holdsworth, 'Sir Edward Coke' (1935) 5 *The Cambridge Law Journal* 332.

[73] Oakley, 'The "Hidden" and "Revealed" Wills of James I' 373.

... *but also* in the political sphere. James's conception that his subjects could not even discuss the royal prerogatives seems like the political equivalent of the philosophical statement that 'What we cannot speak about we must pass over in silence'.[74] This was particularly true here because, for James, to indulge in futile speculations about royal prerogatives was also a crime of treason: 'As it is blasphemy ... it is treason ...'.

We must literarily pass over in silence what is unlawful to speak about, and that is the essence of *legitimate* power. Legitimacy is surrounded by its unfathomable occult nature.

C. The Devil and the King

At this point, however, more than James's conceptions of God in relation to the Crown Prerogative, it may be of great interest for us to analyse his theory of the Devil. According to Orr, James's articulation of divine right kingship also served as a bulwark against the perceived *threat of the supernatural* to his rule, starting from the demonic threat to the peace and stability of his rule in Scotland, and the panics provoked by the spread of witchcraft in 1590–91 and 1596–97.[75]

Stuart Clark[76] was the first one to point out the political dimensions of early modern demonological writings. As we know, James was actively interested in witchcraft at a time when witches were seen as the Devil's sworn servants, tacitly or formally covenanted to a power other than that of God and his lawful lieutenant on earth. Moreover, James was involved in the witch hunt, and in particular in the prosecution of North Berwick in 1590–99, taking a personal role in the interrogation of the accused witches.[77] We cannot overlook this element, as it is well represented by his contemporaries and by Shakespeare, in particular in *Macbeth*. The regicide perpetrated in the drama represents the worst kind of treason because it originated in the prophecy of witches, and in the tacit pact that Macbeth formed with demonic instances in seeking to fulfil that prophecy.

In a way, we can say that James's reflections articulated a fully developed political theory serving to legitimise the king's role as God's chosen instrument

[74] L Wittgenstein, *Tractatus Logicus-Philosophicus* (London, Kegan Paul, 1922) proposition n 7.

[75] DA Orr, '"God's Hangman": James VI, the Divine Right of Kings, and the Devil' (2016) 18 *Reformation & Renaissance Review* 137.

[76] S Clark, 'King James's *Daemonologie*: Witchcraft and Kingship' in S Anglo (ed), *The Damned Art: Essays in the Literature of Witchcraft* (London, Routledge & K Paul, 1977) 159; J Wormald, 'The Witches, the Devil and the King' in T Brotherstone and D Ditchburn (eds), *Freedom and Authority: Scotland, c. 1050–c. 1650: Historical and Historiographical Essays Presented to Grant G. Simpson* (East Linton, Tuckwell Press, 2001) 174–75.

[77] PG Maxwell-Stuart, *Satan's Conspiracy: Magic and Witchcraft in Sixteenth-century Scotland* (East Linton, Tuckwell Press, 2001); PG Maxwell-Stuart, 'King James's Experience of Witches, and the 1604 English Witchcraft Act' in J Newton and Jo Bath (eds), *Witchcraft and the Act of 1604* (Leiden, Brill, 2008) 31–46.

for combating the Devil, in a context where the theory of witchcraft evolved in strict connection with the events closely examined by Maxwell Stuart. We refer in particular to the connection between the circumstances of the North Berwick witch hunt and the troublesome Earl of Bothwell, a detail which also strongly interested Schmitt in his study on Hamlet.[78] In these trials, witnesses were collected to prove that the Devil appeared personally to his adepts, declaring that he hated the king, because James was the greatest enemy he had on earth. It was not then by chance that in his theory of prerogatives, James asserted that the rights of kingship were strictly linked to the king being the child and servant of God.[79]

Indeed, James's *Daemonologie* was written during the panics, a time that can easily be described in modern terms as a prolonged state of exception due to supernatural attacks against the peace of the realm. In his vision, in parallel with the theories of Bodin,[80] the kings enjoy a special immunity from the power of witchcraft by virtue of their divinely ordained offices, such that the witches are disarmed of their occult powers if brought face-to-face with the godly magistrate.

Here, we encounter the issue of control over evil spirits once again at work in political matters, as occurred during the discussions between pope Gregory VII (1010–1085) and emperor Henry IV (1050–1106), when the former denied the latter the authority to practise exorcisms. On this point, James had strong opinions, as he believed that papally licensed exorcists were frauds, the holy water to be at best a cold shower and at worst blasphemous vanity.[81] For him, only inward sincere faith had any efficacy in holding the Devil at bay. But one of James's most intriguing speculations is on the theological justification for the existence of witches and their powers. The *Malleus Maleficarum* (1487)[82]—the most used book of instructions for judges during the witch hunt trials—had emphasised the notion of a divine permission for witchcraft in which God permitted the Devil and his followers to act in the world, but did not actively will them to do evil. Based on this view, it was possible to sustain that the demons that tormented Job were acting with God's permission. James operated consistently with the *Malleus Maleficarum*, asserting that witchcraft depended on the Devil but that his followers were acting as God's 'hangmen' in the world.[83]

[78] C Schmitt, *Hamlet or Hecuba. The Irruption of Time into Play* (S Draghici trans, Corvallis, Plutarch Press, 2006) 16.

[79] Orr, '"God's Hangman": James VI, the Divine Right of Kings, and the Devil' 142.

[80] Orr, '"God's Hangman": James VI, the Divine Right of Kings, and the Devil' 143.

[81] James I, *Daemonologie, in Forme of a Dialogue, Divided into Three Bookes* (Edinburgh, Robert Waldegrave, 1597) 78.

[82] Henricus Institoris (alias Jacob Sprenger), *Malleus Maleficarum* [1487] *The Hammer of Witches. A Complete Translation of the Malleus Malleficarum* (CS Mackay trans, Cambridge, Cambridge University Press, 2009).

[83] L Normand and G Roberts (eds), *Witchcraft in Early Modern Scotland: James VI's Demonology and the North Berwick Witches* (Exeter, University of Exeter Press, 2000) 331; Orr, "God's hangman': James VI, the Divine Right of Kings, and the Devil' 146.

This notion, rightly emphasised by Orr in his study on James, became particularly relevant for a theory of world lordship through the thoughts expressed by the king in his treatise on *The True Law of Free Monarchies*.[84] The treatise can be seen as an attempt to re-legitimise James's kingship in the face of Buchanan's explosive legacy as interpreted by radical Presbyterians as a claim to a right of resistance,[85] some holding that kings could be deposed, exiled, and even executed should they fall into tyranny *or heresy*.[86] Indeed, a real Presbyterian *coup d'état* was attempted in Edinburgh in December 1596 during the witchcraft panic.[87]

The two rival claims, that of the divine right of kings, and that of an equally divine right of resistance against a tyrannical or heretic monarch, came to clash on a supernatural level. In this context, James reaffirmed that the kings were *divinely appointed guardians* charged with combatting the Devil and his servants in the world, and that rebellion was very much like witchcraft, the work of the Devil acting in the world as God's hangman.[88]

This parallel is of extraordinary importance, bypassing the usual analogy traced between the government of heaven and that of the earth, because it emphasises that it is the presence of the Devil that legitimises the prerogatives of the kings. Rebellion and witchcraft are equated, and both are a crime against the king (*not* the church) because the king is appointed in his *political* office as the guardian of demons. The political and the supernatural were perhaps never before so intertwined theoretically as they were in this passage of James's.

What then about the tyrant? James's answer is given in his *Basilikon doron*,[89] where he affirms that only God could judge *wicked* kings and hold them accountable. The king, then, and not the pope or the emperor, becomes the ultimate court on earth who can judge magic and witchcraft. People cannot rebel against a wicked king for the formal reason that they cannot judge magic. Only the king can, and only God can hold him accountable for witchcraft.[90] This is the sovereign's *monopoly*, not of earthly powers but of *supernatural* powers. Magic became the essence of sovereignty as a guardianship of the devils.

[84] James I, 'The True Law of Free Monarchies', in CH McIlwain (ed), *The Political Works of James I* 53 ff.

[85] JH Burns, *The True Law of Kingship: Concepts of Monarchy in Early-modern Scotland* (Oxford, The Clarendon Press, 1996) 234.

[86] Orr, '"God's Hangman": James VI, the Divine Right of Kings, and the Devil' 146.

[87] J Goodare, 'The Attempted Scottish Coup of 1596' in J Goodare and A MacDonald (eds), *Sixteenth Century Scotland. Essays in Honour of M Lynch* (Leiden, Brill, 2008) 311–36.

[88] Orr, '"God's Hangman": James VI, the Divine Right of Kings, and the Devil' 147.

[89] James I, 'Basilikon Doron' in CH McIlwain (ed), *The Political Works of James I* 20.

[90] Orr, '"God's Hangman": James VI, the Divine Right of Kings, and the Devil' 148.

4

Demonological Inversion and the Birth of the Leviathan

I. James I, the Witches and Bodin

A. The Political Sublime and the Legislation on Magic

The aim of this chapter is to analyse the strange interconnections, that we met at the end of the previous chapter, between the rise of the modern concept of sovereignty and the 'political', and the jurisdiction over magic and witchcraft, especially in two different but parallel figures such as King James I of England and Jean Bodin in France. Both authors wrote extensively on witchcraft, the former in his *Daemonologie*[1] and the latter in his *Daemonomanie*,[2] and both helped to craft the key features of the modern political concept of sovereignty, in practice and in theory. As such, this chapter is devoted to rethinking the origin of modernity and its genealogy pointing to the *sublime aspects* of the political, focusing on its ineffable quality.

A concept re-discovered by Edmund Burke,[3] the 'sublime' denotes those features of human sensibility that are 'beyond words' and probably beyond clear and explicit thought. In this way, everything which is at the same time terrifying but attractive, hazardous but seductive, too large but inescapable, is 'sublime'. To capture the idea, it is enough for the moment to remember that from the standpoint of Burke's aesthetics the sunny Mediterranean in daylight is a piece of beauty, but the stormy North Sea wrapped in darkness is sublime.

Our investigation is then about the dark side of the genealogy of the modern political which happened to be denied by rationalism and to fall into latency. Yet this dark side persists as a remnant, a residue, exceeding our capacity to verbalise thoroughly what politics is at the national and international level.

[1] James I, *Daemonologie, in Forme of a Dialogue, Divided into Three Bookes* (Edinburgh, Robert Waldegrave, 1597).

[2] See J Bodin, *De la démonomanie des sorciers* (Paris, Jacques Du Puys, 1580, reprint, Hildesheim, Georg Olms Verlag, 1988); J Bodin, *Les six livres de la Republique* (Paris, Jacques Du Puys, 1576).

[3] E Burke, *A Philosophical Enquiry into the Origin of Our Ideas of the Sublime and Beautiful* (1757) (A Phillips ed, Oxford, Oxford University Press, 1990).

What, then, lies at the heart of our political conceptions? What exactly is defeating rationalism in the domain of politics? What is the existential nature of political decisions? What kind of ghosts are still dominating a globalised world and is the West not, after all, one of the most *exotic* places in the world today?

Of course, having to do with witchcraft and the romantic sublime, our theory deals with the place of heterodoxy within the transformations which shaped European rationalism. I would like to stress the use of the categories of heterodoxy and orthodoxy instead of the more common divide between rationalism and irrationalism. Those who had to do with witches were not irrational at all, they simply had a *social ontology* different from *ours*. It was on this basis that many of them, including Bodin, were condemned as heterodox by the Church.

This chapter tries to supersede the Schmittian paradigm of political theology, as an historical account on the genealogy of modernity which follows the *plot of the fall*. Once there were theological concepts moulding our understanding of the world and the law; these concepts *decayed* into pure political and legal conceptions, and, as a consequence, modern political orders are but broken pieces of a fallen theology, haunted by its memory. These accounts are themselves a form of self-improving theological understanding of the Western political tradition, implying a sense of nostalgia (or even melancholy) for the pre-political world. From this standpoint, they can be labelled 'orthodox', as they still believe in a lost paradise of theological ontology surviving under the surface of modernity.

By contrast, we think that the birth of the political represented a major fracture in the history of the West, and that its origins were much more heterodox than expected. Our main claim is that the origin of modernity had a *demonological* quality, which also lies at the heart of the romantic aesthetics of the sublime. This reverses Schmitt's paradigm, so far as it implies a condemnation of political romanticism,[4] interpreting it as a form of eternal discussion avoiding the central point of *decision*.

Our project is to show how the pure political element in Western thought emerged from the heterodoxy of magic, and that its 'ineffable' dimension was a major concern for romantic aesthetics. This chapter will develop the premises of this argument, and the next chapter will further develop the argument. Here, our attention will focus on two main works: James's *Daemonologie* and Bodin's *Daemonomanie*.

Following this path, in the following sections we shall present the evolution of English legislation on magic to see how it began at the threshold of modernity, and how it *transformed* witchcraft into a *political* crime of high treason. We shall then discuss King James's conceptions of witchcraft *and* the *arcana imperii*, or the mysteries of royal prerogatives. His conceptions will be compared with those expressed by Jean Bodin in the *Daemonomanie* and in his reflections on the

[4] C Schmitt, *Political Romanticism* (G Oakes trans, Cambridge, MIT Press, 1991) 29.

Republic, which led him to his famous definition of sovereignty.[5] Our main point will be that the Church condemned the books of Bodin as *heterodox* precisely because they offered a *political* theory of magic. On this basis, we shall formulate a first tentative conclusion linking demonology, heterodoxy and the aesthetics of the sublime.

The central importance of magic at the emergence of the modern political was illustrated by the inclusion of such a supernatural element into the legislative body of England as a *political* crime. From this standpoint, we then consider the capture of the magic element within English legislation and its evolution over time.

The first striking point to be noted is that it was at the very threshold of modernity that Henry VIII's Act of 1542 (33 Hen VIII c 8) defined witchcraft as a *felony* of high treason, that is to say as a *political* crime. The Act shows the strict parallel that was created at the time between *magic* and *treason* (this latter considered as the political crime *par excellence*). Under the law, witchcraft was considered punishable by death and the confiscation of property. Indeed, it was forbidden to:

> use devise practise or exercise, or cause to be devysed practised or exercised, any Invovacons or cojuracons of Sprites witchecraftes enchauntementes or sorceries to thentent to fynde money or treasure or to waste consume or destroy any persone in his bodie membres, or to pvoke [provoke] any persone to unlawfull love, or for any other unlawfull intente or purpose ... or for dispite of Cryste, or for lucre of money, dygge up or pull downe any Crosse or Crosses or by such Invovacons or cojuracons of Sprites witchecraftes enchauntementes or sorceries or any of them take upon them to tell or declare where goodes stollen or lost shall become.[6]

This Act removed the right known as *benefit of clergy* from those convicted of witchcraft. This was a provision by which reading a passage from the Bible could spare the convicted from the death penalty. This fact transformed the jurisdiction over witchcraft from the sphere of religion to that of politics. Edward VI, the son of Henry VIII, repealed this statute in 1547.

At the beginning of the reign of Elizabeth I, another act called the Act Against Conjurations, Enchantments and Witchcrafts (5 Eliz I c 16) was passed. In some way more merciful than the previous one towards those found guilty, it demanded the death penalty only where harm had been caused, otherwise the convicted would be punishable by imprisonment. According to the Act, anyone who should 'use, practise, or exercise any Witchcraft, Enchantment, Charm, or Sorcery, whereby any person shall happen to be killed or destroyed' was considered guilty of a felony punishable by death, without the benefit of clergy.

In 1604, the Elizabethan Act was reformed and renamed as An Act against Conjuration, Witchcraft and dealing with evil and wicked spirits (2 Ja I c 12). This increased the penalty, making it punishable by death without benefit of clergy for anyone who invoked evil spirits or communed with them.

[5] Bodin, *Les six livres de la Republique*, book 1, ch 8; J Bodin, *Six Books of The Commonwealth* (KD McRae ed, Cambridge, Harvard University Press, 1962) 84.

[6] Linguistic variants are in the original version of the text.

The main goals achieved by the Acts of Elizabeth and James were the reformation of the law of witchcraft by making it a felony, moving the jurisdiction over these crimes from the ecclesiastical courts to the common law courts, where the prosecution of the accused occurred according to ordinary criminal procedure. This shift represents a point of emergence of the modern political and its capacity to expand over religious and spiritual matters, seizing magic within an attempt to create the 'modern'—and we claim, a particularly exotic—model of the European state. This model later developed into a general concept of political theory to be applied all over the world as a global concept.

It is, then, of relevance to remember the attitudes of Elizabeth I and James I towards the royal prerogatives as a key point of the English constitution. According to Blackstone:

> [The matter of prerogatives Royal] was ranked among the *arcana imperii*; and, like the mysteries of the *bona dea*, was not suffered to be pried into by any but such as were initiated in its service ... The glorious Queen Elizabeth herself made no scruple to direct her parliaments to abstain from discoursing of matters of state ... even that august assembly ought not to deal, to judge or to meddle to her majesty's prerogative royal.[7]

King James went further, and in a perfect statement of what has become the theory of political theology he declared that:

> As it is atheism and blasphemy in a creature to dispute what the deity may do, so it is presumption and sedition in a subject to dispute what a king may do in the height of his power: good Christians, he adds, will be content with God's will, revealed in his word; and good subjects will rest in the king's will, revealed in *his* law.[8]

Sovereignty rests upon a mystery and it is blasphemy, and therefore a felony and a *sedition*, to even have a conversation about the royal prerogatives. Here, we face a *hyperbole* of the human prince becoming (ontologically) a mortal god on earth suffused with mysteries that require an initiation to be coped with. Thus, it would not be absurd for this (mortal) god to have jurisdiction over the spiritual and the magic, or for the use of witchcraft to be deemed a crime of felony. More than a fall from the theological to the political, we witness here the rise of the pure political to the sublime sphere of the theological through the control of the commerce with the evil spirits.

If this is what happened at the origin of modernity, and its peculiar institutions, we may perceive how much later rationalism took a different stance when we consider the newer Act that came into force in 1735, when the intellectual landscape had already changed.

While many thinkers of that period considered witchcraft an *impossible* crime, the Witchcraft Act of 1735 (9 Geo 2 c 5) determined a radical change that applied to the whole of Great Britain by punishing even the pretense of witchcraft.

[7] W Blackstone, *Commentaries on the Laws of England, Volume 1: A Facsimile of the First Edition of 1765–1769* (Chicago, The University of Chicago Press, 1979) book 1, ch 7, 230.

[8] James I, 'Speech of the Star Chamber' (1616) in CH McIlwain (ed), *The Political Works of James I* (Cambridge, Harvard University, 1918) 333.

Simply claiming to have the power to cast spells, predict the future, or communicate with spirits was sufficient to subject the person to fines and imprisonment.

Here, the matter is no longer the reality of witchcraft and its insertion within the political domain, but its falsehood. Under the Witchcraft Act of 1735, witchcraft was no longer high treason, but became a kind of fraud. *Pretending* to use it became punishable as such, *not* for its possible use in political struggles and conjurations, but for its deception of the public. This represented a change in the ontology of magic, and its loss of political relevance.

Curiously, the Witchcraft Act of 1735 was repealed only in 1951, with the enactment of the Fraudulent Mediums Act. The repeal of the 1735 Act indicated a shift from prohibiting magic towards regulating fraud. The 1951 Act was repealed in turn by the Consumer Protection Regulations in 2008, which transposed an EU directive targeting unfair sales and marketing practices.

Whatever we may think of the theory of *secularisation* of Western societies,[9] which we shall confront in the next chapter, the legislative history discussed here displays it in its purest form. From the relevance of magical practices as real conjurations with evil spirits, from which sprang its political relevance and its inclusion in the law in the form of felony, we arrived to its irrelevance and therefore toward its exclusion from public law to the domain of private law as a matter of consumer protection. That is to say, it became a matter of market regulation to prevent fraud and protect prospective contractors. This secularisation had less to do with God than the Devil. The Devil was secularised and pushed toward the substantial irrelevance of private law from the standpoint of the political.

B. James's *Daemonologie*

In the previous section, we saw how modernity emerged as a *hyperbole* of the human prince raised to the level of a divine instantiation within the political realm to the point of even having jurisdiction over witchcraft, to the detriment of the ecclesiastical courts. Now we should consider the intellectual construct that accompanied this origin of modern political power in Europe. We will attempt to unveil the heterodox and hidden, behind the orthodox and visible, nature of its institutions by referring to King James's conceptions in his book on witchcraft: the *Daemonologie*.

This book is conceived as a typical allegorical and baroque dialogue between one Philomates and his friend, Epistemon. In the *preface* to the reader, the royal author states:

> The fearefull aboundinge at this time in this countrie, of these detestable slaues of the Deuill, the Witches or enchaunters, hath moved me (beloued reader) to dispatch in post,

[9] On this point see E-W Böckenförde, 'The Rise of the State as a Process of Secularization' in E-W Böckenförde (ed), *State, Society and Liberty: Studies in Political Theory and Constitutional Law* (IA Underwood trans, New York, Berg, 1991) 26.

> this following treatise of mine … to resolue the doubting harts of many; both that such assaultes of Sathan are most certainly practized, & that the instrumentes thereof, merits most severly to be punished … against the damnable opinions of two principally in our age, wherof the one called SCOT an Englishman, deny, that ther can be such a thing as Witch-craft: and so mainteines the old error of the Sadducees, in denying of spirits. The other called VVIERVS, a German Phisition, sets out a publick apologie for al these craftes-folkes, whereby, procuring for their impunitie, he plainely bewrayes himselfe to haue bene one of that profession.[10]

What is striking here is the reaffirmation of the reality of magic by a political authority against those rationalist thinkers like the German Johan Weyer (VVIERVUS). Weyer wrote an elaborate dissertation and was also the target of Bodin.[11] Thus, two of the most outstanding authors of modern theory and practice of sovereignty, James and Bodin, both stood against the rational thinking of Weyer, who denied the reality of spirits. This raises a suspicion that the connection between the new concept of sovereign power and the struggle over witchcraft and its ontological-political status is more than a mere coincidence.

King James divided his book into three parts: the first speaking of 'Magie' generally, and *Necromancie* specifically; the second of *sorcery* and *witchcraft*; and the third containing 'a discourse of all these kindes of spirits, & Spectres that appeares & trobles persones'. This partition is of particular importance if we consider *Hamlet*, which was written in the years of James's ascension. In the first act, it contains a long and detailed discussion with Horace about the nature of spirits and ghosts and the possibility of having a commerce with them. This is precisely what Hamlet finally did, and, perhaps in the conception of the time, was a possible cause of his malaise and in particular his *melancholy*.[12]

Throughout his book, King James makes explicit reference to Jean Bodin as an authority:

> BODINVS Dæmonomanie, collected with greater diligence, then written with judgement, together with their confessions, that have been at this time apprehended. And if he woulde knowe what are the particuler rites, & curiosities of these black arts (which is both vnnecessarie and perilous,) he will finde it in the fourth book of CORNELIVS Agrippa.[13]

Here, Bodin is paralleled to Henry Cornelius Agrippa (1486–1535), who was among the principal inspirers of the Elizabethan occult philosophy according

[10] James I, *Daemonologie* 2.

[11] Johann Weyer or Wier (1515–1588) was a Dutch occultist and demonologist famous during his times for publishing the treatise *De Praestigiis Daemonum et Incantationibus ac Venificiis* (On the Illusions of the Demons and on Spells and Poisons) (Basileae, ex officina Operiniana, 1568).

[12] For the contemporary relevance of the feeling of melancholy, remember R Burton, *An Anatomy of Melancholy* (1621) (TC Faulkner, NK Kiessling and RL Blair eds, Oxford, The Clarendon Press, 1989).

[13] James I, *Daemonologie, sine pagina* but 6.

to Yates,[14] and who crafted her cult in the form of the *Fairie Queene*.[15] Here, King James makes reference to melancholy:

> For as the humor of Melancholie in the selfe is blacke, heauie and terrene, so are the symptomes thereof, in any persones that are subject therevnto, leannes, palenes, desire of solitude: and if they come to the highest degree therof, mere folie and Manie.[16]

Without going into too much detail, his *legal* conclusion deserves to be looked at, since it is precisely that which we have seen in dealing with English legislation:

> Philomates: Then to make an ende of our conference, since I see it drawes late, what forme of punishment thinke ye merites these Magicians and Witches? For I see that ye account them to be all alike guiltie?
>
> Epistemon: They ought to be put to death according to the Law of God, the ciuill and imperial law, and municipall law of all Christian nations.[17]

To state it in today's terms, the conclusion is derived from a comparative law perspective. There is a concordance of the laws of God, of the Empire and of all other positive laws of Christian nations, but this argument becomes immediately theological-political in equating a treason against God with a felony against the sovereign:

> The assise must serue for interpretour of our law in that respect. But in my opinion, since in a mater of treason against the Prince, barnes or wiues, or neuer so diffamed persons, may of our law serue for sufficient witnesses and proofes. I thinke surely that by a far greater reason, such witnesses may be sufficient in matters of high treason against God.[18]

The passage from an earthly feudal authority to the newer figure of the political sovereign to emerge from these steps of early modernity is achieved here by means of a previously unexpected equation between the king and God. Whatever we may think of Schmitt's theory and its uses, we find at work here that typical device of political-theology that he discovered, or better, uncovered from its oblivion.

But what we want to underline here is its genealogy from the jurisdiction over devils. After all, the matter of witchcraft is ontologically and politically relevant as long as the devils do exist and operate in the kingdom. Otherwise, it becomes only a question of consumer protection. Thus, it is just the reality of the Devil, and his capacity to operate through human beings, which is furnishing a base for the king's pretension to be politically able to act politically like a god on earth. In James's theories, the mysterious royal prerogatives are there to protect the subjects first of all against the Devil's powers.

[14] FA Yates, *The Occult Philosophy in the Elizabethan Age* (London, Routledge & K Paul, 1979) 43.
[15] PJ Alpers, *The Poetry of the Faerie Queene* (Princeton, Princeton University Press, 1967).
[16] James I, *Daemonologie*, book 2, ch I, 30.
[17] James I, *Daemonologie*, book 3, ch VI, 77.
[18] James I, *Daemonologie*, book 3, ch VI, 79.

Our own suspicion is, thus, that there is more of a *demonological* than a pure *theological* origin to modern sovereignty; or, to better state it, that the political-theological device is in its own turn the by-product of a deeper political-demonological complex.

In a way, what we try to maintain is opposite to Schmitt's pure theory. It is not the king assuming the function of a *katechon*—'restrainer'[19]—because of his theologisation; rather it is his own political capacity to produce protection that implies, via the ontological-rhetorical experience of his hyperbole, his own newer and modern (non-medieval) status of Sovereign, implying his jurisdiction over devils, his power over them, to the point of judging them for felony and high treason.

In this way, the original device of demonology is the same political apparatus of protection and allegiance. It is because the king can protect us by his laws, even against devils, that we owe him allegiance, just as devils owe him allegiance. Otherwise, they commit treason against him.

Thus, we are transformed into parts of his body as he is assuming, as a Christ, a mystical body which is a body politic. After all, the king, being their judge, can command the spirits. Willingly or not, he simultaneously becomes a kind of Baal-Zebub. At least, we believe that this is the outcome of the parallel traced by James between his political conception of witchcraft and his mystical conception of royal prerogatives.

C. Bodin's *Daemonomanie*

If we now reconsider Bodin's book on witchcraft, the striking parallels and contrasts with the work of James that went previously unnoticed become apparent. The latter entitled his book *Daemonologie*, while the former selected *Daemonomanie*, with a strong emphasis on the *malaise* which afflicted the witches.

Bodin's starting point is worth noticing, as it derives from his own experience as a trial judge, innovating also the iconography of the Devil with respect to his medieval portrait.

> The conclusion of the proceedings against a witch, to which I was summoned on the last day of April, 1578, gave us occasion to take up my pen in order to throw some light on the subject of witches, which seems marvelously strange to everyone and unbelievable to many. This witch was named Jeanne Harviller … who was accused of having caused the death of many people and animals. She confessed without torture although at first she stubbornly denied it and changed her story several times. She also confessed that her mother had presented her at twelve years old to the Devil, who was in the guise of an unusually tall, dark man dressed in black.[20]

[19] C Schmitt, *The Nomos of the Earth in the International Law of the Jus Publicum Europaeum* (GL Ulmen trans, New York, Telos Press Publishing, 2003) 59–60.

[20] Bodin, *De la démonomanie*, book 1, preface; J Bodin, *On the Demon-Mania of Witches* (RA Scott ed, Toronto, Centre for Reformation and Renaissance Studies, 1995) 35.

This account of Bodin is rather peculiar as it represents one of the first instances of the transformation of the Devil, from a medieval monster into a 'romantic' and seductive tall and dark man dressed in black, and this mutation is reported by a direct eyewitness.

Nevertheless, in a rather 'rational' attitude Bodin goes on discussing alternative theories, and especially that of Dr Houllier:

> A doctor, mocking the theologians said at the outset that it was a disease of melancholy ... And because there were some who found the case strange and almost unbelievable, I decided to write this treatise which I have entitled *The Demon-Mania of Witches*, on account of the madness which makes them chase after devils.[21]

This is, of course, a rather intriguing turning point created by Bodin. It is not only that the Devil seduces his victims. It is that they suffer a malaise, melancholy, making them long for dark and lonely places where they can eventually meet the Devil and be seduced by him. If you think of Chapman's *On the Shadow of Night* (1594) and his appreciation of melancholy, and then of Thomas Gray's *Elegy Written in a Country Churchyard* (1750), you can easily grasp the astonishing aesthetic link between pieces of Elizabethan poetry, at the time new and heterodox, and early Romanticism.

In this theory of the malaise of melancholy offered by Bodin it is also rather easy to see at work that other complex of European modernity that has been described by Foucault as the 'birth of the clinic'.[22] Witches become witches because they are sick. They must be cured, even if many times, and to avoid contagion, the best thing to do is to burn them out.

What is most intriguing for us is that Bodin's conclusion is absolutely parallel to that of James: namely that it is necessary to establish a special civil jurisdiction over the witches to the detriment of the ecclesiastical courts. As Bodin states:

> ... It is necessary to establish special magistrates for that purpose, at least one or two in each province. But I do not mean, however, that authority to be removed from regular judges to exercise jurisdiction, either from bias or rivalry, but rather that they will lend mutual assistance ... In earlier times ecclesiastical judges had this authority to the exclusion of lay judges. There is extant a decree of Parliament issued in the proceedings against the bishop of Paris in 1282. But later, authority was granted to civil magistrates while excluding churchmen, by decree of the same Parliament in 1390.[23]

He is relying on an old decree of Parliament to reaffirm the necessity of a civil, namely royal, jurisdiction over witches. But, of course, just as the parallel with James is striking, so is the difference. For Bodin the matter becomes immediately bio-political. The purpose of politics is to cure; the witches are afflicted from a

[21] Bodin, *De la démonomanie*, book 2, ch 3; Bodin, *On the Demon-Mania of Witches* 110.

[22] M Foucault, *The Birth of the Clinic: An Archaeology of Medical Perception* (AM Sheridan Smith trans, New York, Pantheon Books, 1973).

[23] Bodin, *De la démonomanie*, book 4, ch 1; Bodin, *On the Demon-Mania of Witches* 175.

malaise, and then it is a political matter to administer the political body in order to keep it sane.

Once again, we find this 'sublime' original mixture of European modernity made up of political sovereignty, magic, spirits, and the ineffable state of a '*manie*'. The Church was so inspired by the pious desire of fighting against witchcraft, that not only the *Daemonomanie* but also his *Six livres sur la République* were inscribed into the list of forbidden books. What is important for us to understand is why he was condemned by the Church.

The two main accusations against Bodin, brought by one Jesuit, Antonio Possevino, were mainly that he was too pro-Semite and a 'political' (*un politique*) in the sense that he believed in the existence of a realm of politics autonomous from theology and religion. According to the words of Cardinal Maffa, Bodin:

> in vece de' Santi Dottori seguita sempre, o quasi sempre certi Rabinacci.[24]
>
> [Instead of following the doctrine of the Church, he is always, or most of the time, following the teachings of some evil Rabbis].

So the principal accusation was that he was 'a political'.

Indeed, for Bodin the witches are committing not only a sin but also a real public crime against the king's peace. For him, witchcraft was different from heresy. He considered it as a mere matter of interpretation of the true content of the Christian religion. Witchcraft, even if due to a malaise, is more of a threat to the State than to the Church. So the matter was precisely the same as it was for James: the political jurisdiction over witches and devils for high treason came at the detriment of the spiritual power of the Church.

It is hard to overlook the clash that flagged the rise of the modern pure political in European culture and that is perfectly represented by the condemnation of Bodin's work by the Church. As a matter of fact, Bodin's definition of sovereignty,[25] which is the one we are still using, represents a total displacement of the ecclesiastical power, and it is important to report it here, including the reference he made not only to Roman and Greek terms but also to Hebrew terminology, which is often omitted in modern accounts:

> Sovereignty is the absolute and perpetual power of a commonwealth which the Latins call *maiestas*; the Greeks *akra exousia*, *kurion archè*, and *kurion politeuma*; and the Italians *segnoria*, a word they use for private persons as well as for those who have full control of the state, while the Hebrews call it *tomech Shévet*—that is, the highest power of command. We must now formulate a definition of sovereignty because no jurist or political philosopher has defined it, even though it is the chief point, and the one that needs most to be explained, in a treatise on the commonwealth.

[24] For all references, see D Quaglioni, *La sovranità* (Roma, Laterza, 2004) 49–72; see also D Quaglioni, *I limiti della sovranità. Il pensiero di Jean Bodin nella cultura politica e giuridica dell'età moderna* (Padova, Cedam, 1992).

[25] Bodin, *Les six livres de la Republique*, book 1, ch 8; J Bodin, *Six Books of The Commonwealth* (KD McRae ed, Cambridge, Harvard University Press, 1962) 84.

Tomech Shévet or supreme command. It is crystal clear that a pure political conception of sovereignty, and especially of its location in a single authority which dismantled all previous medieval theories of power and its dislocation at different levels and areas of authority, emerged from the intricacies of Christian Kabbala. No more lords, sub-tenants, kings, bishops, emperors and popes sharing different powers at different levels, but one political locus of the sovereign as the *locus* of supreme command, particularly in connection with the decision over treason. This decision in terms of friends and foes is the domestic equivalent of the international decision over war and peace.

Thus everything which is so peculiarly contemporary and Schmittian is already contained in Bodin's theory (as it is in James's):

> For he is absolutely sovereign who recognizes nothing, after God, that is greater than himself. I say, however, that power of the sovereign. Thus declaring war or making peace is one of the most important points of majesty, since it often entails the ruin or the preservation of a state.

To a large extent, the Schmitt's 'Concept of the Political'[26] appears to be an intricate gloss to the ideas that Bodin developed as a trial judge in witchcraft cases. And it is a climax of irony that this concept can, at least in part, be traced back to a kind of pro-Semitism that caused its author to be condemned as heterodox in the very moment he was establishing the modern political orthodoxy of the West.

II. Leviathan's Ambiguity

A. The Heterodox Sea-Monster

It is precisely in the context delineated in the two preceding sections that we may underline the role played by heterodoxy in the unfolding of modern sovereignty in strict association with the mysteries pertaining to the indefinite and unfathomable royal prerogatives.

This occult philosophy of sovereignty and its link to the mystic of the *Dominus* surfaces explicitly in several authors' works. In Edward Hyde, we find the dazzling statement that 'The Name *Adonai* is given to God for this reason, quia *Dominus Mundi*, because he is the Lord of the World … and that he is also the head to govern it'.[27] This is a clear expression of the fact that even the name of the

[26] C Schmitt, *The Concept of the Political* (G Schwab trans, Chicago, The University of Chicago Press, 2008).

[27] E Hyde, *The True Catholicks Tenure or a Good Christian Certainty which He Ought to Have for This Religion, and May Have of His Salvation* (Cambridge, John Field, 1662) 375: 'Adonai haholam Dominus Mundi, dunque condidit, sustentat & gubernat'.

Lord, *Adonai*,[28] derives from the status of being *Dominus* and his overall world government and possession. Few statements could be more explicit on the point.

Hobbes himself described the pope as 'the *Ghost* of the deceased Roman Empire, sitting crowned upon the grave thereof',[29] and it is, of course, in his famous frontispiece that we then find the most dramatic representation of the modern temporal and spiritual supreme authority, as well as the most thrilling demonic reversal of the old theological complex linked to the Lord Paramount of the World. So many reconstructions have been offered of Hobbes's frontispiece that it is certainly presumption on our side to try to discuss this subject once more. Nevertheless, it is of such importance to Schmitt's enquiry[30] into the modern political, so closely analysed by Agamben,[31] and so intimately linked to the *Dominus Mundi*, that it would be frivolous to skip it altogether.

Hobbes's frontispiece represents what is clearly the portrait of a demon with the face of a king and a body composed of his subjects to form a unique 'corporate entity' governing, from atop a mountain, a city and its surrounding space. As portrayed in Image 3 and Image 4, the Leviathan here is represented as a monster adorned with all the symbols of spiritual and temporal powers.

Our main question in this chapter is then: how could the King of England accept as a present a book with a frontispiece portraying him as a devil?[32]

What kind of heterodoxy could have been transforming the old liturgy of the presence of a power on earth parallel to that of God, into the blatant exhibition of a demonic icon? How could a devil become the Saviour? And last, but not least, why do we find a sea serpent atop a mountain?

This final detail, in the tradition of iconology, could well reveal itself to be the most fundamental of all. Many scholars have approached the frontispiece from more immediately striking conceptual and political features; but if we try to see it essentially for what it is, an image, an icon, an emblem, it must be analysed through its details, especially those that are out of place.[33]

The frontispiece is full of iconic details of dazzling relevance, including the enigmatic presence of small figures in the city wearing plague doctor masks. This detail possibly derived from Hobbes's translation of Thucydides, where the

[28] Indeed Adonai is *not* a name; it means Lord, but it is used in the rabbinic reading of the Hebrew text of the law to avoid pronouncing the sacred name of YHWH. Henceforth our bibles started to be edited substituting 'The Name' (Hashem) with the term *Adonai* rendered as the Lord with a capital L.

[29] T Hobbes, *Leviathan*, part 4, ch 47, § 21 (N Malcolm ed, Oxford, Oxford University Press, 1996) 411.

[30] C Schmitt, *The Leviathan in the State Theory of Thomas Hobbes: Meaning and Failure of a Political Symbol* (G Schwab and E Hilfstein trans, Chicago, The University of Chicago Press, 2008).

[31] G Agamben, *Stasis. Civil War as a Political Paradigm* (N Heron trans, Stanford, Stanford University Press, 2015).

[32] Remember that the earlier edition of the Leviathan was prepared by Hobbes for Charles II, having the faces in the Leviathan's body turned toward the royal reader. See H Bredekamp, *Thomas Hobbes Der Leviathan Das Urbild des modernen Staates und seine Gegenbilder. 1651–2001* (Berlin, Akademie Verlag, 2012) 54.

[33] See MM Goldsmith, 'Picturing Hobbes's Politics? The Illustrations to Philosophical Rudiments' (1981) 44 *Journal of the Warburg and Courtauld Institute* 232.

Hobbes's Earlier Version of Frontispiece[34]

Hobbes's Frontispiece[35]

[34] Abraham Bosse, Frontispiece of Thomas Hobbes, Leviathan, 1651. Copy on parchment. British Library, Mss Egerton, 1910; <scalar.usc.edu/works/observations-on-a-blazing-world/earlier-frontispiece-leviathan>.

[35] Thomas Hobbes, Leviathan, Crooke, London 1651. Frontispiece of the First Edition, public domain; <artsone-test.sites.olt.ubc.ca/files/2016/05/Leviathan_Frontispiece-Wikimedia-PD.jpg>.

plague of Athens is considered the origin of civil disorder in the city (ἀνομία). But there is one further detail that we should note: that the sea-monster is standing over a mountain. A long association of images and metaphors has linked the Leviathan to the waters and the sea, just as the Behemoth was associated with hills and mountains.

Now, undoubtedly, Hobbes associated Leviathan with a mountain, provoking an iconographic inversion, parallel to the normative inversion of portraying the monarch as a monster and a demon. Of course, our major interest lies in the *permanence* of such an inversion, to the point that it is not even thematised by most of the learned authors who confronted it.

What we shall try to do in this section is, first, to reconstruct the interpretative tradition that caused Leviathan to be identified with the Great Enemy as well as associated with the sea. Then, we shall try to rebuild an alternative tradition which can justify Hobbes's frontispiece from the standpoint of new conceptions of sovereignty. Finally, we shall reappraise the frontispiece with the extant legal notions that Hobbes could have had at hand, along with the iconological devices of the Column of Antoninus (Image 1) and Dante's eagle (Image 2) that we have shown in the preceding chapters. Our claim is to cast light on the esoteric and heterodox background of modern theories of sovereignty, emphasising the inversion that happened on the threshold of modernity between theological and demonological elements, as they have always been structurally within the pervading ambiguity of the notion of world lordship.

As it is rather well known, the two biblical monsters to whom Hobbes devoted two of his works[36] appear in the Book of Job. They have been the subjects of long and contradictory exegeses of a rather occult and hermetic nature.[37]

One of the clearest and at the same time most embarrassing points—and for exactly that reason, the object of particular speculations[38]—is that the two monsters were thought to be evidence of the almighty nature of God. It is amidst the Book of Job that we are told that 'He maketh the deep to boil like a pot: he maketh the sea like a pot of ointment' (Job 41:31); and that no creature on earth is stronger than the Leviathan: 'Non est super terram potestas quae comparetur ei' (Job 41:25), who is the king of the children of pride: 'Ipse est rex super universos filios superbiae'.

The starting image of chapter 41 of the Book of Job (41:1–2) clearly depicts the Leviathan as a formidable sea-monster: 'Canst thou draw out leviathan with an hook? Or his tongue with a cord which thou lettest down? Canst thou put an hook into his nose? Or bore his jaw through with a thorn?'. Other lines on this

[36] T Hobbes, *Behemoth* (P Seaward ed, Oxford, Oxford University Press, 2014); Hobbes, *Leviathan*.

[37] M Bertozzi, *Thomas Hobbes: l'enigma del Leviatano* (Ferrara, Bovolenta, 1983); C Scott McClure, 'Hell and Anxiety in Hobbes's "Leviathan"' (2011) 73 *The Review of Politics* 1.

[38] CH Gordon, 'Leviathan: Symbol of Evil' in A Altmann (ed), *Biblical Motifs. Origin and Transformation* (Cambridge, Cambridge University Press, 1966) 1–9; C Peri, *Il regno del nemico. La morte nella religione di Canaan* (Brescia, Paideia, 2003) 125.

king of the children of pride heavily influenced its representation and interpretation. The first is the peculiar question (Job 41:13): '*Who can discover the face of his garment?*', which is peculiar because Hobbes showed his face and it was that of the King of England. A second crucial point consists in the assertion (Job 41:23) that: '*The flakes of his flesh are joined together: they are firm in themselves; they cannot be moved*', an assertion supporting the iconographic rendition in the frontispiece of his 'corporate' body. Then there is a third ambiguous statement (Job 41:10) made directly by God about His relations with the monster: '*None is so fierce that dare stir him up: who then is able to stand before me?*'. This latter pronouncement is dazzling because it blurs the distinction between good and evil. Is the Leviathan the great enemy, or is he a symbol of the Lord's omnipotence?

Both meanings are indeed generated by the phrase. One is that nobody on earth can confront the Devil, so that nobody can dare to confront God, who is stronger than the Devil. The other may be that God is so powerful that he even created this monster as a sign of His supreme majesty. If we cannot resist this creature of His, how could we try to resist the Lord? In both cases it is rather clear that God, *because* of His power, is the Lord of the Universe to whom we must bow.

B. St Jerome's Tradition

In his comment on the Book of Job,[39] St Jerome (347–420 CE) established the tradition of reading the Leviathan and the Behemoth as symbols of the Enemy. Leviathan is the Satan who, at the beginning of the book, is tempting Job to give in and abandon his faith in God. It is intriguing that in Jerome's comment it is Behemoth who is interpreted as a plural,[40] rendering this monster a creature with a body composed of many devils: '*Proinde inimicus diabolus cum toto corpore satellitum suorum hoc loco a Deo describitur*' (So the enemy devil is described by God in this place with all the body of his guards). Here the Devil is depicted as a *corporation*, a corporate body made up of his cronies, the men and angels whom he has subjugated. For Jerome, a typical sign of the demonic nature of Behemoth is his uncontrollable luxury. Behemoth is slave to his '... *ventris voluptas, vel carnis luxuria*' (throat pleasure or body lust).

In St Jerome, Leviathan is a term that is always used to denote the demonic entity. The only difference between the two monsters is their opposite locations: Behemoth on the land, and Leviathan in the sea as a '*magnus draco*' (great drake). Such description of Leviathan establishes a link with the Beast of the Sea of the book of Revelation (Revelation 13:1 10) and with the Psalm 74 (Psalms 74:12–14) [KJV]:

> For God is my King of old, working salvation in the midst of the earth.

[39] St Jerome, *Commentarii in Librum Job*, in 26 PL clm 619–802.

[40] In Hebrew, the termination in *–oth* normally denotes feminine plurals, something which does not imply that some words or names can end in *-oth* without being plurals.

> Thou didst divide the sea by thy strength: thou brakest the heads of the dragons in the waters.
>
> Thou brakest the heads of leviathan in pieces, and gavest him to be meat to the people inhabiting the wilderness.

Moreover, the human impossibility of drawing out the Leviathan with a hook becomes associated with Ezekiel (17:20) [KJV]:

> And I will spread my net upon him, and he shall be taken in my snare, and I will bring him to Babylon, and will plead with him there for his trespass that he hath trespassed against me.

In this case, the 'hook' by which Leviathan can be drawn out is interpreted as Christ and His Cross, and the 'net' is patently His teaching.

It is not without importance that Ezekiel's text is thought to make reference also to the Pharaoh, as we find in Bodin the same analogy between the sea-monster and the tyrannical lord of Egypt:

> Son of man, set thy face against Pharaoh king of Egypt, and prophesy against him, and against all Egypt: Speak, and say, Thus saith the Lord God; Behold, I am against thee, Pharaoh king of Egypt, the great dragon that lieth in the midst of his rivers, which hath said, My river is mine own, and I have made it for myself. (29:3–4 [KJV])
>
> …
>
> Son of man, take up a lamentation for Pharaoh king of Egypt, and say unto him, Thou art like a young lion of the nations, and thou art as a whale in the seas: and thou camest forth with thy rivers, and troubledst the waters with thy feet, and fouledst their rivers.
>
> Thus saith the Lord God; I will therefore spread out my net over thee with a company of many people; and they shall bring thee up in my net (32:2–3 [KJV])

In this kind of ancient parallel reading of texts in search of word-links, the context or the real historical meaning is, of course, irrelevant. It is a method completely opposite to that of philology.[41] What is essential to this method is that a given collection of books, the canonical Bible or Justinian's *Digest*, form a nested set of phrases, each of which can open a link toward another part of the collection. Reading is the art of seeing these marks and following these links as if they were contrived corridors that the reader must enter to capture their meaning.

A powerful political association linked to these texts was that of an intrinsic correspondence between the Devil and the lord of Egypt. Bodin is following this tradition when he equates Leviathan to the great crocodile Set in the Nile.[42] The Leviathan and the evil king are one and the same thing, and both appear patently

[41] See J Gordley, 'Humanists and Scholastics' in CM Carmichael (ed), *Essays on Law and Religion, The Berkeley and Oxford Symposia in Honour of David Daube* (Berkeley, University of California, 1993) 13.

[42] Bodin, *De la démonomanie*, book 1, ch 1, 5; Bodin, *On the Demon-Mania of Witches* 48.

as a representation of the lordship of the Devil on earth. Leviathan, the Pharaoh, and the apocalyptic dragon represent the evil and arbitrary government of the world.

The final evidence that the Leviathan is a symbol of the Devil and of the evil kingdom (Egypt) is offered by St Jerome with reference to its attribute of being '… a *king over all the children of pride*' (Job 41:34 [KJV]). It is this passage which constitutes the unifying factor that links Leviathan to the Pharaoh and the Devil.

Jerome's interpretation has been very successful, influential and far reaching. It is sufficient, here, to remember the image of the Lord as a fisher-king, and of the Christ and His cross as a lure and a hook for the big fish. In such images, the Leviathan is deceived by the apparent fragility of the hook such that Christ can finally overcome it. This is an image perfectly represented in an illumination of the *Hortus Deliciarum* of the Abbess Herrade von Landsberg[43] upon which Schmitt also placed his attention.[44] But we may also find other typical images corresponding to these conceptions, such as those contained in the *Liber Floridus* (circa 1120),[45] where we see Behemoth mounted by a horned devil and the Leviathan portrayed as a serpent saddled by the Antichrist.

Moreover, Jerome's reading of the monsters as a corporation of rogues was consciously used by John of Salisbury in his *Policraticus* (circa 1159) in opposition to the good republican government. In his appraisal, all the evil men form a compact corporate body to fight against the Lord and His Christ: '… *convenerunt in unum adversus Dominum et adversus Christum ejus*'.[46] This image, of course, conveys the precise opposite concept of that illustrated in Hobbes's frontispiece, where it is the legitimate government that is a corporation of devoted subjects forming the unitary body of the sovereign, as we may also see represented in Dante's corporate eagle. For us, the magic performed by Hobbes was that of mixing the two images in a new and extravagant compound, reversing the old meaning of the Leviathan as a monstrous sea-serpent.

In John of Salisbury, we face the rogues forming a corporation to fight the Almighty: the strict, compact alliance of villains which is well represented by the thick skin and scales of the Leviathan, but which Hobbes inverted into the opposite concept.

> Canst thou fill his skin with barbed irons? Or his head with fish spears?
>
> (Job 41:7 [KJV])
>
> …

[43] See for example the image portrayed in G Cames, *Allégories et symboles dans l'Hortus Deliciarum* (Leiden, Brill, 1971) 40–42, picture 35.

[44] See C Schmitt, 'Die vollendete Reformation. Bemerkungen und Hinweise zu neuen Leviathan—Interpretationen' (1965) 4 *Der Staat* 68–69.

[45] J Poesch, 'The Beasts from Job in the Liber Floridus Manuscripts' (1970) 31 *Journal of the Warburg and Courtauld Institutes* 41.

[46] John of Salisbury, *Policraticus*, VI, 1, in 199 PL clm 589–92.

> His scales are his pride, shut up together as with a close seal.
>
> One is so near to another, that no air can come between them.
>
> They are joined one to another, they stick together, that they cannot be sundered
>
> (Job 41:15–17 [KJV])

This empire of evil, unbeatable because of the consistency of his corporate body, is an enormously efficient image, but how could this tradition of reading, from Jerome to Salisbury, be reversed? How could the great Pharaoh, as a symbol of the Devil and of tyrannical government, become Hobbes's specular opposite image of the sovereign-saviour to whom we owe our lives and our political existence? What kind of an 'inversion of all values' could have taken place between John of Salisbury and Thomas Hobbes?

C. Calvin's Re-elaboration

If we delve into the genealogy of Hobbes's frontispiece, we should consider the role played by Calvin (1509–1564), because it was he who rather abruptly reversed the whole tradition attributed to St Jerome.[47]

In his work,[48] Behemoth is identified with an elephant, when most other accounts referred to it as a hippopotamus, and Leviathan is a whale rather than a sea serpent. Both are deemed to be symbols of God's power, *not* the Devil's.[49]

The shift in the bestiary is not without meaning here. It is much more acceptable to have a whale as a symbol of the majestic power of God, than to try to convince someone that God's power can be mirrored on earth by a sneaky slithering slimy water serpent. An elephant is also a rather more acceptable political emblem. So Calvin is, we presume, rather consciously changing the standard imagery of the Leviathan, completely transforming it. The two beasts, here, cease to be emblems of the Devil to become manifestations of the '*puissance de Dieu*', or the power of God. After all, was God not saying (Job 41:10 [KJV]) that no one is so fierce to dare stir up Leviathan when He said '… who then is able to stand before Me?'. This phrase can well be interpreted as indicating that Leviathan is a manifestation of His transcendent powers. And isn't the Psalmist saying (Psalms 104:25–26 [KJV]) 'So is this great and wide sea, wherein are things creeping innumerable, both small and great beasts. There go the ships: there is that Leviathan, whom thou hast

[47] On the relationship between Calvin and Hobbes, see JJ Edwards, 'Calvin and Hobbes: Trinity, Authority, and Community' (2009) 42 *Philosophy & Rhetoric* 115; AP Martinich, *The Two Gods of Leviathan: Thomas Hobbes on Religion and Politics* (Cambridge, Cambridge University Press, 2010) 334.

[48] J Calvin, 'Sermon CLXI' in E Cunitz, J-W Baum and EWE Reuss (eds), *Joannis Calvini Opera Quae Supersunt Omnia* [Corpus Reformatorum] vol 35 (Brunsvigae, CA Schwetschke, 1863) clm 463–476, at 464–65.

[49] Bertozzi, *Thomas Hobbes: l'enigma del Leviatano* 5.

made to play therein'? If the Lord is playing every morning with Leviathan, can he be evil?

Of course, Calvin did not displace the older interpretation all at once. As we noted, Bodin, in his *Daemonomania* (1581), still portrayed Leviathan as a symbol of the Pharaoh, the arbitrary and tyrannical ruler, as well as of the Devil.[50] In his analysis, Leviathan is not satisfied by devouring men's bodies only, he is also in search of their souls, to seduce them, and for this reason it is impossible to make a covenant with him. He is the absolute enemy, and he represents an admonishment to all those who plan to have commerce with arcane spirits. Also Joseph Caryl, whose commentaries were certainly known and appreciated by Hobbes,[51] still interpreted Leviathan as a figure of evil, affirming that under the name of '… that great Leviathan' are to be included all of the enemies of Christ and the Church,[52] reproducing the image of a corporate society of villains assembled in a unitary body. This is done, again, by pointing to his impenetrable scales, so perfectly connected to one another, and taking for granted that the name of the beast is to be traced back to the Hebrew root *Lavah*, meaning 'united' or 'associated'. This may be why the Leviathan was interpreted as a society or an association.[53]

At this point, it is clear that Hobbes was following a minor and heterodox interpretative current, which transmuted the Leviathan into an emblem of the Lord's world rule. At the same time, it is evident that there is a strong parallel between Hobbes's reading and that of Calvin.[54] In order to fully appreciate this interpretative inversion, we can précis for the reader the last three chapters of the Book of Job.

In chapter 40, God shows Job His might, reminding him that He has created such a marvellous monster as Behemoth, and in chapter 41 He mentions His even more spectacular other creature, the Leviathan, before whom nothing on earth can stand, and who—because of this irresistible power—is said to be the king of all that are proud. In this context, God explicitly states (Job 41:11) that everything under heaven belongs to Him. God *is* the *Dominus Mundi*. Is, then, Leviathan the sign of His lordship?

We want to emphasise this point. God is the Master of the World, *Adonai*, which could imply that Leviathan is a kind of God's lieutenant, made to compel the proud to pay respect to Him. God's argument proved to be effective, and finally, in chapter 42, Job bows irrevocably to God's mysterious will and projects, acknowledging that He can do all things. In this sense, God is the Lord of the Universe, and the emblem of His lordship on earth can precisely be the Leviathan as the ultimate

[50] Bodin, *De la démonomanie*, book 1, ch 1, 5; Bodin, *On the Demon-Mania of Witches* 48.

[51] WH Greenleaf, 'A Note on Hobbes and the Book of Job' (1974) 14 *Anales de la Cátedra Francisco Suárez* 21.

[52] J Caryl, *An Exposition with Practicall Obseruation upon … the Books of Job* (London, L Fawne, H Cripps and L Lloyd, 1647) 141, 374.

[53] WH Greenleaf, 'A Note on Hobbes and the Book of Job' 22–23, 25.

[54] On the Calvinism of Hobbes, see Martinich, *The Two Gods of Leviathan* 46.

appearance of God's power, to whom even the righteous but quarrelling Job must eventually bow.

Given this succession of chapters, it may appear that, though a heterodox reading, Leviathan could be interpreted as the political aspect of God. The Leviathan could be His sovereign aspect: that power than no man can dare to resist, which is precisely what Hobbes tried to portray in his frontispiece through the citation of Job 41:24 [Vulg.]: '*non est super terram potestas quae comparetur ei*'. There is no power *on earth* that can be compared to his.

As we may easily grasp, Hobbes's citation is at the end of God's speech, when Leviathan is proclaimed the king of all children of pride and Job ends his questioning. The book ends in chapter 42 with the acknowledgment by Job of the powers of God, so that the climax is reached in chapter 41 through the revelation of Leviathan as the emblem of God's power.

III. The *Dominus Mundi* and Hobbes's Frontispiece

A. Hobbes and His Sources

The parallel between Calvin's and Hobbes's readings can hardly be denied, but what could have been its political meaning in the English context at the time? Was Hobbes simply dissociating Leviathan from the Devil, or was he reversing the values associated with tyranny and the republic? Or was he not giving a peculiar new depiction of the nature of political power opposite to classical political theology, who tailored the sovereign as an image of God on earth?

The two lines of argument to be followed here are intermixed: on one side, they concern the interest of Hobbes in occult and magic; on the other side, they pertain to Hobbes's use of classical legal sources of previous authors.

Although Hobbes asserted that ideas of demonic possession had abated in his time, his observation may be considered, according to Stark, as 'utterly absurd' given the sheer number of witchcraft trials and discussions about contemporary cases of demonry occurring throughout the seventeenth century.[55] While it is true—as Starck oberves—that the Anglican Church terminated its office of exorcism in 1550, this act did very little to diminish the belief in demonic possession. Rather, as we have seen, this marked the politicisation of witchcraft trials as crimes of treason.

Additionally, it is worth noting the unsceptical interest that scientists displayed for cases of possession. For example, William Whiston, the successor of Newton

[55] See RJ Stark, *Rhetoric, Science, and Magic in Seventeenth-Century England* (Washington, The Catholic University of America Press, 2009) 28 ff.

in the Lucasian chair of mathematics, perceived demonic possessions as a normal event in the world, in the same way that gravity was a normal event.[56] Demonic activities are not to be denied simply because we cannot, at present, give a direct explanation of them, which looks like sound epistemological advice. His argument goes so far as to trace a parallel between possessions and occult events and scientific theories: magic events, as well as Boyle's experiments on the elasticity of the air, or Sir Isaac Newton's demonstrations about the power of gravity, are not to be denied, only because neither of them are to be solved by mechanical causes.

We know that Hobbes was discussing magic with his noble protectors, but also that he always displayed the greatest incredulity toward alleged demonic manifestations.[57] Quite surely, he could have thought that after the turbulences which afflicted Charles I's reign and brought him to his execution in 1649, a viable way out could be represented by the establishment of a strong central government.

If it is so, the title that he gave to his work on the civil war would be the evidence that he was playing with the symbols of a long-established tradition of political metaphors surrounding the two monsters, as others such as Bishop John Bramhall were doing.[58]

Indeed, he could have found in the *Historia Ecclesiastica* a connection between Leviathan and the king (*rex*) and Behemoth and the people (*populus*).[59] Following this parallel, Behemoth—the beast made up of a multitude of beasts—could well have represented the rioting multitude and its representatives, unbound in their luxury for passions and power, and by contrast, Leviathan could have represented their reunion in an ordered political body. This explanation, based on the idea that Behemoth and Leviathan can be seen as the constantly potentially present and clashing forces of state and revolution is not wholly convincing per se. As we have seen the Leviathan was always anyway surrounded by a sinister aspect of demonic power, with the strong and important exception of Calvin, to whom Schmitt makes no reference in his enquiry. Other scholars have traced back the device of opposition, instead of complementarity, between Behemoth and Leviathan in the apocalyptic myths, envisaging a final struggle of the former against the latter.[60] It is almost taken for granted that Hobbes depicts[61] the end of monarchy in terms of a regression of civil society toward the primeval chaos of violence and civil war, such that he could prefer the 'evil' of a monarch, which was more tolerable than the chaos of a long-parliament Behemoth.[62]

[56] W Whiston, *An Account of the Daemomaniacks, and the Power of Casting Out Daemons* (London, Boyle's Head, 1737) 74; RJ Stark, *Rhetoric, Science and Magic in Seventeenth-Century England* 28.

[57] A Pacchi, *Convenzione e ipotesi nella formazione della filosofia naturale di Thomas Hobbes* (Firenze, La Nuova Italia, 1965) 48–49, fn 27.

[58] SI Mintz, *The Hunting of Leviathan* (Cambridge, Cambridge University Press, 1962) 110–23.

[59] See J Chanteur, 'Note sur les notions de "Peuple" et de "Multitude" chez Hobbes' in K Koselleck and E Schnur (eds), *Hobbes* (Berlin, Forschungen, 1969) 223–36.

[60] L Drewer, 'Leviathan, Behemoth and Ziz' (1981) 54 *Journal of the Warburg and Courtauld Institutes* 148.

[61] Hobbes, *Leviathan*, part 3, ch 42, § 125.

[62] Bertozzi, *Thomas Hobbes: l'enigma del Leviatano* 22.

As can be seen from these references, the use of metaphors with an occult meaning is so pervasive in these interpretations of the Book of Job, that it must be thematised. Hobbes's relations with occult philosophy remain an obscure matter. Radical in his rejection of metaphysics and spirituality, he nonetheless shared with Bacon and Sennert a basic concern about the vocabularies of magic. Hobbes's 'anxiety about occult tropes'[63] appears most obviously in *The Leviathan* when he complains about 'the use of Metaphors, Tropes, and other Rhetorical figures, instead of words proper'.[64] Hobbes dismisses obscure and ambiguous expressions because they are often of a 'mystical' nature, though his polemic against figurative language may sound rather odd since *The Leviathan* itself appears to be a rather prolonged metaphor on a demonic figure.

Hobbes was never invited to join the Royal Society, partly because his materialism and scepticism 'went too far down the road of disbelief'[65] and many scholars of the time, including Bacon, remained entirely *non-sceptical* on the topic of witchcraft. Browne maintained that the Devil does possess some men, the 'spirit of melancholy' others, and still others are possessed by the spirit of delusion.[66] Here we find, once again, that deep association between witchcraft and melancholy which connoted Bodin's conceptions expressed in the *Daemonomanie*. There is a malaise, a melancholy, of the spirit, which either resembles that of the Devil, or makes people inclined to be hooked by the Devil. This is an association underlined even by Hobbes, though in a more materialistic mood, when he declares

> there were many Daemoniaques in the primitive Church, a few Madmen, and other such singular diseases; where at these times we hear of, and see many Madmen, and few Daemoniaques, proceeds not from the change of Nature; but of names.[67]

The point in this passage displays a certain degree of nominalism where folly and possession can become interchangeable depending on our lexicon, strengthening the need for the use of 'words proper'. How can, then, Leviathan be a proper name for the Sovereign?

This monstrous association happened in the context of a strong opposition that was developed against what may be called the *preternatural* rhetoric—made of strange metaphors, suggestive allusions or conceits—in favour of a plain English *scientific* use of the language. This polemic reached its height in the eighteenth century, when '… deism and Sadducism as forms of cosmology, took root as appropriate methodological starting points for scientific enquiry'.[68] The opposition to the occult rhetoric—which parallels that of the occult philosophy, but perhaps

[63] Stark, *Rhetoric, Science, and Magic in Seventeenth-Century England* 25–26.

[64] Hobbes, *Leviathan*, part 1, ch 5, § 24.

[65] Stark, *Rhetoric, Science, and Magic in Seventeenth-Century England* 27.

[66] T Browne, *Religio medici* (1643) (New York, John B Alden, 1889) 60, on whose influence see K Murphy, 'The Physician's Religion and "salus populi": The Manuscript Circulation and Print Publication of "Religio Medici"' (2014) 111 *Studies in Philology* 845.

[67] Hobbes, *Leviathan*, part 4, ch 45, § 9.

[68] Stark, *Rhetoric, Science, and Magic in Seventeenth-Century England* 29–30.

going deeper in its charge since language precedes abstract reasoning—that lay at the foundation of the plain style as the *organon* of scientific enquiry raises many problems in relation to Hobbes and his political vision. It was Glanvill in *Sadducismus Triumphatus* (1681), a text likely edited by Henry More, who openly directed the charge of scepticism against '... those Hobbians [*sic*] and those Spinozians, and the rest of that Rabble, who flight Religion and the Scriptures, because there is such express mention of Spirits and Angels in them ...'.[69]

Notwithstanding his proclaimed scepticism toward witchcraft, Hobbes's text is entirely constructed around occult metaphors, from the apparition of the Leviathan to the final chapter on the Kingdom of Darkness, and the long discussion of what is a 'fairy'.[70] If we pay due attention to the *text* it may become more apparent to what extent the modern theory of the political has been formulated in a frame of occult rhetoric, tropes and images, though Hobbes himselfy openly complains about the use of metaphors '... and the Rhetoricall figures, instead of words proper'.[71] This passage is of a peculiar importance, since it places words *proper*, probably as the correct designation of realities, in opposition to tropes and 'ambiguous expressions' which are often of a mystical nature. We find in this passage a condemnation of figurative language as improper and an association of it with the enchantments deriving from magic. Now what is at stake in the complaints about the use of metaphors is perhaps the striking inner contradiction which is revealed within Hobbes's text, leading him to deny on the surface what is actually pursued in depth.

Can the inventor of the frontispiece and of the most overwhelming demonic trope of political modernity condemn his work as unscientific? Or, is there a sublime irony in condemning the *true* nature of government as demonic? Hobbes himself declared that 'The Light of Human minds is Perpicuous Words, but by exact definitions first snuffed, and purged from ambiguity'.[72] And what is the Leviathan, if not the most ambiguous possible portrait of the Sovereign?

At this point, it would be hard to separate the matter of witchcraft from language *and* government. As Stark reports,[73] active participation of demons could provide an explanation for how certain tropes and phrases seemed to work together. Tropes may have natural magical force. Modern theory conceptualises rhetoric as an adornment rather than a charm, but the opposite idea could persist, that it should be possible to master tropes as an inherently enchanted vocabulary.

Now the vocabulary of sovereignty and the tropes invented by Hobbes are perhaps there just to prove the extent to which this 'enchanted vocabulary' can

[69] J Glanvill, *Sadducismus Triumphatus or, Full and Plain Evidence Concerning Witches and Apparitions* (London, J Collins, 1681) 16.
[70] Hobbes, *Leviathan*, part 4, ch 47, § 21.
[71] Hobbes, *Leviathan*, part 1, ch 5, § 24; Stark, *Rhetoric, Science, and Magic in Seventeenth-Century England* 25.
[72] Hobbes, *Leviathan*, part 1, ch 5, § 20. See P Pettit, *Made with Words. Hobbes on Language, Mind, and Politics* (Princeton, Princeton University Press, 2008) 53.
[73] Stark, *Rhetoric, Science, and Magic in Seventeenth-Century England* 23.

dominate our own political imagination for centuries. If this is true, there is an inherent occultism in the modern philosophy of politics that cannot easily be overthrown. In order to understand this fact, we should simply remember that words have a meaning which bypasses their reference. If we reduce words to the referred objects we deny their inner power, especially in an age strongly imbued with the concept of the operativeness of the Power of Names. What we mean is that the *connotation* of words is as important as their *denotation*. Moreover, as long as the matter is politics and the public discourse, and the referential plan is constituted of invisible entities—such as law, sovereignty, state or the nation—connotation becomes *more* important than denotation, for the simple reason that the denoted entities are almost entirely constituted by word chains, which also appeal to feelings and emotions.

In a way, Hobbes was perceived as a champion of mechanicism and because of this was accused of Sadducism, or the disbelief in the existence of spirits characterising the Sadducees in the Gospels, in a time when even the new scientists did not consider the belief in angels and devils as superstitious. What we may notice is the surprising parallel accusations directed toward Bodin and Hobbes, conceived as they were with a flavor of antisemitism. The former was condemned as a *politique* having too many dubious contacts with Rabbis and their literature, and the latter was deemed a stubborn *Sadducee*, unable, for his innate materialism, to accept revelations pertaining to angels and spirits. This may sound somewhat ironic, given that Bodin referred to contacts with a 'good angel',[74] and that Hobbes dealt, to a certain length, with occult metaphors to the point of evoking a sea-serpent to portray the proper nature of the sovereign as the lord paramount on earth.

Nevertheless, we think that some major philological problems remain to be clarified pertaining to Hobbes's use of the Bible and the *Digest* as two of his main sources. As we will show, this operates from a specific use of the 'corporal' metaphor as already adopted in the history of political thought by Baldus, St Augustine and Fortescue. It is starting from this imagery that we have to depict the demonological inversion which characterises so profoundly the hidden framework of Western political thought on law and sovereignty.

B. Hobbes, Baldus and Fortescue

One of the major points in Hobbes's vision of monarchy is that, though monarchy derives from a covenant, this covenant is irrevocable. Once the monarchical *Dominium* is established, it cannot legitimately be reversed. This is indeed a strange point in the system, since normally what is given can be taken back,

[74] See CR Baxter, 'Jean Bodin's Daemon and His Conversion to Judaism' in JH Franklin (ed), *Jean Bodin* (London, Routledge, 2006) 301; ML Kuntz, *Venice, Myth and Utopian Thought in the Sixteenth-century: Bodin, Postel and the Virgin of Venice* (Ashgate, Aldershot, 1999).

especially in case of necessity. Nonetheless, this is precisely the argument on the irrevocability of the transfer of power from the people to the emperor as *Dominus Mundi*, and that we already encountered in Baldus.[75]

The reasons why Baldus holds that the *Lex Regia*—the law conferring the power from the people to the emperor—is irrevocable are contained in his theory of imperial and papal jurisdiction.[76] For Baldus, the *Lex Regia* was the necessary human instrument that instituted the perpetual and universal empire sanctioned by divinity and approved by Christ. The people gave general legislative power to the emperor through the *Lex Regia*, and the question of whether—in his days—the Roman people could legislate received a negative reply from Baldus, who interpreted the Roman text as a *traslatio imperii*, ie an irrevocable transfer, conveyance and alienation of authority such that the *populus* lost its original power and authority and thus did not retain any residual claim over the power given to the emperor.

In his commentary, Baldus clearly holds the *populus* to be a 'corporate entity' distinct from its human members, and considers this corporate unit to be the sovereign within an independent city-republic.[77] The sovereign is the lord and prince of its citizens and the source of jurisdictional authority.

From Baldus's highly complex point of view, there are three different units to consider: one, a corporate entity possessing sovereignty: the *citizen-body*; two, the citizens as corporal members of this entity partaking in *its* sovereignty; and three, the citizens taken as individuals in the position of subjects. The 'people'—as the set of all private citizens—is the subject of the 'people as a corporation', and this corporate whole is the body politic of the reunion of all private citizens.

As can easily be perceived, the parallel between Baldus's explanation of the *Digest* and Hobbes's frontispiece is dazzling: the corporate unity formed by the human members is superior to its members and assumes the face of the superior sovereign to whom the people 'as a whole', as a *corporation*, conferred all his powers. It is a vivid, almost motion-like image, visualising the movement of the private citizens toward the constitution of the corporation of their body politic.

This visual passage, which highlights the identification of the people and the ruler as a single body, is dominant in Baldus's treatment of the *podestà* and the *popolo* (the mayor and the people) in the context of Italian city-republics. He depicts the city authorities as being the 'head' of the citizens' corporate body, such that their presence personifies the whole city.[78] Baldus's definition of *populus* is crucial for his understanding of the fundamental question of whether and how

[75] Baldus [X 1.2.8].

[76] J Canning, *The Political Thought of Baldus de Ubaldis* (Cambridge, Cambridge University Press, 2003) 59.

[77] Canning, *The Political Thought of Baldus de Ubaldis* 204.

[78] Baldus [X 2.2.28, n 2] 'Ubi sunt anciani, sive decuriones, qui sunt caput civitatis, tota civitas esse videtur'.

the people can act and will something political.[79] Baldus demonstrates that the people is at the same time a set of real men *and* an abstract entity distinct from its human members. He considers that the abstract entity and the real members are but two aspects of the same thing: the people *as* a corporation. The members are the physical expression of the abstract entity of the corporation, which acts through the instrumentality of these members. The people is, then, an abstract entity which is, legally speaking, one person. The dual nature of the people is captured in the expression of a universal person or *persona universalis*.[80]

This image of a head and a body of the political unit as a universal person constitutes indeed a complicated conceit, a prolonged *metaphor* transformed into a synecdoche. The head makes present and visible the body which sustains it, and the mystical union forming a body politic is rooted into the very legal notion of corporation. Such a conceit became a standard theory in the civil law, but what was new in Hobbes is, of course, the association of it with the figure of the Leviathan, transforming it further into something that is as occult as it is sublime.

Nevertheless, at this point it becomes clear that if Hobbes assembled together both of these well-known passages from Baldus, the idea of Leviathan as a corporate body and the Calvinist reading of it as an emblem of the power of God on earth, then his illustration could follow as a logical consequence.

Even the formula by which a mortal or corporal god may exist in the world in the form of a corporate entity made up of his subjects can be traced back to Baldus.[81] This corporal god was therefore already present in the continental tradition even if it was inserted in a comment to the feudal law. The feudal customs were collected as *Libri Feudorum* and added to the fifth volume of the Corpus Juris as an appendix to the imperial Novels.[82] We must also recall that the readers of the time, especially when building up a political theory, were certainly not engulfed by modern academic disciplines willing to frame it according to modern departments of Roman, Canon or feudal matters.

This argument was not unknown in England nor alien to the English mind, to the extent that the metaphor used by Baldus—that we have also seen poetically visualised by Dante in his image of the 'corporate eagle'—not only expressed civilian theories on the body politic; these metaphors, rooted in the theological tradition, were also reported by Fortescue in his *De Laudibus Legum Angliae* with reference to St Augustine (St Austin). Fortescue's argument flows as follows.[83]

[79] W Ullmann, 'De Bartoli sententia: Concilium repraesentat mentem populi' in D Segoloni (ed), *Bartolo da Sassoferrato. Studi e documenti per il VI centenario* (Milano, Giuffrè, 1962) 707–33.

[80] Canning, *The Political Thought of Baldus de Ubaldis* 189.

[81] Baldus [Feud 2.55]; Baldus, *In Usus Feudorum* (Augustae Taurinorum, Nicolai Beuilaquae, 1578) 80, sub-s *De prohibita feudi alienatione per Federicum*, *Praeterea si inter duos*, n 23–24.

[82] A Padoa Schioppa, *A History of Law in Europe. From the Early Middle Ages to the Twentieth Century* (C Fitzgerald trans, Cambridge, Cambridge University Press, 2007) 169.

[83] J Fortescue, *De Laudibus Legum Angliæ* (circa 1470) (A Amos trans, London, Butterworth, 1825) 36 ff.

In his book *De Civitate Dei* (1.19) St Augustine stated that a people is a body of men joined together in society by a consent of right, by a union of interests, and for promoting the common good. According to Aristotle, whenever a multitude is formed into one body or society, one part must govern, and the rest be governed. For this reason, where a company of men combines and forms themselves into a body politic, it is necessary that someone should preside as the governing principal, who usually goes under the name of king. A human body is formed in this order, as out of an embryo, with one head to govern and control it. So, from a confused multitude is formed a regular kingdom, which is a sort of mystical body, with one person as the head to guide and govern. And according to the philosopher, just as in the natural body the heart is the first thing that lives, having in it the blood, which it transmits to all the other members, thereby imparting life, growth and vigour. Thus, in the body politic, the first thing which lives and moves is the intention of the people, having in it the blood, that is, the prudential care and provision for the public good, which it transmits.

The result of all these metaphors based on the body is that if we start from the *Lex Regia* we may have a monarchical government originally derived *from* the people in accordance to God's will. This government is a government *by* the people, as long as the *universalis persona* is the corporate body composed of its members and made visible and present through the presence of its 'head'. Quite naturally, it is also a government *for* the people, being directed to their salvation.

The firm and strictly connected body of the Leviathan as the emblem of God's power on earth can be apprehended positively because of the Calvinist inversion of St Jerome's interpretive tradition. As a consequence, the Leviathan can become the image of this corporate association which is the state as a corporal, and consequently mortal, god—a god whose power is supreme as his figure is moulded upon that of the *Dominus Mundi*.

We want to further stress that in Baldus and other civilians the *Lex Regia* was approved by Christ for the salvation of the people, such that the Leviathan's government, if grounded on this particular Calvinist interpretation of its Roman sources, is not only a government of the people and by the people, but also *for* the people, because the final task of the sovereign, as Hobbes clearly states, is to proclaim that 'Jesus is the Christ'.[84] It is based on this mixture of Calvinism and civil law that the impressive inversion of the Old Serpent into a Saviour could emerge as almost natural, as the monstrous and demonological parallel of the *Dominus Mundi*.

Our view is that Hobbes worked on his civilian, English and Calvinist sources and combined in a single illustration the theory of the conferment of power of the *Lex Regia*, the theory of corporation, and the heterodox reading of the Book of Job with the dazzling result of producing a demonological inversion of the imagery

[84] Hobbes, *Leviathan*, part 3, ch 34, § 13.

of the *Dominus*. The next step will be, then, a *close reading* of the biblical passages concerning the impressive figures of the Leviathan and Behemoth, which will demonstrate in turn a new philological perspective on the meaning of these common, yet mysterious, symbols. Occultism, witchcraft, government of souls, and the mystic prerogatives of the royal will all appear to be linked together, each of them intertwined upon the *demonological* roots of modernity.

C. The King Over the Water

Now that we have reconstructed the two clashing lines of interpretation of Leviathan attributed to St Jerome and Calvin, and shown the importance of civilian metaphorical speculations on the nature of the body politic, we will next approach the particular use made by Hobbes of the biblical text from which he derived his frontispiece.

We can better frame our problem if we consider the extreme variance which distinguishes the Greek and Latin versions of the Book of Job, the former being known as the *Septuagint* and the latter as the *Vulgata*. The Book of Job was likely composed in the sixth century BCE to become a book in the Ketuvin section of the Tanakh (the so-called Hebrew Bible) whose authoritative Hebrew and Aramaic text was established between the seventh and the tenth centuries CE. According to tradition, the *Septuagint* was composed in the third century BCE by 72 sages enclosed in a tower by Ptolemy II, to be of use for Greek-speaking Jewish communities of the Western diaspora.[85] The *Vulgata* was the translation of the Old Testament done by St Jerome himself in the fourth century CE (circa 384), using a variety of Hebrew, Aramaic and Greek sources. Both the *Septuagint* and the *Vulgata* were constantly copied and printed at the time and used by learned scholars, but the puzzling difference between the two versions[86] has been strangely overlooked by many authors who wrote about the frontispiece.

Now, the passage that must eminently be scrutinised commences in chapter 40 of the Book of Job (Job 40:1) when God eventually answers to Job's critique of His justice:

> Repondens autem Dominus Iob de turbine [*Vulg*]
>
> καὶ ἀπεκρίθη κύριος ὁ θεὸς τῷ Ιωβ καὶ εἶπεν [*Sept*]
>
> And God replied to Job from amidst the tempest [*KJV*]

[85] JB Gabel and CB Wheeler, *The Bible as Literature. An Introduction* (Oxford, Oxford University Press, 1990) 167.

[86] Notice that even the number of chapters and verse may vary between the Greek and the Latin versions and they will be indicated when they do not match.

God the *Dominus* shows to Job His creations and creatures and, as we said, Behemoth appears in the Latin version at Job 40:10:

> Ecce Behemoth quem feci tecum, fœnum quasi bos comedet [*Vulg*]
>
> ἀλλὰ δὴ ἰδοὺ θηρία παρὰ σοί χόρτον ἴσα βουσὶν ἐσθίει [*Sept*]
>
> Behold now Behemoth, which I made with thee; he eateth grass as an ox [*KJV*]

'Behemoth' as a name is completely missing in the parallel Greek version (Job 40:15) where it is simply rendered with a plural for *beasts* (θηρία) eating grass 'like oxes' (ἴσα βουσὶν).

The simple reason for this variance is that the Hebrew text refers to a plural generic name for a kind of wild and huge animal, as indicates the termination in '*-oth*'. In this way, the Greek version maintains the generic reference of the Hebrew text, whereas St. Jerome decided to leave that word untranslated, and so, *invented* 'Behemoth' as a proper name for some unknown mythical monster; a marvelous beast generated in the translation from a Hebrew common plural root, into a singular *untranslated* term.

The same happened for the name Leviathan.[87] The name of Leviathan appears in the Latin version, which is simply rendered as *drakonta* (δράκοντα) in Greek. Once again, we have a generic name for serpent in one version and a non-translated term, Leviathan, in the text of St Jerome, becoming the proper singular name of a monster. In sum, we have in the text of St Jerome the non-translation of Hebrew words, which are transformed into proper names for fabulous monsters, names that are not present as such in the Greek text.

We can say that the creation of Behemoth and Leviathan as monsters having proper names was the work of St Jerome as a translator, mixing his own interpretation of Hebrew and Greek sources. This is absolutely consistent with the translation of the Psalm 104 as the other major locus where the Leviathan appears.[88]

In St Jerome's Latin version, we find:

> Hoc mare magnum et latum manibus ibi reptilia innumerabilia animalia cum grandibus
>
> Ibi naves pertranseunt
>
> Leviathan istum plasmasti ut inludere ei.

In the *Septuagint* version, we have:

> αὕτη ἡ θάλασσα ἡ μεγάλη καὶ εὐρύχωρος, ἐκεῖ ἑρπετά, ὧν οὐκ ἔστιν ἀριθμός, ζῷα μικρὰ μετὰ μεγάλων·
>
> ἐκεῖ πλοῖα διαπορεύονται, δράκων οὗτος, ὃν ἔπλασας ἐμπαίζειν αὐτῇ.

[87] 40:25 [*Vulg*]; 41:1 [*Sept*].
[88] Psalms 104:25 [*Vulg*]; Psalms 103:25 [*Sept*].

An English translation from the Greek would be as follows:

> [So is] this great and wide sea: there are things creeping innumerable, small animals and great.
>
> There go the ships; [and] this dragon whom thou hast made to play in it.

As we know, the King James version has:

> So is this great and wide sea, wherein are things creeping innumerable, both small and great beasts.
>
> There go the ships: there is that Leviathan, whom thou hast made to play therein.

It is easy to see that modern versions followed St Jerome's translation, and not the older Greek version of the text. In this way, the simple serpent or generic 'dragon' of the Greek text becomes a real character, a specific unique monster known as Leviathan. It is absolutely unclear if it was created by God 'to play in it' as a bizarre creature, or 'to play therein', to play *with* it, as a pleasure for God, as an enjoyable creature, a sort of pastime like swimming with a dolphin. Another possible interpretation is, also, that Leviathan *enjoys* the sea and plays in it. Nevertheless, the creation of Leviathan as such, not simply a dragon or a big fish but a creature-character with its own name written capitalised, is probably a transliterated Hebrew word (*livyathan*) meaning 'twisted' or 'coiled'. This term is sometimes used to denote a serpent or a crocodile, or sometimes as a metaphor to denote the reign of Egypt as a 'crooked serpent' (Isaiah 27:1), but it is never used as a proper name. This is a transformation in translation which is accentuated in most modern versions, where it is normally taken for granted that Behemoth and Leviathan are proper names for fabulous beasts. This matter is of direct importance for our argument and for a parallel reading of the Bible and the *Digest*, as was used in medieval interpretations.

In what is Job 41:2 in Latin and 41:3 in Greek, God uses the example of the two powerful beasts to reaffirm what is written in Deuteronomy (10:14), namely that:

> Omnia quae sub cielo sunt mea sunt [*Vulg*]
>
> πᾶσα ἡ ὑπ᾽ οὐρανὸν ἐμή ἐστιν [*Sept*]

Here it is clear in all versions that God is the *owner*, the *dominus* of all things on earth, and that (Deuteronomy 10:17) God is the God of gods and the Lord of lords.

> Quia Dominus Deus vester ipse est Deus deorum et Dominus dominantium [*Vulg*]
>
> ὁ γὰρ κύριος ὁ θεὸς ὑμῶν οὗτος θεὸς τῶν θεῶν καὶ κύριος τῶν κυρίων [*Sept*]
>
> Indeed your Lord is the God of gods and the Lord of lords [*KJV*]

It would be hard to believe that such a tremendous parallel between the *Digest* and the sacred texts of the Old Testament did not make an impression on readers accustomed to handling both of these sources because of their education.

The Roman emperor and God are making precisely the same assertion that they are *Domini Mundi*, and in a sense much deeper than that etherised by Bartolus with reference to respecting private property. In these passages, we have a literal dominion of all things that are under heaven, including the many gods and lords alluded to in the text. Most importantly, the reason given in the Book of Job for the Lord's property of all things consists in His might. His might is evidenced by His creation of beasts such as the personified great hippopotamus (Behemoth), devouring forests and riding atop the hills, and the personified great crooked creature dominating the seas (Leviathan).

Moreover, the strict connection between God's lordship and the two monsters is openly stated in the *Septuagint* at 40:19 (*Vulgata* 40:14) where it is said of Behemoth that:

> τοῦτ᾽ἔστιν ἀρχὴ πλάσματος Κυρίου, πεποιημένον ἐγκαταπαίζεσθαι ὑπὸ τῶν ἀγγέλων αὐτοῦ [*Sept*]
>
> Ipse est principium viarum Dei: qui fecit eum applicabit gladium ejus [*Vulg*]
>
> He is the chief of the ways of God; he that made him can make his sword to approach unto him [*KJV*]

In the Greek text there is a textual reference to God's messengers (*angels*) which is completely omitted in St Jerome's version, upon which the English version depends. The Greek passage could be translated as follows:

> This is the beginning [chief] of the creation of the Lord; made to be played with by his angels [messengers].

But can the angels play with Behemoth? Can the angels rejoice with the great serpent? Can the angels rejoice with the pharaoh or the big crocodile of Egypt?

This is not only a matter of philology, but of orthodoxy. Of course, we cannot find such a reference in St Jerome and the *Vulgata*. No angel may play with the Leviathan or Behemoth in Jerome's interpretation. This is a classical case where interpretation constructs the text to be constructed. On the contrary, if Leviathan is not a monster but the symbol of Lord's power as the Lord Paramount of the universe—The Lord of the lords—it becomes natural that angels may play with it.

Nonetheless, the most important difference between the Greek and the Latin versions concerns exactly the phrase selected by Hobbes for his frontispiece (Job 41:24–25 *Vulgata*; Job 41:25–26 *Septuagint*).

> Non est super terram potestas qae comparetur ei
>
> Qui factum est ut nullum timeret
>
> Omne sublime videt
>
> Ipse est rex super universos filios superbiae [*Vulg*]

The King James version translates this as:

> Upon earth there is not his like, who is made without fear.
>
> He beholdeth all high things: he is a king over all the children of pride [*KJV*]

Here we have the key to interpreting the Leviathan as the Devil, as the prince of demons and as the Old Serpent, because he is *rex super universos filios superbiae*—he is a king over all the children of pride. But why, then, is he beholding *all high things*? Why can he see *omne sublime*, all the sublime things? Is the sublime demonic?

In Greek, the whole passage sounds rather different:

> οὐκ ἔστιν οὐδὲν ἐπὶ τῆς γῆς ὅμοιον αὐτῷ πεποιημένον ἐγκαταπαίζεσθαι ὑπὸ τῶν ἀγγέλων μου·
>
> πᾶν ὑψηλὸν ὁρᾷ, αὐτὸς δὲ βασιλεὺς πάντων τῶν ἐν τοῖς ὕδασιν.[*Sept*]

This can be translated as:

> There is nothing upon the earth like to him, formed to be sported with by my angels.
>
> He beholds every high thing: *and he is king of all that are in the waters.*

At the very end, if we follow the Greek version, Leviathan *sports* with angels and knows all that is sublime, as he is *king over the water*. These two texts could hardly have been more different. It is not important here which text is closer to an original of the sixth century BCE. Both versions (third century BCE and fourth century CE) can, indeed, be consistent with the Masoretic text (seventh–tenth century CE) where it is said that Leviathan is king over all the *b*ᵉ*né šāhas*. This word (*šāhas*) appears only twice in the biblical Hebrew and both times in the Book of Job. In Job 28:8, in connection with *šāhal*,[89] it seems to indicate all insolent or arrogant creatures (υἱοὶ ἀλαζόνων in Greek), in line with St Jerome's translation of Job 41:26b. But this etymology is contested, as there are no other occurrences of it in the Hebrew text. That is why the Greek version could translate the same expression with reference to '*all* (the proud beasts) that are *in the waters*' in Job 41: 26b (πάντων τῶν ἐν τοῖς ὕδασιν).

What matters is that we may have an answer to the question of why Charles II could have received that frontispiece as a present. Hobbes could have been 'ironically' making reference to the sovereign as the 'King over the Water', as the Greek version of Job maintains that Leviathan is 'king of all that is in the waters', and in clashing parallel to the *Digest* (14.2.9) affirming that the Roman emperor is the 'owner of the land' and the 'rule of the sea'.

Hobbes's play on the strategic use of the Latin and Greek versions of the text allowed for the conclusion that the Leviathan is not a demon or the tyrannical pharaoh, but the sublime emblem of God's power as *Dominus Mundi* and as Lord of the Sea.

This is, of course, speculation, but may be a consistent interpretation. We know that Hobbes was perfectly acquainted with Greek[90] and citing the Latin, he could

[89] S Mowinckel, 'sahal' in D Winton Thomas and WD McHardy (eds), *Hebrew and Semitic Studies presented to Godfrey Rolles Driver* (Oxford, The Clarendon Press, 1964) 95–103.

[90] Hobbes used to extensively translate ancient Greek works, like Aristotle's *Treatise on Rethoric* and Thucydides' *The Peloponnesian War*.

well have alluded to the Greek in order to *exclude* the '*hoi polloi*' from understanding. Hobbes does not conclude the phrase in the frontispiece. He just cites the beginning: '*Non est super terram potestas quae comparetur ei*'. Certainly, in the Calvinist appraisal of the Leviathan, Job understood the emblem, because it is after this vision that he exclaims (42:5):

νυνὶ δὲ ὁ ὀφθαλμός μου ἑόρακέν σε [Sept]

Nunc autem oculus meus videt te [Vulg]

now mine eye seeth thee [KJV]

Job *sees* the Lord through the Leviathan's appearance. What we then have at the end is this dazzling and mystifying experience of the transmutation of the image of the *Dominus* into that of the Leviathan. The Old Serpent of St Jerome, this emblem of the association of rogues, becomes the icon of the body politic of the sovereign, the corporal god of Baldus.

The luminous detail of the mountain upon which the Leviathan rises in its entire majestic figure can then receive a consistent interpretation. The English title denoting the king can be, as we all know, that of Lord *Paramount*, a word patently derived from the Norman-French *paramont*, meaning above the mountain. Just as the king is the lord of lords who also governs the seas, the sea serpent is in the highest position on the mountain, and also rules the waves. He is the lord paramount and king over the water.

From this perspective, the frontispiece would represent a sovereign claim on land and the sea through a cryptic reversal toward a demonological and occult imagery. The cryptic dimension was certainly not alien to the sort of royal occultism that can be traced in Jacobean reflections on witchcraft, the government of souls and the mystic of prerogatives royal. If something can display the *demonological* origin of the modern political, it would be the transfiguration of the Leviathan operated in the heterodox line of interpretation followed by Hobbes. The perturbing novelty of the frontispiece could well have been created to illustrate the global claim to universal dominion through the heterodox interpretation of the Leviathan in the context of the mystic of royal powers. Certainly, if this theory holds, and there was a reversal of the imagery styling the sovereign in a way perturbing the old orthodox political theology, a major consequence could be to have the Schmittian paradigm dismantled at its very root.

D. Conclusions: The Heterodox and Demonological Origins of Modernity

In the third chapter, we saw to what extent King James was concerned about witchcraft and that at the same time he developed a mystic of the royal prerogatives hyperbolising the nature of the king to the point of having jurisdiction even upon magic. In this chapter, we developed the parallel between King James and

Jean Bodin, who gave the modern definition of sovereignty and, as James did, defined witchcraft as a political crime. His theories caused him to be condemned by the Church as a heterodox. Our main point is, then, that the politicisation of magic lies at the threshold of modernity, producing a sovereign who can command and judge the devils and humans having commerce with them.

We tried to show the extent to which the politicisation of the 'dark arts' reversed the traditional imagery linked to sovereignty, producing the stunning frontispiece of the Leviathan as the icon of the modern political. Though the emblem designed by Hobbes can be deconstructed as a skilful use of previous sources, including the *Digest* and heterodox interpretations of the Book of Job, there remains in it an irreducible excess, which marks a dramatic turning point in political imagination.

The tentative conclusion is, then, twofold. One point is the *demonological*, and as such exotic and heterodox, rather than theological and level headed, origin of the modern Western concept of the political. If something can establish the demonological origin of this modern concept of the political, it would certainly be the transfiguration of the Leviathan: the tremendous transformation of the major of devils into the emblem of political salvation.

The other point, to be further developed in the next chapter, is the *sublime* nature of this transfiguration. By sublime, we mean that element of astonishment, personal initiation and attraction for darkness which characterises both the theory of Bodin about melancholy as the malaise of witches, as well as the mystic of the *arcana imperii* of James I as a form of royal occultism. This sublime element will form the subject matter of our final chapter in the context of the romantic quest for the wistful and the ineffable that resides in exceptionality. In this way, we shall try to reach an understanding of the importance of political romanticism well beyond its denial and condemnation by Schmitt as the mere ideology of the liberal middle class of the nineteenth century. On this ground, Schmitt's theory of political romanticism, as it is associated to world government, will appear to be a typical ideological construct.

5

Sublime Dissolution

I. The Collapse of Modernity

In the first chapter, we tried to delineate two models of law, one based on global sovereignty and the other on fracture and exception. Under the first 'compact' model, the whole globe could be thought to be under a unitary and *uniform* legitimate political authority, a world without an inside or an outside because the overall sovereignty of a *Dominus Mundi* would be all-encompassing. The second model, on the other hand, could be represented by the 'fracture' of the global space into different political sovereign units without any legally possible lordship over the entire planet. Such a world, as we said, would be based on a variety of disjunctures between land and sea and between spaces, dominated by the binary of inside and outside. It would be, as Kissinger has pointed out, a world of *political diversity*.[1]

We have seen the extent to which the Roman Empire tried to affirm the first model through the transcendence of the emperor, seen as the most manifest of gods, especially in the Eastern part of the empire. Such model evolved into a real refined political theology in the Byzantine Empire, by the encounter of classical political thought with Christian revelation. The whole apparatus of imperial hegemony was then devised to express what we have called a 'liturgy of the presence', referring to the presence of the *Dominus* in the world as an *icon*, an ontological image of God. This model may be deemed to represent in its purest form that kind of expression of the transcendence of political power that Schmitt placed at the root of his conception of the law, and that still influences the paradigm of many of his epigones, including Agamben.

In addition, we have stressed that, according to Byzantine conceptions, since the royal presence is always miraculous, there is not really any room for the exception. As long as miracles are a suspension of the established order, if the order is already miraculous it is immaterial to speak of its miraculous suspension. This is a form of pure political theology where, in contrast to Schmitt's theory, sovereignty does not need to be exceptionally connected with miracles, because its connection with the miracle is normal.

[1] H Kissinger, *World Order* (London, Penguin Books, 2016) 365.

A further consequence of this model is that there is no need for an eschatology of power in itself. In this model, the *Dominus Mundi*, as actually present, is the all-mighty parallel of God on earth. The sovereign is already God's political manifestation.

Our endeavour has then been to analyse the two major revivals of the notion of *Dominus Mundi* which marked the Western juridico-political tradition. The first occurred at the time of Frederick Barbarossa (1122–1190) and the second at the brink of the possibility of a real universal empire during the reign of Charles V (1500–1558). In this way, in the second chapter, we scrutinised how the Byzantine models came to be variously imitated in the West. A first key point was represented by the revival of the notion of *Dominus Mundi* in the context of the Diet of Roncaglia (1154–1158), when Frederick Barbarossa endeavoured to define the complex of his royal prerogatives, and as such, the nature of his global sovereignty.

Two different and contrasting conceptions could prevail. One we have called *legal Spinozism* and it was represented by the rise of legal studies in Bologna. If the world is completely legally defined, and social relations are completely legally framed, there is no longer any real room for a pure political decision: a solution to any problem will be found in the reasoning and the subtle distinctions of the jurists. From a theological perspective, this arrangement of human relations in pure legal terms always tends toward a kind of Spinozism in the sense of equating God with His own order. In such a logical universe, the space of exception tends to evaporate and disappear, as it becomes neutralised within the formal scheme of the law. In this case, the *Dominus Mundi* has no real power, as it is more of an abstraction, an entity almost nullified in its personality through its own assimilation into the legal order. A peak in this imagination of a personal but impersonal world order could be found in Dante's eagle, representing Justinian in paradise in the form of a corporate body of the souls of his subjects, where the very body of the emperor becomes the sublime political body of his subjects in an effort of legitimation and representation of a sanctified legitimate government.

Notwithstanding such a powerful, and enduring, ideology of empire and the law, a rather opposite direction was taken by Barbarossa in his assertion of being the Lord of the World. This was a rather stirring move that we have termed *imperial messianism*, as a special form of a Western eschatology of power. In this case, far from being nullified, the emperor becomes the active agent of salvation, but, contrary to the Byzantine model, he assumes the role of destabilising the world to reach the world's end. The sovereign is like one of the possible interpretations of Christ, who has to destabilise this world and bring it to an end to realise salvation. Now, if the *Dominus* is a Christ in this sense, then he must assume an eschatological stance politically, and exceptionalism starts to be embodied within the structure of a power which is at once sovereign and subversive.

This sovereign ambiguity and the clash of different models reached an apex in the reign of Frederick II (1194–1250). In a dramatic turn of events, Frederick II came to be condemned, excommunicated by pope Gregory IX and deposed by

Innocent IV as an Antichrist. Such a dramatic reversal of the *Dominus* effectively showed the possibility of the *exceptional* intervention of the pope in political matters. Thus, a theory of exception could develop within the disjuncture between the temporal and the spiritual dimension of sovereignty.

These vicissitudes offered Kantorowicz the possibility of a romanticisation of sovereignty and its mysterious characters. These same vicissitudes offered Saint Bonnet the basis for his historical interpretation of the birth and evolution of the theory of the state of exception within Western culture. This theory stressed the coexistence of two powers: the *potentia absoluta* (absolute power) and the *potentia ordinata* (the ordered or constituted power), the former being informal and never completely definable, the latter assuming the forms of apparent and publicly-exercised powers. The canonical theory of exception then points toward a supposed level of global sovereignty that remains in its state of pure potentiality up to the point when it can be triggered into action by some urgent state of necessity.

From these studies and interpretations can emerge a deeper uncanny layer of Western politics, especially if we consider them in parallel with Bloch's thorough study on the magic of kingship, in the proper aspects displayed by the 'royal touch' and other miracles, or wonders, that could be performed by the kings of France, England and Castille.

The circumstances surrounding Frederick II's deposition reveal the duplicity of imperial sovereignty, where the *Dominus Mundi* can be both a Christ and an Antichrist in the context of undefinable powers of emergency and an eschatological conception of politics and power. At the same time, from Bloch's considerations may emerge an atheological or heterodox feature of kingship.

This mystic of royal prerogatives resurfaced when the Spanish emperor Charles V possessed the practical means (fleets to navigate the oceans and gunpowder) to effectively realise a world rule and dominion. His attempt did not succeed and because of the Thirty Years' War (1618–1648) between Catholics and Reformers, the world space became divided into independent political units, the states. The Treaty of Westphalia (1648) represented a global form of compromise and coexistence in implying mutual recognition of states and the right for them to make war for the acquisition of new territories.

The tentative *Dominium Mundi* of Charles V also left other residues in the form of an occult philosophy of the political and in mystic considerations of the royal prerogatives. Such a philosophy of the political had to be filtered through a revision of the classical schemes of political theology. Thus we could encounter a Gelasian model of papacy and a Lutheran Augustinism.

The Gelasian solution allowed for a temporal sphere for law and justice independent from the spiritual, but subject to the *indirect* authority of the pope. In contrast, Luther maintained that as temporal laws cannot have any validity in the spiritual order, so too evangelical norms cannot be invoked against the prince's laws. Civil authorities have been instituted to preserve the peace by the sword, not by the gospel. The civil authority, whether an emperor, a king, a prince or a parliament, is supreme for the very legal and technical reason that no action can be filed against it by a superior authority. If the real legal problem is always '*quis judicabit?*', Luther's answer is that there is no judge to hear a case against the king. A political case is *never* justiciable. Since everything which is temporal is political, there cannot be a judgement over the political. The two realms are completely separated: politics cannot command the souls; spiritual powers cannot interfere in civil governments.

Amidst these classical controversies between Catholics and Reformers, we maintained that a newer kind of heterodox and ambiguous political theology emerged in England and France and brought us to the threshold of modernity. In a nest of complex speeches and acts, James I eventually elaborated a mystic of the absolute and ordinary power of kings based on what we have called a real *political occultism*, where it is impossible for the subjects, and even for parliaments, to discuss the nature and qualifications of the king's prerogatives. They become unspeakable.

Operating in a context of spiritual crisis provoked by the supposed spread of witchcraft, James came to develop the theory that the kings were divinely appointed guardians charged with combating the Devil and his servants. For him, rebellion was very much like witchcraft, the work of the Devil.

This parallel is of extraordinary importance, bypassing the usual analogy traced between the government of heaven and that of the earth, because it emphasises that it is the presence of the Devil that legitimises the prerogatives of the kings. Rebellion and witchcraft are equated, and as a consequence, witchcraft must fall under royal jurisdiction. Witchcraft was no longer a sin against the Church, but high treason against the king, acting as a spiritual and temporal lord.

We would emphasise this reversal of grounds transforming the classical political theological parallel into an almost demonological basis of royal legitimacy. But for the work of the Devil, the mysterious power of the kings would be dispensable. It is the Devil giving a sense to the world of politics.

Far from being an isolated case, James's evolution is paralleled in French political thought in the work of Jean Bodin. He too was deeply involved in witch trials, wrote extensively on the matter of witchcraft and is thought to have invented the modern notion of sovereignty as the locus of supreme power which cannot tolerate any superior power. Like James, Bodin also reached the conclusion that witchcraft had to be considered a *political crime*. That Bodin's elaboration of the modern notion of sovereignty was deemed heterodox is easily shown by the fact that the Church condemned his book on witchcraft, the *Daemonomanie*, as well as his books on the commonwealth.

We could then advance the theory that at the threshold of modernity there was a structural interconnection between the role of magic and the birth of the modern independent sphere of politics. It was in a sense the appropriation of the realm of souls and spirits that allowed the modern structures of power to emerge outside of the control of ecclesiastical authorities. For this reason, we have called this turn of events a *demonological* turn.

Thus, we argue, the sovereign became not he who could perform the *miracle* of the state of exception, but rather he who could command the spirits. The sovereign is he who can trigger the *magic* of the exception.

For these reasons, at the end of the previous chapter we needed to examine in detail that most impressive icon of modern political power that emerged in the emblem of the Leviathan portrayed on the frontispiece of Hobbes's work. How could he produce such an outstandingly new image of sovereignty? And most of all, how could the King of England, to whom the book was presented, accept being equated with the figure of the Old Serpent? Does this not entail a dramatic hidden turn in the conception of the political?

Our enquiry proceeded then to examine the interpretive tradition that framed the Leviathan in demonic terms. We could trace this tradition back to St Jerome, who translated the Bible into Latin, producing a version of it known in the Middle Ages as the *Vulgata*. According to this translation, the Leviathan is to be the sire of demons as it is not only the strongest creature on earth but also the 'king of the children of pride': '*Ipse est rex super universos filios superbiae*' (Job 41:25).

As such, in this orthodox line, Leviathan represented the unity of the wicked, the association of the evils. Its body is thick and cannot be hooked, thus reproducing the image of a corporate society of villains assembled in a unitary impenetrable body. For Bodin, the Leviathan, being a water monster, is associated with the image of the Great Crocodile of the Nile, the emblem of the tyrannical government of the Egyptian pharaoh.

On the other hand, Calvin developed an alternative heterodox, interpretation of the Leviathan as an agent of God. Based on the structure of the Book of Job and other passages, for Calvin, Leviathan represents the power of God. God is so powerful that He could even create such a huge and terrible creature. It is after the vision of the Leviathan that Job surrenders unequivocally to God's omnipotence and stops questioning God's justice. The importance of this interpretation is revealed if we revert to the Greek version of the Book of Job known as the *Septuagint*. Hobbes could have easily been acquainted with this version, given his knowledge of Greek displayed in his translations of Aristotle and Thucydides. In this version, we find that the Latin phrase cited by Hobbes on his frontispiece sounds very different in Greek, with no connection whatsoever with the sin of pride. In the Greek version, completely different from that translated by St Jerome, Leviathan is to be sported with by God's angels, it beholds every high thing (*omne sublime videt*) and it is *king over the water*. This last mention in particular makes rather evident a possible *positive* connection with English sovereignty, as it was to be exercised over the seas.

What remains of this philological discussion is then a reversal of imagery, from the corporate eagle of Dante as a representation of Justinian (the *Dominus Mundi*) in paradise, to the monstrous representation of the new state sovereign through the emblem of the corporate body of the sea serpent. Here the demonological turn in the representation of the modern political becomes apparent. A mystic eagle flying in Heaven is one thing; the creeping body of a huge snake mounting a hill as the paramount lord of all is another.

To sum up our theory, the body of the *Dominus* collapsed and the world came to be inhabited by Leviathans, representing the states as new political units. Thus, the old political theology, with its unitary conception of the world legitimate government represented by the *Dominus*, faded in favour of an opposite imagery linked to the new international conditions of warring independent states, each with its own legitimation. We can then interpret modernity as the parable of the rise and fall of the *Dominus*, and our current times as those of its ghostly resurgence in the ideal of a global rule as vengeance against the state-Leviathans that had taken its place. What, then, must be our direction of enquiry going forward?

Our theory of the demonological origin of modernity can represent an alternative to Agamben's outline[2] of two opposing conceptions of secularisation in terms of disenchantment (Max Weber) or political theology (Carl Schmitt). For us, the political world did not cease to be enchanted, but the old scheme of political theology cannot be maintained any longer because of the demonological fracture that occurred at the beginning of modernity. Thus, the world of politics continues to be under the spell of its own too-muchness, its excess of signification, but this excess can no longer be captured by the categories of political theology. Our current world appears to be that of the ghost of the *Dominus* with an excess of transcendence that continues to operate, though no longer through the theological apparatus.

How can we name this intangible aspect of politics? If we truly think that the appearance of the Leviathan marked a new age in the history of politics, we can recall that the Leviathan can 'behold every high thing'; it can grasp the sublime. Is there a sublime side of the political world order that supersedes any disenchantment and remains irreducible to theological elements? Is there a too-muchness of hegemony that is not theological?

II. New Monsters and Good Feelings

David Kennedy's book on the dark sides of the human rights discourse[3] becomes an essential feature in this part of our book, since it links the concepts of hegemony, human rights—as the new foundation of a possible legitimate world order—*and* the sublime. For Kennedy, human rights occupies the field of emancipatory possibility *through* its *hegemonic* character, and his claim is that this institutional

[2] G Agamben, *The Kingdom and the Glory: For a Theological Genealogy of Economy and Government* (L Chiesa trans, Stanford, Stanford University Press, 2011).

[3] D Kennedy, *The Dark Sides of Virtue: Reassessing International Humanitarianism* (Princeton, Princeton University Press, 2015) 3.

and political discourse makes other valuable emancipatory strategies *less* available.[4] As a dominant and fashionable vocabulary for thinking about emancipation, human rights discourse crowds out other ways of understanding harm and recompense, and occupies the field by implicit or explicit delegitimisation of other emancipatory strategies.

From his point of view, the vocabulary and institutional practice of human rights promotes an unduly abstract idea about people, politics and society. A one-size-fits-all emancipatory practice reduces the possibility for variation. Indeed, political diversity, the major trait of the old international system,[5] tends to disappear when a global standard of legitimation such as human rights comes into being.

Human rights effectively becomes the cornerstone of the dismantling of political diversity, not only from a right-wing point of view but also from a leftist one. On both sides of the political spectrum there can be a *melancholy* for sovereignty. Human rights can dismantle sovereignty, but they can also make a revolution impossible. Can a revolution be conducted without some violations of human rights? Could a revolution be scrutinised in international courts?

After all, no people's revolution could be allowed in a jurisdictional world granting a wide protection of human rights. A new *dominium mundi* can then be achieved not only, as Legendre has it,[6] through a domination of technocrats and sponsored economists in the hands of private corporations; it can also be achieved through human rights activists *against* other forms of emancipation.

In Kennedy's account, if we leave aside the long preparation and background of this evolution before the First World War and in the years of the League of Nations, it has become common sense that the second half of the twentieth century can be described as the 'Age of Rights.'[7] This characterisation reflects the view that with the end of the Second World War, the idea of human rights has become a universal political ideology and a central aspect of an ideology of constitutionalism.[8] Moreover, we know rather well that in the 1990s, humanitarian interventionism became a major and widespread doctrine allowing intervention from outside into local political realities, dismantling the inside-outside distinction of classical international law, and therefore globalising, or making the world space *imperial*. According to Kennedy, it is precisely in this disjuncture in the history of international law that we may pick up the dark sides that arise when humanitarianism, political, and military policy makers all come to speak the same pragmatic vocabulary.

[4] Kennedy, *The Dark Sides of Virtue* 8.

[5] Kissinger, *World Order* 11.

[6] P Legendre, *Dominium mundi: L'empire du management* (Paris, Ed Mille et une nuits, 2007).

[7] L Henkin, *The Age of Rights* (New York, Columbia University Press, 2002).

[8] Kennedy, *The Dark Sides of Virtue* 278; LF Damrosch, L Henkin, RC Pugh, O Schacter and H Smit (eds), *International Law. Cases and Materials* (St Paul, West Group, 2001) 586.

Against this dominant discourse David Kennedy's language becomes autobiographical, at the end of his book, while pointing at the same time toward a *sublime* dimension:

> We have made policy while turning our eyes from the darker consequences of our work … Imagine a humanitarianism which embraced the act of decision—allocating stakes, distributing resources, making politics, governing, ruling … deciding in the exception … It can be pleasurable—but it is also frightening.[9]

That which is *pleasurable but also frightening* is, of course, the *sublime* character of the political in the establishment of the world order.

It is not by chance then that he adds that there is also a *terrible* responsibility in humanitarian activism: deciding for others, causing consequences which '… *elude our knowledge but not our power* … The darker sides of our nature and our world confronted, embraced, and accepted, rather than denied' (emphasis added).[10] Here we touch on a major point implicit in the ideology of the *Dominus* from its very beginning: *that which eludes our knowledge though not our power.*

In his autobiographical approach, Kennedy tells us that this consciousness derived from his own 'disenchantment', a word certainly not selected by chance given its reminiscence of Weber and Weber's theories of secularisation. But how can we conceive the secularisation of a secularisation? Would it be something like a squared disenchantment? Is this melancholy not the residue of a political repressed figure that returns as a haunting ghost? Does it not represent the consciousness that *even* the rule of law and human rights can become a tool of the Devil?

Given this reminiscence of Weber in Kennedy's narrative, we should not be surprised to find a direct link to a Schmittian image in the last page of his work: 'Modern humanitarianism is a Gordian knot of participation in power and denial'.[11]

David Kennedy seems to make a hidden reference to the famous dialogue between Ernst Jünger and Carl Schmitt,[12] where it is indicated that the essence of the political is the capacity to cut the knot by a decision as strong as a sword; a decision needed to end an infinite discussion on an intricate issue *assuming* the risk of the political. What could be, then, the meaning of this Gordian metaphor? Is it a reference to the technology of power?

We will now investigate the modern role of metaphors, and especially of metaphors associated with technology, as applied to the legal and political domain. Are these metaphors not, after all, a way to deny the relevance of transcendence

[9] Kennedy, *The Dark Sides of Virtue* 354–55.

[10] Kennedy, *The Dark Sides of Virtue* 355.

[11] Kennedy, *The Dark Sides of Virtue* 357.

[12] C Schmitt, 'Die weltgeschichtliche Struktur des heutigen Weltgegensatzes von Ost und West. Bemerkungen zu Ernst Jüngers Schrift, "Der Gordische Knoten"' in A Mohler (ed), *Freundschaftliche Begegnungen: Festschrift für Ernst Junger zum 60. Geburtstag* (Frankfurt, Klostermann, 1955) 136–67.

and exception? Are they a continuation of the *artificial*[13] nature of the mortal god of Hobbes?

One possible way of framing the issue is through the concept of 'political technology', which has been recently defined as an attitude or mindset and a method.[14] The mindset of political technicians is meant to capture the way engineers think and act in political contexts. Such instrumentalism is reflected in current notions of statecraft as the efficient and up-to-date use of power.

Frankenberg singles out four paradigms of political technology as a bundle of political techniques for executing power. The first is individualised as the *method Machiavelli* and its scheme, dominated by the technicity of the acquisition and conservation of the prince's power, subverts the clear distinction between regular order and exception and allows for a variety of authorities and even dictatorial techniques, which foreshadows the informality of current techniques of governing.[15] Properly speaking, this scheme is not even concerned with the distinction between normalcy and emergency and the corresponding separation of competences, as it is unhampered by moral or legal constraints.

In contrast, the *method Hobbes* is aligned with more complexity. Hobbes designs a 'physics' of power against the chaotic context of England torn apart by religious wars and power struggles. Since here sovereign authority is linked to a central political goal, the protection of life, Hobbes attributes for the first time the essential aspects of a security calculation to a political technology. The techniques employed by the state turn out to be security technology. Even if the Hobbesian fear-driven theory of sovereignty lacks the conceptual space for a worldly state of exception that is different from the norm, it becomes apparent[16] that the superior purpose of security suggests a distinction between 'the greatest inconvenience that can happen to a commonwealth',[17] and everyday conflicts.

The third paradigm, according to Frankenberg, is the *method Locke* where the protection of property, liberty and security of the individual is associated with a protection of the 'body politic'. In this paradigm, the elements of security are reorganised around a parliamentary sovereignty finding its limits in the fundamental natural rights to property and personal freedom. The principles of security

[13] See C Schmitt, *The Leviathan in the State Theory of Thomas Hobbes. Meaning and Failure of a Political Symbol* (G Schwab and E Hilfstein trans, Chicago, The University of Chicago Press, 2008) where the author defines the State in Hobbes as the first product of modern technology using the phraseology of *machina machinarum*.

[14] G Frankenberg, *Political Technology and the Erosion of the Rule of Law: Normalizing the State of Exception* (Cheltenham, Edward Elgar, 2015) 5. See JP McCormick, *Carl Schmitt's Critique of Liberalism: Against Politics as Technology* (Cambridge, Cambridge University Press, 1997).

[15] JP McCormick, *Machiavellian Democracy* (Cambridge, Cambridge University Press, 2011).

[16] Frankenberg, *Political Technology* 16; about the 'demonic' root of Machiavellian politics see D Sternberger, 'Machiavellis "Principe" und der Bergriffs des Politischen' in D Sternberger (ed), *Schriften*, vol 3 (Frankfurt am Main, Insel Verlag, 1980) 29.

[17] T Hobbes, *Leviathan* (N Malcolm ed, Oxford, Oxford University Press, 1996) part 2, ch 18, § 18, 138.

are reorganised, shifting from the potentially rebellious citizenry to potentially arbitrary and despotic state power and its incursion into the sphere of property and liberty. One could add, from a Schmittian viewpoint, that what is changed is the potential enemy around which the theory is built. Nevertheless, in this context the law-rule is meant to guarantee the normalcy of lawful government, but there is a 'dark side' to this paradigm, though: the prerogatives of the monarch. Locke recognises the explicit emergency powers as deviations from regular law, or more precisely as exceptions. They appear as deviations and indicate the illiberalism woven into the fabric of the liberal paradigm and its political rationale.

A fourth paradigm is indicated by Frankenberg as the *method Foucault*. It opens a new and critical perspective on the other *methods*. Though centred on the illiberal security paternalism designed by presumed liberal political philosophy, its major turning point is directed toward the *bodies* and the ongoing mechanism to exercise power over them through continued monitoring, control and registration as well as discontinuously via the tax system or other devices. The *method Foucault* outlines the ensemble of discursive and non-discursive disciplinary techniques and practices where the unitary conception of sovereignty dissolves into various manifestations of disciplinary power.[18]

From Foucault's perspective, the Hobbesian concept of ultimate authority emerges with the 'self-exemption of the sovereign' from these systems of control and discipline.[19] This, we may add, would be even truer on a global scale: after all, could the Master of the World be submitted to a jurisdiction higher than his own? And could the divine, or political theology, have been a tool to discipline him? To a certain extent, we think they have been used to discipline the sovereign. Being king, by the grace of God, has always meant that God could judge the king. As long as the matter is '*quis judicabit?*', if the word of God is in the hands of the Church, this latter could judge and depose even the *Dominus Mundi*, as we saw at the time of Frederick II.

Moreover, as Pennington noted, lawyers can define property in a way that leaves practically no real possession in the hands of the *Dominus*, rendering its own dominion rather irrelevant. In such a scheme, even the Master would not be indifferent to practices of discipline, all pervasive, objective and ever-expanding as they are. Only in the exercise of his or her absolute prerogatives can the sovereign exempt him or herself from discipline.

Naturally, these sovereign practices of self-exemption from discipline, the undisciplined and undisciplinable feature of overall lordship lies in the voidness

[18] See M Foucault, *'Society Must Be Defended': Lectures at the Collège de France, 1975–1976* (D Macey trans, M Bertani and A Fontanta eds, New York, Picador, 2003) 23 ff, lecture of 14 January 1976.

[19] N Luhmann, 'Metamorphosen des Staates' in N Luhmann, *Gesellschaftsstruktur und Semantik. Studien zur Wissensoziologie der modernen Gesellschaft* (Frankfurt am Main, Suhrkamp Verlag, 1995) 101, 108.

of exceptional cases. As Frankenberg observes, the average reaction of lawyers to these cases has been maintained between negation and juridification of the state of exception,[20] a rather vain attempt if we think that it is, by definition, that which can never be normalised. But the question is precisely how to locate the thinkers of the absoluteness of the state of exception, such as Schmitt and Agamben, within this framework?

Frankenberg's analysis is conducted under the rubric of 'apocalypse and the politics of fear',[21] displaying the particular inclination of these theories toward the sublime that we have emphasised throughout this text. For Frankenberg, Schmitt is essentially an author who *succumbed to the fascination of the exceptional*, cultivating a focus on the state of exception that is nothing other than a preference for the extraordinary, a symptom of his own disenchantment with the normal everyday life of democracy and the law-rule. Schmitt and his epigones are tempted to perceive the world as revolving around the state of exception and to reserve regular law for issues of lesser importance. This might be caused by fears triggered by a feeling of homelessness in secularised systems. They, like the witches of Bodin, suffer from a form of *Daemonomanie*, or a melancholy for something they cannot express in any way other than a mystic and mystifying manner.

The language Frankenberg uses on the point is particularly precise, though allusive: succumb, fascination, the extraordinary, disenchantment, secularisation. It is almost patent that the sub-text of his analysis is Weberian in the sense of the rational thought that must emerge as disenchantment of the world in the time of its secularisation.[22] The use of this lexicon by Frankenberg supports our idea that these theories of the exception share an intimacy with the vocabulary of witchcraft (succumb, fascination) and that of the romantic sublime, that is, the exceptional or the extraordinary, which is linked at the same time with spell and fear.

For him, Schmitt becomes one of 'the most prominent inhabitants of this island of fear'.[23] Schmitt, the apocalyptic, uses the triad of states of exception, sovereignty and decision as a 'magic formula' to placate his own *Weltangst*, and so he justified the empty place of the sovereign as a 'miracle' to deny the despised modern age any legitimacy.

Certainly, there are precursors to this doctrine of the *priority* of the exception. Schmitt, however, enters the history of state theory as 'spokesman of the exceptional' via his *Political Theology*, revealing in *The Concept of the Political* the explosive implications of his theory with the emphasis on the existential decision about war and peace.

[20] Frankenberg, *Political Technology* 25.
[21] Frankenberg, *Political Technology* 100.
[22] See M Weber, *The Protestant Ethic and the Spirit of Capitalism* (S Kalberg trans, Oxford, Oxford University Press, 2010).
[23] Frankenberg, *Political Technology* 101.

In a passage, which Frankenberg labels as 'pompous kitsch', Schmitt reveals his romantic unconditional preference for the exceptional:

> The exception can be more important [to it] than the rule, not because of a romantic irony for the paradox, but because the seriousness of [such] an insight ... The exception is more interesting than the rule. The rule proves nothing: the exception proves everything.[24]

Indeed, there is always a subtle threshold between that which is sublime and that which is pompous kitsch. Frankenberg indicates the source of Schmitt's political existentialism in Kierkegaard,[25] to the point of accepting the apparent paradox suggested by McCormick[26] to define Schmitt as a 'political romanticist', as it was Schmitt who condemned political romanticism as the ideology of the despised *clase descudidora*, the parliamentary bourgeoisie.[27]

In short, we find in these theories of the political a sentimental-apocalyptic romanticisation of the exceptional—something which leads Schmitt to surpass the *method Locke*: a paradigm where there may be room for the special prerogatives of the monarch *within* the legal system.

Of course, Schmitt's move tends towards a critique of his arch-opponent Kelsen, who also allowed these prerogatives to exist within, and only within, the well-framed government by the law. On the contrary, Schmitt wants to show that—like Frederick II (!)—the sovereign situates himself *between* chaos *and* the legal order, so that he simultaneously resides outside *and* within the law.

Indeed, Frankenberg's conclusion leads toward a condemnation of Schmittian escape through aesthetics. Schmitt's use of aesthetics represents an attempt by a legal scholar to obtain the authority of an artist writing *as a romancier*. There are no good reasons for him to follow Carl Schmitt into the darkroom of his fears and the supposedly ideal world of the past, or to celebrate his *Political Theology*, let alone his preference for the state of exception.

We strongly agree with Frankenberg. Yet, it is because we agree with his depiction of Schmittian aesthetics that we think that there are good reasons to enter his darkroom, namely, to see that that room is not only *dark* but also filled with ghosts and remnants.

Schmitt was not alone, but rather one author in a long history of political fascination, and his psychology cannot explain his embarrassing and enduring presence. It is precisely because the aestheticisation of the political is enormously hazardous that we need to investigate it, from St Jerome, through Hobbes's occult

[24] C Schmitt, *Political Theology: Four Chapters on the Concept of Sovereignty* (G Schwab trans, Chicago, The University of Chicago Press, 1985) 18.

[25] S Kierkegaard, *Repetition and Philosophical Crumbs* (MG Piety trans, Oxford, Oxford University Press, 2009).

[26] JP McCormick, 'Irrational Choice and Mortal Combat as Political Destiny: The Essential Carl Schmitt' (2007) 10 *Annual Review of Political Science* 315.

[27] C Schmitt, *Political Romanticism* (G Oakes trans, Cambridge, MIT Press, 1991) 27.

metaphors to Schmitt's epigones. Romanticism has remained the hidden unresolved spectre of modernity; a *refoulée* which returns. Perhaps the sentimental revolution brought forth by romanticism has been a serious attempt to cope with what Christian Joerges has called the darker legacies of law in Europe,[28] and David Kennedy terms the dark sides of virtue. The kingdom of darkness cannot easily be overpassed by disregarding Schmitt as a *romancier*, though he has been its major voice in the last century. From a heterodox point of view, as maintained in this book, this 'kingdom of darkness' may effectively lie at the foundation of European modernity and its *apparent* Enlightenment.[29] After all, could we not gain something by reconsidering romanticism, and in particular the political consequences of the sublime?

Frankenberg is right again in indicating in Agamben the real continuation of the fascination for the extraordinary which marked the terrific nature of Schmittian exception. In so doing, Agamben reveals himself as even more romantic than Schmitt. Whereas Schmitt conceptualises the state of exception as the 'coronation hall' of the sovereign, Agamben translates it into the *dark phantasmagoria* of the 'bare life that cannot be sacrificed yet may still be killed'.

Following Walter Benjamin, Agamben locates the state of exception in the 'gloomy realm' of purpose-free power, in the emptiness of law. But in so doing, from our standpoint, he locates sovereignty in an 'anomic space'; a space without law—a morgue, so to speak.[30] Perhaps this morgue is the morgue of Santner's royal remnants.[31] For Benjamin, this state of exception is determined not by the violence or power (*Gewalt*) that generates or maintains the law (*Rechts-Gewalt*), but by a *fearsome divine power*, which is certainly sublime in its own terms.[32] Agamben, far beyond the liberal paradigm and the conservative tradition, undertakes a radical disjunction of the law-rule on the one hand and the state of exception on the other. Using what Frankenberg defines as a 'rather vague metaphor', he describes the exception as 'a threshold at which logic and praxis blur with each other and a pure violence without logos claims to realise an enunciation without any real reference'.[33] It is in this way that for Agamben the paradoxical nature of the state of exception consists in the fact that 'it is impossible to distinguish transgression of the law from execution of the law, so that what violates a rule and what conforms to it coincides without any remainder'.[34]

[28] C Joerges, *Darker Legacies of Law in Europe: the Shadow of National Socialism and Fascism over Europe and its Legal Traditions* (Oxford, Hart Publishing, 2003).

[29] M Horkheimer and TW Adorno, *Dialectic of Enlightenment: Philosophical Fragments* (E Jephcott trans, Stanford, Stanford University Press, 2009).

[30] Frankenberg, *Political Technology*; Agamben, *State of Exception* 6, 69.

[31] EL Santner, *The Royal Remains: the People's Two Bodies and the Endgames of Sovereignty* (Chicago, The University of Chicago Press, 2012) preface, xi.

[32] W Benjamin, 'Critique of Violence' in W Benjamin, *Reflections. Essays, Aphorisms, Autobiographical Writings* (E Jephcott trans, New York, Schocken Books, 2007) 287, 295.

[33] G Agamben, *State of Exception* (K Attel trans, Chicago, The University of Chicago Press, 2010) 40.

[34] G Agamben, *Homo Sacer: Sovereign Power and Bare Life* (D Heller-Roazen trans, Stanford, Stanford University Press, 1998) 57.

In contrast to Schmitt, who locates the exception somehow in between law and chaos, for Frankenberg, Agamben insists on an 'enigmatic' neither-nor, in other words, the state of exception is determined neither as a factual nor as a legal situation. Indeed, for Agamben, the state of exception is the device that must ultimately articulate and hold together the two aspects of the juridico-political machine by instituting a threshold of un-decidability between *anomie* and *nomos*, between life and law, between *auctoritas* and *potestas*.[35]

Frankenberg's conclusion about Agamben parallels the one he reached about Schmitt: Agamben shares Schmitt's *fascination with the extraordinary* and his preference for the exceptional. Agamben is a romantic and his theories are suffused with the aesthetic of the sublime; they are not philosophy in the strong sense of the word, but a philosophy of strong words.[36]

The whole of Frankenberg's critique is well grounded but, as we have said, romanticism is not something that we can simply disregard, since it addresses the unspeakable side of politics and hegemony. What is misleading in Agamben is his methodological continuation of the political theological paradigm, to the point of purporting a kind of messianism from below to disrupt the yoke of the law. But we can reach a completely different interpretation of the undeniable sublime-kitsch side of the modern political if we think neither in terms of disenchantment nor in terms of political theology, but rather in terms of the demonological turn which transformed the *Dominus* into the Leviathan. In our terms, what is needed is to give a different appraisal, a different consciousness of the domain reached by the *angelos tes anomias* (the angel of lawlessness) as the occult side of modernity.

III. The Political *Refoulé*

A. Superseding Political Theology

The ideal of a world legitimate order, as we have seen, involves the plans of transcendence and hegemony in the spatial partition of the earth, as well as a feeling of *nostalgia* and *melancholy*. 'Political theology', for us, has been but one attempt to formulate these connections between geopolitics and the law. In particular, we maintain that Schmitt's appeal to political theology perverted the political discourse with the illusion of a permanence of the theological which was reversed into a heterodox occultism of sovereign powers. What we should do now is reappraise the theories of secularisation as one of the key features of modernity,

[35] Frankenberg, *Political Technology* 114.
[36] Frankenberg, *Political Technology* 112.

and analyse the field of international relations and the world order from a different perspective.

In an important locus of his works, Agamben sketches two alternative models of secularisation.[37] The first is the Weberian model which interprets it as the *disenchantment* of the world and the Schmittian appraisal of political theology. In the Weberian model, the world is eventually reduced to the domain of pure rational decision and behaviour.[38] The second is Schmitt's conception of the theory of political theology as a reaction, claiming that our conceptions of law and the political are still embedding their previous theological meanings. But there is, perhaps, the possibility of a third approach, which would be neither Schmittian nor Weberian, and that we try to maintain here: that of a demonological normative inversion which occurred at the threshold of modernity. In this case, the world of politics would not be a disenchanted flat world, nor would it be dominated by previous theological concepts. Rather, the ancient theological orientation reverted into its opposite, remaining an uncanny excess by which the notions of sovereignty and international order are still constantly characterised.

What we mean is that the imagery surrounding the political and the function of government is as important as the wording by which they are located within the scientific discourse. Of course, what is always at stake in this imagery is the struggle for hegemony and legitimacy. The globalist challenge to sovereignty arouses that sense of melancholy for a world order centred on nation states. We cannot simply rebuff the current resurgence of sovereignty, and the feelings associated with it, as mere populism, as this label reinforces the impression that the power has been taken away from the people in favour of mysterious and unaccountable global institutions. If we want to defeat what we polemically label as populism, perhaps we should delve into more sophisticated analyses of the feelings associated with the political and the *repression* of those feelings. At the same time, we think, we can no longer inhabit the Schmittian paradigm as it is both politically hazardous and conceptually untenable. We should, rather, reconsider the political *beyond* this paradigm.

In his outstanding work on the *People's two bodies*, Santner argued that the complex symbolic structures and dynamics of sovereignty that informed medieval and early modern European monarchies did not simply disappear from the space of politics once the body of the king was no longer available as the singular embodiment of the principles and functions of sovereignty. Rather, these structures and dynamics migrated into a new *location*, which thereby assumes a turbulent and disorienting semiotic density previously concentrated in the 'strange material and physical presence' of the king.[39] His analysis is centred on the mystic element of the flesh of political bodies as the one which holds the *surplus of immanence*

[37] Agamben, *The Kingdom and the Glory* 3.

[38] D Leshem, *The Origins of Neoliberalism: Modeling the Economy from Jesus to Foucault* (New York, Columbia University Press, 2016) 5.

[39] Santner, *The Royal Remains* 245.

implied by legitimacy and power. By 'flesh' he means the '.... *übersinnlich element that fattens the one who occupies the place of power*'.[40]

This phrase is dense, and it is revealing that the author has to revert to an ambiguous German word to express what he means. *Übersinnlich* can indicate, at the same time, something which is extrasensory (beyond sensation) or something that is more than *sinnlich* (beyond signification), and also something which is supernatural not because it is *übernaturlich* but just because it encompasses the limits of our senses and our capacity to signify. For us, of course, the most important point is the sequence, allowed by the German language, between what is beyond meaning as well as beyond sense. Is there any better way to try to capture what we mean by magic and sublime, by spell and witchcraft, especially as applied to the *Dominus* as the Lord of the World?

If the sublime is by definition beyond signification as it operates in a mysterious way upon our sensibility, Santner may offer a modern key to understanding the too-muchness of the king's body, letting us speak consistently about his immaterial political body. To use his words, 'biopolitics came to be charged with the care taking of the sublime flesh of the new bearer of the principle of sovereignty, the People'.[41] In describing the king's body, he says it is both *sublime* and *entsetzlich* flesh, using another German term that can be translated as *dreadful, appalling, hideous, terrible, awful*. What is there more sublime, being at the same time *übersinnlich und ensetzlich*, supernatural, beyond words and terrible, than the Leviathan? Does it not indeed have a corporate body? And are we not supposed to be his flesh?

If we understand Santner's work correctly, he uses flesh to denote the extrasensory side of the biopolitical dimension of bodies, the sublime as it is attached to a material earthly presence, precisely as in the case of the presence on earth of the *Dominus*. Here, the matter of biopolitics transcends human bodies to confront the much more decisive question of non-humans and their dominion in world affairs. Santner grasps the too-muchness of the political situation, linked to sovereignty and bodies, which we try to manage through the technical languages of law and economics, but that we can never successfully capture without a residue. It always remains as a hidden mode of thinking that governs us more than we can govern it.

What we maintain, then, is the possibility to read the Leviathan and its demoniac aspect through the category of *political sublime*.

B. Political Sublime

The locus where Schmitt should have confronted the theory of the sublime is his book on *political romanticism*, a historical study that offers a political critique.

[40] Santner, *The Royal Remains* 82.
[41] Santner, *The Royal Remains* 34.

His critique is mainly brought against the passivity that would be entailed by the romanticisation of experience. As has been perfectly stated by Oakes in his introduction,[42] the first aim of the book is to show that romanticism represents a secularisation, subjectification and privatisation in which God is replaced by the modern emancipated private individual. As it were, the whole world decays to an occasion for the subjectivity of the subject. From these premises, Schmitt proceeds to assault political romanticism as an attack on the European bourgeoisie, characterised as the historical bearer of the movement. The more specific target of Schmitt was nevertheless Adam Mueller,[43] as the representative of the German liberal romantics. He sees in them the affirmation of the ideology of the *clase descudidora* (ever-talking class),[44] that is to say, of the rising middle class who found political expression in the practice of parliamentarianism. In this precise sense, romanticism is conceived by Schmitt as an 'endless talk' fit for a bourgeoisie incapable of real political action, where for him this constitutes a neutralisation and a denial of the true essence of the political, as long as it rests on the capacity to decide.

This idiosyncratic view of romanticism led Schmitt to consider authors such as Burke, the author of the aesthetics of sublime, and Goethe, in their own turn, as mere *romantic figures*, as *Handlungsgerüsten* (plot-characters), only 'characters' of the English or the German romanticism. In the first edition, Schmitt practically omits Burke only to add a simple footnote dedicated to him in the second edition[45] stating that:

> The romantic elements are not decisive for Burke's political view. They mediated the great impact on romanticism, and thus the reception of conservative ideas as well. *I did not emphasize* this point sufficiently in the first edition, and in this regard I am indebted to M.J. Bonn's essay on Burke (Frankfurter Zeitung, July 10 and 12, 1897), *which I did not become acquainted with until later*, for an important suggestion. (emphasis added)

Notwithstanding the absolutely extravagant notion that the romantic element was not *decisive* for Burke's political view, Schmitt goes on to say that there is an important 'suggestion' to be derived from Burke:

> Burke's aesthetics is also of great interest here. In his work, *the dark appears as the new sign of the sublime* ... The stream of ideas that flows from Burke divides into the historical conception of the world and political romanticism in the strict sense. In Burke, both are united. (emphasis added)[46]

[42] Schmitt, *Political Romanticism* iv ff.

[43] Adam Heinrich Muller (1779–1829) was a German literary critic, political economist and theorist of the state.

[44] A Spanish term derived from the catholic thinker Donoso Cortes, and meaning 'a class which shifts all political activity onto the plane of conversation'. See C Schmitt, *Donoso Cortés in gesamteuropäischer Interpretation: vier Aufsätze* (Berlin, Duncker & Humblot, 2009).

[45] Schmitt, *Political Romanticism* 165.

[46] Schmitt, *Political Romanticism* 165.

This footnote, which normally goes unnoticed, is hugely significant, having been written by an author whose theory of law can certainly be described as abysmal. At the very end in writing the first edition Schmitt was not aware of Burke's aesthetics, to the point of acknowledging, in the *second* edition, that it appeared to be important. Here, Schmitt credits Burke for having played a decisive role in the unfolding of romanticism, to the point of signaling 1799 as a turning point because that was the year when Schlegel read Burke.[47]

This late acknowledgement of the aesthetic of the sublime does not change Schmitt's position. For Schmitt, political romanticism is nevertheless to be condemned because *it was* revolutionary, and then *became* conservative, to return revolutionary in 1830. These swings display the possibility of changing political views as a direct consequence of the occasionalism of political romanticism. Romantic aesthetics transform the whole world, including the world of politics, into an opportunity for self-expression, which can change because it has no fixed stuff. The core of romanticism lies in its political passivity derived from its transmutation of the world into a narrative of the self.

For Schmitt, it is this *passive* attitude toward self-expression that nourishes the fundamental link between romantic aesthetic and political parliamentarianism as an endless discussion where political facts are degraded to a mere opportunity for argument. The roots of romantic ideology of sublime are to be found in its incapacity to decide, to take position. Romantic thinkers build a world of their own and then use it as a chance to express their emotions. Their sublime derives from their occasionalism.

This theatrical gesture of Schmitt aims at neutralising Burke and the sublime. Burke—for Schmitt—is a deep thinker, but the bulk of romanticism lies in its lack of depth, in its avoidance of world problems, transforming them into personal problems of feelings and expression. What is, then, the aesthetics of the sublime and how is it linked to the political?

An aesthetic of the sublime, reactivated in post-modern terms by Jean-François Lyotard,[48] was introduced in the first century CE by the Greek scholar of rhetoric, Longinus. As it is commonly received, sublime may denote a sensation, a concept, object, or experience if it is breathtaking, unique, incomparable, and *beyond words.* Kant, in the *Analytic of the Sublime*, reverted to something which can be described as a sense of the unlimited and its immense potential power: 'the boundless ocean set into a rage'.[49] In its modern reprisal, the sublime became attached, especially by Schiller, to a particular feeling of that which remains in 'the contemplation of

[47] Schmitt, *Political Romanticism* 167–70.

[48] JF Lyotard, *The Postmodern Explained: Correspondence, 1982–1985* (D Barry trans, Minneapolis, Univeristy of Minnesota Press, 1992) 71.

[49] I Kant, *Critique of the Power of Judgement* [1790] (P Guyer ed, Cambridge, Cambridge University Press, 2008) § 28, 144.

nature where people give themselves up to the play of fantasy',[50] especially the attempt to express what is absent *but* present as occupying an 'empty space'. Something like a gothic mansion that, whilst abandoned, is still haunted by the spectral presence of the ghostly ancestors.[51] There is in all of this the discovery of a strange association between fear and attraction, very proximate to the effect of a demonic seduction in the terms of Bodin, who, as we know, dedicated a whole work to the knowledge of things sublime.[52]

Nevertheless, such an aesthetic effect of the sublime was not popularly identified in the terms used here until John Dryden and Nicolas Boileau-Despreaux in the seventeenth century, and then various other authors concurred in revitalising the aesthetics of the sublime.[53] Joseph Addison noted this relationship between fear and attraction in his *Essay on the Pleasures of the Imagination* (1712) which was to be influential for both Kant and Burke:

> When we look on such hideous Objects, we are not a little pleased to think we are in no Danger of them. We consider them at the same time as Dreadful and Harmless; so that the more Frightful appearance they make the greater is the Pleasure we receive from the sense of our own safety.[54]

John Dennis traced a list of objects that inspire terror and attraction, including not only 'Thunder, Tempests, raging Seas, Inundations, Torrents,' or 'Earthquakes' but also 'Spirits and Souls of Men', 'Fire', and 'War'.[55] In *An Essay on the Sublime* (1747), John Baillie linked the sublime also to works of destruction and ravaging when performed by extraordinary men such as Alexander the Great,[56] and very similar images were later used by Schiller to reconstitute the *truth of the sublime*, or the truth of its terrifying political actuality.[57] This is, of course, of particular interest in our reconstruction of the Leviathan as an *inversion* of the old *Dominus* and its related theology.

Such association is indeed directly marked by the greatest of the reinventors of the sublime: Edmund Burke in his *Philosophical Enquiry into the Origins of Our Ideas of the Sublime and the Beautiful* (1757).[58] In this work, sublimity remains

[50] F Schiller, 'On the Sublime (Toward a Further Development of some Kantian Ideas)' in F Schiller, *Essays* (W Hinderer and WO Dahlstrom eds, London, Continuum, 1993) 29 ff, 38.

[51] CH Hinnant, 'Schiller and the Political Sublime: Two Perspectives' (2002) 44 *Criticism* 121.

[52] J Bodin, *Colloque de Jean Bodin; des secrets cachéz des choses sublimes, entre sept sçavans qui sont de differens sentimens* (reprint, Paris, L Tenin, 1914).

[53] E King, 'Quinquennial Terror: Machiavelli's Understanding of the Political Sublime' (2013) 3 *Open Journal of Political Science* 70.

[54] J Addison, *The Miscellaneous Works of Joseph Addison*, vol 2 (New York, Harper & Brothers, 1837) 149.

[55] J Dennis, *The Critical Works of John Dennis*, vol 1 (EN Hooker ed, Baltimore, Johns Hopkins University Press, 1939) 361. See Hinnat, 'Schiller and the Political Sublime' 127.

[56] J Baillie, 'An Essay on the Sublime' in A Ashfield and P de Bolla (eds), *The Sublime: A Reader in British Eighteenth Century Aesthetic Theory* (Cambridge, Cambridge University Press, 1996) 93.

[57] Hinnant, 'Schiller and the Political Sublime' 128–32.

[58] E Burke, *A Philosophical Enquiry into the Origin of Our Ideas of the Sublime and Beautiful* [1757] (A Phillips ed, Oxford, Oxford University Press, 1990).

strongly dominated by *natural* phenomena, such as hurricanes, volcanoes, mountains and stormy seas.[59] Nonetheless, Hinnat claims that at the centre of Burke's analysis of the sublime there can be a *political* example of 'state terror', the gruesome torture and execution of Robert Damiens, the would-be assassin of Louis XV.[60] In a way, Burke's aesthetic inquiry is not only devoted to the grandiose prose of that which is exceptional, but actually starts with the political example of a regicide in the gothic atmosphere of a mysterious state of exception.

Burke's theory of the sublime is strongly based on an opposition between beauty, as that which is well-formed and pleasing, and sublime, which is ugly, fearful *but also* desirable, all at once.[61] Beauty, is that which we perceive with pleasure, sublime is that which truly moves us. This opposition concerning the limits of the imagination and the senses in contrast to the power of reason had a deep impact on romantic authors and certainly bypassed the bourgeois ideology of parliamentarianism as an endless politically inconclusive talk.

But what was the relation of Burke's aesthetics to his political views? As we know, Burke never wrote a work truly devoted to the principles of politics. His ideas are exposed in speeches and letters devoted to specific problems with a rather practical intent, even if he seems to have stuck to the same principles for all of his life.[62] Those principles appear to have inspired his campaigns in favour of the American colonists, or the Irish Catholics, and *against* the French Revolution. Burke's stance against the Revolution is perhaps his most meaningful reflection on politics, also because it does not follow the path of continental reactionary thought represented by Donoso Cortés (1809–1853) or De Maistre (1753–1821), who so deeply influenced the works of Schmitt.[63] It is consequently even less understandable why Schmitt attributed so little weight to Burke in his *political romanticism,* notwithstanding his theory that it was the French Revolution that determined the opposition between friends and enemies in Europe for almost a century.[64]

This point of Burke's doctrine on law and politics has been of particular importance especially for Hayek's theory of the preeminence of the common law.[65] Burke stood against the radical French revolutionaries because they transformed an exception into a rule, that is to say, because they considered as normal what can be valid only in extreme cases. Burke condemned the French Revolution since it elevated the extreme case to the rank of a paradigm. It elevated the remote possibility of the revolution to the normal condition of the possibility to rebuild society

[59] SH Monk, *The Sublime: A Study of Critical Theories in XVIII-Century England* (Ann Arbor, University of Michigan Press, 1935) 8.

[60] Hinnant, 'Schiller and the Political Sublime' 128.

[61] PA Shaw, *The Sublime* (London, Routledge, 2017) 48.

[62] See F Dreyer, 'The Genesis of Burke's Reflections' (1978) 50 *The Journal of Modern History* 462.

[63] See A Spektorowski, 'De Maistre, Donoso Cortés, and the Legacy of Catholic Authoritarianism' (2002) 63 *Journal of the History of Ideas* 283.

[64] Schmitt, *Political Romanticism* 28–29.

[65] FA Hayek, *Law, Legislation and Liberty: A New Statement of the Liberal Principles of Justice and Political Economy*, vol 1 (Chicago, The University of Chicago Press, 1976) 22–23 and 152.

from scratch through political action *and* legislation. This should have been of interest to Schmitt's theory of the case of exception, rendering his omission of Burke even more inexplicable.

For Burke, 'French philosophy' was to be condemned not so much for having created the conditions for the Revolution, as for having perverted the notion of the law,[66] making the exception the paradigm. For him, the people are not the masters of the constitution, but its creatures. The law can never be reduced to the king's will or the people's will, as it transcends both. Therefore, it is not possible to rebuild and redesign the whole legal order, as the French Revolution did. This pretension amounts to an *abuse* of reason. These legal-political consequences of Burke's thoughts are, for us, strictly connected to his aesthetic of the sublime and are associated with an exaltation of the *unwritten* English constitution, as may be clearly indicated in his chapter on 'power'.

We know that for Burke the sensation of the sublime is based on the feeling of astonishment, pointing out the kindred emotions which attend fear and horror. Astonishment is that state of the soul in which all its emotions are *suspended*, with some degree of horror. He states:[67]

> In this case the mind is so entirely filled with its object, that it cannot entertain any other, nor by consequence reason on that object which employs it. Hence arises the great power of the sublime, that, far from being produced by them, it anticipates our reasonings, and hurries us on by an irresistible force. Astonishment, as I have said, is the effect of the sublime in its highest degree.

Sublime bypasses our reason in that suspension produced by awe, amazement, and fear. Day is beautiful, but night is sublime. In the same passage and by his words:

> Whatever therefore is terrible, with regard to sight, is sublime too, whether this cause of terror be endued with greatness of dimensions or not; for it is impossible to look on anything as trifling, or contemptible, that may be dangerous.

From the standpoint of political theory, it is hard to avoid the connection between Burkes' description of the sublime and Hobbes's description of the Leviathan when he states that the force of the natural law by which God reigns on humankind derives from His *irresistible* power.[68] Leviathan is sublime *ante litteram* as it is horrific, irresistible and governs our feelings. Its appearance dominates and produces an overwhelming seduction, which, given its nature, cannot but be demonic. It represents a heterodox *demonic* fascination with *the power of God.*

The aesthetic of the sublime in political matters represents precisely the fascination with what governs our sensibility beyond our reason and that leads us to

[66] See L Strauss, *Natural Right and History* (Chicago, The University of Chicago Press, 2008) 299, in chapter 6, explicitly dedicated to Burke. See E Burke, *Reflections on the Revolution in France: A Critical Edition* (JCD Clark ed, Stanford, Stanford University Press, 2001).

[67] E Burke, *The Writings and Speeches of Edmund Burke*, vol 1 (TO McLaughlin and JT Boulton eds, Oxford, The Clarendon Press, 1997) 230.

[68] Hobbes, *Leviathan*, part 2, ch 31, § 5.

admire God for His power, as well as death or the Devil for their darkness. Burke's comment on Milton's description of the power of death as the king of terrors, and the undoubted fascination that such power may exercise on the human mind is illuminating:

> [Milton's] description of Death in the second book is admirably studied; it is astonishing with what a gloomy pomp, with what a significant and expressive uncertainty of strokes and colouring, he has finished the portrait of the king of terrors ... In this description all is dark, uncertain, confused, terrible, and sublime to the last degree.[69]

Sublime points to that abysmal and shapeless ontological beyond, which always transcends any objectivity or any logical constitution of the world. But why, then, did Burke condemn the French terror? Was the exceptional terror of the Revolution not one of the most perfect realisations of a political sublime in history?

What disturbs Burke about the French Revolution is that it was done in the name of Reason. French revolutionaries acted out of the desire to accomplish the principles dictated by Reason. They were rationalists, and their monstrous acts were therefore so monstrous just because they were an offspring of rationalism used to rebuild human society through politics and law. The Revolution was monstrous because it aimed to realise a political upheaval in the name of enlightened rationality.

This line of thought led Burke to his most successful political elaboration: the sharp distinction between the English Revolution of 1688 and the French Revolution of 1789. It is indeed important to remember that before Burke's considerations, English liberals, and he was among them, were sympathetic to the French Revolution, tracing a parallel between contemporary events and those which occurred in England a century before. The French were realising what the British had already done. The analogy between the two revolutions was, then, for them rather natural. It was Burke who created an alternative theory to distinguish and mark a deep opposition between the two revolutions. For him, as we said, French Revolution was *unique* and unparalleled. It had no common traits with any of the other revolutions that occurred in Europe, because it was first of all a revolution of doctrine and of theory. The political contest had become doctrinal.[70] It was the first *total and philosophical revolution.* It stretched the concept of the political beyond its limits to the point of imagining a redesign of the whole of society. Nothing of this kind ever happened in other revolutions, least of all in England.

[69] Burke, *Writings and Speeches* 231.

[70] H Kissinger, *A World Restored: Metternich, Castelreagh, and the Problem of Peace, 1812–22* (Boston, Houghton Miffin, 1957) 4.

It is important to underline the evolution of Burke's thoughts on the argument. Initially, Burke did not condemn the French Revolution. In a letter written to Lord Charlemont on 9 August 1789, he had not yet taken a position:[71]

> England gazing with astonishment at a French struggle for Liberty and not knowing whether to blame or to applaud! The thing indeed, though I thought I saw something like it in progress for several years, has still something in it paradoxical and Mysterious. The spirit it is impossible not to admire; but the old Parisian ferocity has broken out in a shocking manner.

Two months later, on 10 October, after riots had provoked the reclusion of Louis XVI at the Tuileries, he wrote to his son Richard in terms of the *dissolution* of all the constitutive elements of civil society in France. The Revolution was provoking a 'world of monsters', where Mirabeau could govern as the 'Great Anarchist' in the place of the destitute Great Monarch; grandiose prose adopted in a tone of open disapproval. His first public condemnation came on 7 November 1790 in reply to the favourable speeches of Pitt and Fox. For Burke, the French showed themselves to be the greatest architects of the world's ruin. In a very brief span of time they levelled to the ground their monarchy, the church, aristocracy, laws, wealthy, army, navy, commerce and industries, realising a ferocious, bloody and tyrannical democracy.

It was, then, in the debates of the Revolution Society, devoted to celebrate the English Glorious Revolution of 1688, that Burke definitively refined his theory of a direct opposition between the 'abstract metaphysics' of the rights of man and the concrete 'historical tradition' of the common law. The English Revolution was made *to preserve* the ancient constitution, and the ancient laws and liberties of the English people. For him, the very idea of the fabrication of a new government had to raise our *disgust* and *horror*:

> We wished at the period of the Revolution, and do now wish, to derive all we possess as an inheritance from our forefathers. Upon that body and stock of inheritance we have taken care not to inoculate any cyon alien to the nature of the original plant. All the reformations we have hitherto made, have proceeded upon the principle of reference to antiquity.[72]

Never before had the historical and local dimensions of rights been so eloquently defended or received a greater poetic expression. This is particularly true given that the only argument adduced by Burke is to follow the paths of the forefathers. A new law sounds like something alien and absurd to him. You inherit your rights, you do not create them. The law remains something that you can inherit, but you cannot invent. Reason in the field of law feeds monsters. The history of

[71] E Burke, *The Correspondence of Edmund Burke*, vol 6 (TW Copeland ed, Cambridge, Cambridge University Press, 1958–78) 10.

[72] E Burke, *Reflections on the Revolution in France* (WL Arnstein ed, Lexington, DC Heath and Company, 1993) 121.

the common law, by contrast, is romanticised. It is the romantic of the 'long ago and far away': ancient charters are but repetitions of even more ancient laws, up to a mythical gothic past of kings and knights. The law governs us more than we can govern it, remaining always partially ineffable. As such, there is no contrast between Burke's aesthetics and his political views. On the contrary, the political sublime is constituted as the main feature of the ancient constitution and of English law. It is striking that Schmitt shared a parallel abysmal view of the law and the political, but Burke displaces the exception in another nation. Its proper locus is France, and exception can never be paradigmatic. There can scarcely be room for miracles in English law, even if its nature is unfathomable. Here in Burke we face a sublimity which is very different from that of political theology. The point is that there is always more than that in the constitution and the law, a surplus of immanence that cannot be captured and mastered at our will, but which is sublime rather than theological.

Moreover, another author who is peculiarly missing from Schmitt's political romanticism is Friedrich Schiller (1759–1805). Alluded to only three times,[73] he is just cited for his theory on the melancholy of lost childhood and sentimental poetry.[74] But Schiller has been indeed the one author who most worked on the paradox of terror and attraction, essential to the theory of sublime. Additionally, his political attitude toward the French Revolution changed dramatically, as did that of Burke.

According to Schiller,[75] an object is theoretically-sublime insofar as it brings with it the notion [*Vorstellung*] of infinity, something the imagination does not feel capable of depicting. An object is practically-sublime insofar as it brings with it the notion of danger we do not feel ourselves capable of overcoming with our physical powers. We succumb in the attempt to grasp the idea [*Vorstellung*] of the theoretically-sublime or to resist the force of the practically-sublime. A peaceful ocean is an example of the former, a stormy ocean an example of the latter.[76]

As long as we have a representation [*Vorstellung*] of a frightening object, if this representation is 'vivid enough,' it will set 'the preservation instinct in motion and the result' will be 'something analogous to what the actual sensation would produce'.[77] On this double movement rests not so much a distinct experience of its own, but rather the repetition, on a different tune, of the feeling of actual fear.

All of this points to something more than the simple feeling of being overwhelmed by the aesthetics of the extraordinary. For Frankenberg,[78] Agamben

[73] Schmitt, *Political Romanticism* 15, 36 and 69.

[74] F Schiller, 'On Naive and Sentimental Poetry' in HB Nisbet (ed), *German Aesthetic and Literary Criticism: Winckelmann, Lessing, Hamann, Herder, Schiller, Goethe* (Cambridge, Cambridge University Press, 1985) 177.

[75] See Hinnant, 'Schiller and the Political Sublime: Two Perspectives' 122.

[76] Schiller, 'On the Sublime' 24.

[77] Schiller, 'On the Sublime' 30.

[78] Frankenberg, *Political Technology* 114–15.

shares Schmitt's fascination with the extraordinary, so that both are overwhelmed by their emotions. For us, what are at stake here are not emotions, but *what remain occult in the political.* There is perhaps an excess, a residue of the political which Schmitt failed to exhaust, just because of his own reference to theology.

Indeed, for Schiller this feeling of fear-and-attraction—which is assumed to be a central element of the sublime experience—is far from simple even if, for us, it closely mirrors the feelings associated with melancholy as analysed by Bodin in relation to witches: it is that particular kind of seduction which is exercised by the Devil.

As we know, Schiller gave a romantic explanation of the seduction of terror in terms of a *detachment* of the subject from the hazard of the situation. As Paul de Man says in his essay on Kant and Schiller: '[i]f Reason can take on the attribute of Terror, then Nature will be able to take on the attribute of tranquility, and you will be able to enjoy with a certain tranquility, the sublime violence of Nature'.[79] What is thrilling here is precisely this sort of fascination for the sublimity of Nature's *violence.* Is this not, ultimately, an argument strictly parallel to that of the Book of Job? Is it not the sublime terrific aspect and potential violence of the Leviathan that convinces Job to eventually bow to the Lord? And was Hobbes not—we may say—attracted by the potential violence of the sovereign?

It is important to note that this cult of violence does not entail a cult of success through violence. It is a rather different feeling strongly associated with melancholy, the disease of witches. In Schiller's example,[80] Hannibal was magnificent from a theoretical point of view, since he forged a passage over the untrodden Alps to Italy. He was magnificent in a practical sense, but he became sublime only *in misfortune.* Hercules is magnificent because he undertook and completed his 12 tasks, but Prometheus is sublime because, fettered to the Caucasus, he did not regret his deeds and did not acknowledge having done anything wrong. An individual can display magnificence in good fortune, but sublimity in misfortune. This is a melancholic aspect of violence and of history. Great men reach sublimity in their disillusionment more than in their ascension.

Clearly, in our appraisal, the sublime supposes comprehension of some kind of awe-inspiring, destructive power, but *also* a positive evaluation of melancholy as a state of superior consciousness or knowledge of men's destiny. As we have tried to show, this was precisely an attitude of occult philosophy and of Bodin's depiction of the devil and his appearances. This feeling, related to the unfortunate fate of Prometheus—which was so important to Shelley[81]—represents a form of aesthetic consciousness of the abyss which may be evoked by a thunderstorm,

[79] P de Man, *Aesthetic Ideology* (A Warminski ed, Minneapolis, University of Minnesota Press, 1996) 136.

[80] Schiller, 'On the Sublime' 35; Hinnant, 'Schiller and the Political Sublime: Two Perspectives' 123 ff.

[81] PB Shelley, *Prometheus Unbound—A Lyrical Drama in Four Acts* (London, C & J Ollier, 1820) viii. Shelley, in the preface of this work, draws an analogy between the figure of Prometheus and Satan. Indeed the latter is 'resembling in any degree' the former in his 'opposition to omnipotent force'.

a flaming volcano, or a looming mass of rock about to fall upon us; a storm at sea, a bitter winter in the polar regions, a summer in the tropics, ferocious or venomous animals, a flood. All of these and more are the sorts of natural forces in the face of which our capacity to resist counts for nothing; natural forces that contradict our physical existence.[82] Now it is patently clear that this evocation of the abyss may indeed have a demonic character as it is well testified by numerous writings on romanticism.[83] What is most extraordinary is that Schmitt completely omitted not only any accurate reference to Burke, as we have seen, but completely bypassed this particular feature of romanticism, reducing it to the parliamentary attitude of the middle class incapable of real political decision.

Reducing the aesthetic of the sublime and the abyss to the feebleness of the middle class is a typical ideological *manœuvre* provoking a false consciousness of historical changes. But when an ideological *manœuvre* is adopted it normally hides an embarrassing discomfort.

Once again, in the case of Schiller as well as in the case of Burke, we cannot underestimate the political side of their aesthetics. Indeed, Schiller explains this unexpected feature of human sensibility by reverting to a fable of origins,[84] sounding very similar to Hobbes's account of the terror that dominates in the state of nature before the institution of civil government. Originally, according to this fable, in each unexpected appearance of nature, people see an *enemy* armed against their existence. In this age of origins, the preservation instinct is the people's unbridled master and, since this instinct is anxious and cowardly, human existence is dominated by terror and fear.

Through this fable on the infancy of human kind, Schiller marks the secret truth of the sublime: the primordial threat is posed less by natural forces than by other humans. Hostile nature, here, is seen *as an enemy*, which is a *political concept*. The original hazard is political more than natural. For Schiller, early history becomes the disclosure of a genealogical link between the sublime and terror; a link, to cite Hinnant, 'ignored by a tradition that seeks to segregate aesthetic appearances from political actualities'.[85]

C. Schmitt's Denials

Our question, then, is what brought Schmitt to omit references to such features of romanticism so apparently parallel to his abysmal theory of politics? Why did Agamben also overlook romanticism? A possible *structural* answer may be found in the fact that an aesthetic of sublime may render the whole project of political theology unattainable.

82 Schiller, 'On the Sublime' 37.
83 M Praz, *La carne, la morte e il diavolo nella letteratura romantica* (Milano, La Cultura, 1930).
84 Schiller, 'On the Sublime' 38.
85 Hinnant, 'Schiller and the Political Sublime' 126.

As we have noted, authors like Burke and Schiller are rather disturbing both for the Weberian as well as for the Schmittian paradigms of secularisation. Their romanticism contradicts any disenchantment of the world, but it also escapes the theological. This kind of romanticism represents almost a sort of reversal of orthodox values, as may easily be apprehended through Milton's Lucifer or Shelley's Prometheus, where he who revolts against the world ruler assumes the heroic features of a charismatic revolutionary leader. What we try to mean, very imperfectly, is that this form of romanticism must be fully appreciated in terms of its transmutation of political values.

We could say in this case not so much that Schmitt succumbed to a fascination of the extraordinary,[86] but that he did not succumb to it enough.

His critique of political romanticism was simply inconsistent, and transmitted this inconsistency to his epigones. As strange as it may appear, he retracted himself from the abyss he saw, and preferred a restoration of a kind of Byzantine liturgy of the *Dominus*, as surviving behind the surface of modern rationality, rather than confronting the revolutionary implications of the romantic sublime.

From this point of view his work on *political romanticism* and that on *political theology* appear eventually strictly correlated. What is more romantic indeed than asserting that normality does not prove anything and the exception proves all? This assertion looks like the reprisal of the typical romantic theory of the *genius*. Only the exceptional genius can speak, and that is why only geniuses may be poets or artists, and why history itself becomes a history of heroes and of heroes' worship.[87]

This would be, indeed, the meaning that we should attribute to the central role assigned by Schmitt—and Agamben—to exceptionality. But could we, then, still maintain that political romanticism is the ideology of bourgeois parliamentarianism? A shallow ideology fit for the endless talks of the middle class?

This is, as we have said, pure ideology in the sense of a false consciousness of the real; and this ideological nature of the Schmittian paradigm condemns it without appeal.

Given the abysmal attitude of Schmitt, his downgrade of romanticism and his omission of the sublime, with all its potential subversiveness, probably represents a mysterious but conscious *denial* in favour of the reassuring permanence of theology under what he perceived as the political anomie of modernity. Schmittian political theology appears as a grandiose but nostalgic withdrawal.

If we, then, dismantle Schmitt's theory in this way its paradoxical construct may start to shine evident. His writings display a constant sort of melancholy for that kind of sovereignty which belonged to the idealised *Dominus* of theological origins and *at the same time* exhibit a clear nostalgia for the kind of international

86 Frankenberg, *Political Technology* 117.

87 T Carlyle, *On Heroes, Hero-Warship and the Heroic in History* (London, Chapman and Hall, 1840).

order openly based on terror and fear, on threats, self-help and the potentiality of war that emerged as a consequence of the consumption of the *Dominus*.

His concept of the political tries, unsuccessfully, to keep together the typical purely political decision for friends and foes which characterised the European world order, and the typical theological foundation of sovereignty that preceded the advent of the political.

In other words, he shows himself to be under the spell of two inconsistent fascinations succumbing contemporarily to both: a fascination for the Byzantine *Dominus* of theological origin and also a fascination for the anomie of the international order of Leviathans; a compulsion for the god of the *nomos* of the earth, and one for the angel of anomie, together with a logically consequent contempt for any kind of bourgeois disenchantment. His world is that of the *Dominus* and that of Belial *at the same time*—something which is, of course, untenable.

The unifying element for these two opposite melancholies for Schmitt was to be found in the exception and its assimilation to miracles. The constant crises and exceptional cases of international politics, and the exception as the void around which the apparent rational legal order is built, could in this way be transfigured into grandiose theological appearances. Epiphanies due to the personal intervention of the sovereign paralleling the personal intervention of God in history. But also this is, of course, an *ideology* of exception that can be reversed on itself if only its link with miracles is broken. After all—as has been noted above—comparing a coup d'état, the *eighteenth brumaire* or the burning of the Reichstag to miracles is a way to nobilitate them. All our interpretations change if we see them not as miracles but as wonders, the products of the dark arts of government.

According to us, the key point operated by Schmitt consists in the omission of the sublime as an atheological alternative to interpret the too-muchness, the excess of signification intrinsic to political upheavals. But as we have tried to show, this alternative is not only possible, but it reveals the inner arbitrariness of Schmitt's intellectual performance—an arbitrariness which is even stronger in his epigones. Affirming that exceptions are irruptions of a *theological* transcendence in history vis-à-vis the disenchantment of the world, presents the apparatus of political theology as the *only* way to cope with the too-muchness of the political fields. But it is not so.

Considering the two opposite melancholies afflicting the Schmittian paradigm—that for the Sovereign, and that for the anomie of the international order based on friends and foes—we can fully appreciate, in their disconnection, the fracture which intervened with modernity, that demonological turn which supplanted the theology of the *Dominus* with the occultism of the Leviathans. We shall then have on one side the theological political parallel legitimising the world rule of a *Dominus*, and on the opposite side we have the anomie of the political: decision and war among sovereign states. And, of course, there is no longer any miracle that can pack them together.

The excess of meaning that is left, that intangible side of power and hegemony that goes beyond words, that surplus of immanence, must then be appraised in terms of sublime, with all its threatening but revealing consequences—a spell that returns as a residue. On one side there is the phantom of the *Dominus*, the spectral ghost of a legitimate world sovereignty, and on the other side the infernal anomie of the modern political.

IV. The Ghost of the *Dominus*

A. Property, Sovereignty and Ecology: The *Dominium* of the *Dominus*

At the end of the previous section we reached the main focus of our theory: a picture of the modern political as a world of Leviathans spawned from the corpse of the *Dominus Mundi*, whose ghost returns to claim his vengeance. But what sense can his revival have in a world so dominated by global markets and economic institutions? Is there still room for him to be *remembered* in current projects of global governance?

We have already confronted many of these points, but one remains to be considered, and it pertains to the notion of *dominium* to the extent that it encompasses both the politics of sovereignty and the economics of property. After all, the assertion that there was a single Master of the World also had strong economic consequences, as was well perceived by Baldus and Bartolus. Does this assertion imply a sort of economic monopoly, or a planned government of all resources? Or does it say something about the central role of economics from the standpoint of sovereignty and the world order?

Schmitt never really confronted economy, whereas today Agamben tries to theologise its genealogy, reverting to the Christian notion of the 'economy of salvation'.[88] This notion has been recently analysed in full detail by Dothan Leshem, who—also correcting many of Agamben's remarks—has shown its fundamental link with the ideal of infinite growth that seems to so deeply characterise the Western economic ideal.[89]

All of this is particularly important from the standpoint of a theory of *dominium mundi* as it was immediately understood by Bulgarus and Martinus in their fictitious dialogue with Barbarossa on his royal prerogatives,[90] which we discussed earlier. As Koskenniemi recently concluded, sovereignty and property

[88] Agamben, *The Kingdom and the Glory* xi.

[89] Leshem, *The Origin of Neoliberalism* 6.

[90] K Pennington, *The Prince and the Law, 1200–1600: Sovereignty and Rights in the Western Legal Tradition* (Berkeley, University of California Press, 1993) 12.

have indeed always operated together to create the structure of power that is, at any moment, the real government of the world. From this angle, the proprietary side of the *dominion* renders being in favour of or against sovereignty or property nearly meaningless, if, as Koskenniemi suggests, every sovereignty relies on a complex network of private property relations and all property relations are supported by some type of public power. These nested and complex relations determine a form of governance, and as such determine who will rule us.[91]

These considerations are strengthened by the observation that 'corporations'—in a mixture of hybrid powers—have assumed a major political role in comparison with states. A silent takeover happened and the corporations took control of the planet earth.[92] This remark led Mattei and Capra to state that the 'true political', the Leviathan, escaped the form of the state to incarnate itself into the corporate bodies of private global agents.[93] Their argument represents the latest version of the complex of metaphors adopted, with different scopes, by Dante and St Jerome.

The recipe which is then invoked by Mattei and Capra to avoid a final breakdown is based on the loss of importance of the political circuit—elections and government budgets—in favour of the economic circuit. As a consequence, what we should do is divert our attention away from polls and the voting booths and direct it towards corporate boardrooms. We should, so to speak, cease to focus on ballots and start to buy shares to cast our votes in corporate meetings, because it is the corporations and no longer the parliaments that have become the *locus* of power and decision.

From our perspective, the most relevant point in Mattei and Capra's discourse is that the political element (decision and power) had been *transferred* from the states to the private corporations. In these terms, it is not that the political has ended; rather, it has traded its place. It went out from the corporate body of the state to instantiate itself within the corporate body of private entities. The state is the old Leviathan, now deprived of its prerogatives and which has become a void form, because the New Leviathan lives in the private corporation.

We face here both the persistence *and* the transformation of the imagery linked to the demonological inversion of the sovereign. In one way or another we are still in search of a heterodox salvation. Since we are consuming more resources than the earth[94]—*the Dominium of the Dominus*—can produce and absorb, our need to preserve the planet can be better achieved as shareholders rather than as citizens. It is quite obvious that Mattei and Capra keep a strong faith in the public

[91] M Koskenniemi, 'Sovereignty, Property and Empire: Early Modern English Contexts' (2017) 18 *Theoretical Inquiries in Law* 355.

[92] N Hertz, *The Silent Takeover: Global Capitalism and the Death of Democracy* (London, Cornerstone Digital, 2013).

[93] F Capra and U Mattei, *Ecology of Law* (Oakland, Berrett-Koehler Publishers, 2015).

[94] Capra and Mattei, *Ecology of Law* ch 10.

company and its democratic functioning. After all, if you search for salvation you need a faith, and their faith is based on the belief that a shareholders' meeting can become the proper *locus* of democracy.

Nevertheless, we concur with their approach, even if we may not share their faith. Mattei and Capra's thesis affirms that the political has been *excarnated* from the states to be reincarnated into public companies, where the wandering spirit of the political changes bodies without changing its nature. This 'political' looks indeed like a *dybbuk* that in Jewish folklore wanders in search of bodies to possess, because God started to create it late on Friday and could not complete the work before the Sabbath. The 'political' is like a *demon* wandering in search of bodies. The world that was inhabited by the *Dominus* and then by the *Leviathans* is now starting to be populated by non-Westphalian creatures, animated by the ever-reincarnating spirit of the intangible side of the political.

If we look at this theory attentively, linked as it is to the proprietary aspect of the *Dominus Mundi*, we may also find a good consonance with the illustration made by David Kennedy of the 'mystery' of global governance. According to him, across the legal field, people are re-imagining the nature of law outside and among states, which is significant in itself because it reflects how little we actually know about how we are governed. Global governance remains a mystery because so much about global society itself eludes our grasp:

> Are the worlds of politics, markets and cultural influence held together in a tight structure or is it all more loose and haphazard? Are there more than one global order—how much, in the end, is simply chaos, how much the work of an invisible hand?[95]

The mysteries of global governance for Kennedy largely depend on the lack of 'workable maps' of global power:[96] some form of cognitive control over global political life. This is exactly the point that we would suggest: our incapacity to grasp the excessive meaning of global government and its sublime aspect which escapes not only words but our own cognitive capacity.

Quite naturally, Kennedy's faith lies in the multiplication of spaces for discussion and reversal. Our objective should be to carry the revolutionary force of the democratic promise, of individual rights, of citizenship, of community empowerment, and participation in the decisions that affect one's life to the sites of global and transnational authorities. If we multiply these sites and open up spaces for conflict and struggle we could put into motion newer utopian heuristics for 'a political remade'.[97] To appreciate these faiths, Mattei's, Capra's and Kennedy's, we will develop the point of what we call the demonological turn of modernity.

[95] D Kennedy, 'The Mystery of Global Governance' (2008) 34 *Ohio Northern University Law Review* 827.

[96] Kennedy, *The Mystery of Global Governance* 857.

[97] Kennedy, *The Mystery of Global Governance* 859.

B. The *Demonological Turn*: Hegemony, Legitimacy and the Ineffable

What we share with the previously cited authors is a strong critical attitude towards any kind of false consciousness of the political, the market or of the international order. For this reason, we take from Gramsci the notion of hegemony[98] as that which bypasses the explicit devices of disciplinary powers, becoming invisible just because it is commonly accepted: that ideological invisible by which discipline can work. If we reframe Gramscian theory of hegemony in these terms, we may perceive how it is very close to what we call the political sublime. It is like that uncanny dimension of government that now, no longer captured in a precise form, has been left free to wander in the international space, fluctuating and reincorporating itself in various subjects, agencies or agents, and in multiform shapes. O'Gorman has defined the political sublime a 'free-floating force' that speaks only unpredicated power, and, for this reason has labelled the political sublime as an oxyomoron.[99] But for us, far from being an impossibility, it really captures the uncanny dimension that we have seen at work in James I and in Bodin as a predecessor of Hobbes.[100] In these terms, when we have spoken of the sublime we always meant that *surplus of immanence* which is nested in politics and in the law, making them both valid and effective.

What we want to maintain is what we said on Gramsci's theory and the 'mystery' of hegemony made explicit by Duncan Kennedy.[101] Hegemony remains a mystery and there is little sustained or serious discussion on what might be meant by it. What we add is that this mystery, as David Kennedy argued with regard to global governance, is not to be assumed as a failure of understanding but as a distinct feature of modernity. It is a trait of that occultism which lays at the foundation of the rise of the modern conception of sovereignty.

As a consequence, our attempt in this book goes a step *further* than postmodern theories. It is not only a matter of undecidability between the sovereign and the beast, as in Derrida,[102] nor is it a mere question of the sovereign being captured in a threshold of ambiguity as in Agamben, being at the same time within and without the legal order.[103] It is rather a story of a deactivation. After all, the existence of a legitimate *Dominus* of the world has been a kind of legal revelation

[98] A Gramsci, *Prison Notebooks*, vol 1 (JA Buttigieg ed, New York, Columbia University Press, 2010) 265.

[99] N O'Gorman, 'The Political Sublime: An Oxymoron' (2006) 34 *Journal of International Studies* 889.

[100] WA Dunning, 'Jean Bodin on Sovereignty with Some Reference to the Doctrine of Thomas Hobbes' (1896) 11 *Political Science Quarterly* 82.

[101] Du Kennedy, 'Antonio Gramsci and the Legal System' (1982) 6 *ALSA Forum* 32.

[102] J Derrida, *Séminaire: la bête et le souverain* (Paris, Galilée, 2010).

[103] Agamben, *Homo Sacer* 28–29.

that was revitalised many times in history, but was then disabled during the modern age, leaving us with the phantom of its *refoulé*.

As it were, the presence of the *Dominus* has been turned into the *nothingness* of its revelation,[104] something still effective even if no longer *meaningful*. What is the meaning of such a reversal that lies behind both globalism and the opposition to it? What is this form of validity without meaning, which characterises the term 'Law', and which risks dominating world affairs and international relations? And in the secularised world of globalisation, where is the proper *locus* of the sublime hegemony of law and the political?

Our modern political and juridical conceptions seem to have been the result of a completely 'demonological turn' which encompasses the hidden side of power, exception and transcendence, the uncanny side of the hegemonic order that shows its face only to avoid a complete rational knowledge of its force. Needless to say, the answers to these questions imply a deep rereading of the classical tradition, as nested as it has become in the apparently commonsensical oppositions between 'friend' and 'enemy', 'theological' and 'secularised', 'sacred' and 'profane'.

Such an uncanny and 'excessive' nature of the law and the political leaves us with the problem of a surplus of immanence in the domain of legitimacy. One of these forms may be traced, as we said, in Morgenthau's insistence on the intangible side of power politics as irreducible to pure scientific treatment.[105] Another instance—as strange as it may appear at first glance—can be found in the economic field in Hayek's approach, both in his theory of the ineffability of the overall order of society as something which always defeats our capacities of expression, and in his position against the abuses of reason. Today, this complex approach may well sound like a direct attack on the rational constructivism of neoliberal institutions and their conscious design of legal reforms to promote growth and development through an active role of legislation.[106]

Our discourse tries to retain this particular point raised by Hayek—different from most current neoliberal assumptions—on the limits of our language to cope with the law and its notions.[107] If our language is limited in describing legal and political relations, it follows that there is an *excess* that our words cannot capture without a *residue*, and that the political world remains partially unfathomable.

In this respect, the parallel between Morgenthau and Hayek is striking. For Hayek, the attempt to manage the overall order of society is doomed by the fact that no single group of minds can control the trillions of pieces of information needed to cope with singular situations. For Morgenthau, there are intrinsic limits

[104] On the possible interplay between meaningfulness *and* revelation, see Santner, *The Royal Remains* 231, making reference to Gershom Scholem.

[105] HJ Morgenthau, *Scientific Man Versus Power Politics* (Chicago, The University of Chicago Press, 1965).

[106] R Ptak, 'Neoliberalism in Germany: Revisiting the Ordoliberal Foundations of the Social Market Economy' in P Mirowski and D Plehwe (eds), *The Road from Mont Pèlerin: The Making of the Neoliberal Thought Collective* (Cambridge, Harvard University Press, 2009) 124–25.

[107] Hayek, *Law, Legislation and Liberty*, vol 1, 26.

to our scientific design of the world order, because of its 'existential' nature. Both put the calculability of the political sphere, especially at a global level, into serious question.

So, our point, as we have tried to develop it through this book, is the impossibility of ontologising the political, and therefore the existence of a political excess that can never be captured without a residue. This residue is that which is always beyond words. For this reason, this too-muchness of the political can be defined as *sublime*. As we said, this is not a neutral label, rather it represents the conscious establishment of a parallel with the language of witchcraft and magic. In this sense, our theory is that the world has not been disenchanted as Weber described, nor has theology survived in political and legal concepts as Schmitt expressed. Rather, the orthodox legal political theology has been reversed into the heterodoxy of political modernity.

Through the vocabulary used by Agamben made of *signatures*, *captures*, *residues*, *thresholds*[108] and of the dialectic of visible/invisible that characterises the ambiguity pervading human institutions, we want to point to what we call the 'too-muchness' *device*. In other words, we try to show that the semantics of political action transcends our verbal capacity, leaving space for remnants and *refoulés* to fluctuate as the haunting ghosts of a global world.

The *Dominus Mundi* is thus the perfect emblem of what could be defined as the inner ambiguity of Western institutions, due to the encounter of classical political theory with the Christian revelation, displaying in its various characterisations the unfathomable threshold of what is godly and what is demonic in the world order. We tried to show that the entire construction of the *Dominus Mundi*, with his claim to govern—as a real or ghostly presence—the whole world under the strict categories of law, hides a deep ideological assumption that emerges from every attempt to actualise it. Indeed—as we said—the very idea of a legitimate world ruler can be seen, after all, as the hegemonic complex *par excellence*.

C. The Locus Absconditus of Change

Our investigation has been centred on the dark side of the modern political which was denied by rationalism. It fell into latency, but persisted as a sublime remnant, exceeding our capacity to govern it. Our enquiry brought us to underline the role played by the politicisation of the 'dark arts' in unfolding modern conceptions of sovereignty, deeply marked by the sublimity of its hidden prerogatives. As such, these observations led us to cope with the place of heterodoxy within the transformations that shaped European rationalism, presented as a standard for global orthodox governance, in the appraisal of the political and legal domain.

[108] A lexicon linked to Paracelsus (1493–1541), see G Agamben, *The Signature of all Things: on Method* (L D'Isanto and K Attell trans, New York, Zone Books, 2010) 34.

From this angle, we tried to undermine political theology as an account of the transcendent dimension of law and legitimacy, to the extent that this account is based on the 'Plot of the Fall'. According to this account, there once were theological concepts rendering our understanding of the world and the law meaningful. These concepts *decayed* into pure political and legal conceptions, and, as a consequence, modern political orders are but broken pieces of a fallen theology. As we may perceive, these accounts are themselves a form of self-improving theological understanding of our political tradition, implying a sense of nostalgia or *melancholy* for the pre-political world. From this standpoint, they can be labelled orthodox as they prolong the faith in a lost paradise of theological ontology surviving under the surface of modernity.

On the contrary, we think that the birth of the modern political represented a major fracture in the history of the West, and that its origins were much more heterodox than expected. Our main claim is, indeed, that of a *demonological origin* of modernity, which reverses Schmitt's paradigm and its denial of the sublime.

What is at stake here is that all along the history of the parable of the *Dominus Mundi* and its reversal into the demonic figure of the Leviathan—via the transformation of witchcraft into a political crime of high treason—we have witnessed a legal and political history of the West which is even more abysmal than any political-theological account: a history whose internal devices of meaning production and influence are yet to be investigated in depth.

What we have tried to reconstruct here is a lineage which tries to overcome the denial of one of the most important features of romanticism, and that lies in the theory of the sublime. What we mean, by reference to sublime, is, indeed, that political reactions are never predetermined by what is happening. Facts do not determine politics, because of the excess embedded in them which is reflected in their sublimity. One of the major problems affecting the Schmittian paradigm lies precisely in its inner inconsistencies. It promises to disclose the abyss of the occult origins of modernity while hiding their real features. Condemning political romanticism for contingent reasons, Schmitt precluded himself and his followers a deeper understanding of the occult exoticism and heterodoxy at the root of modern sovereignty. This preclusion became structural in Schmitt's paradigm, creating an intrinsic inconsistency at its centre.

For all these reasons, this book has been an investigation on the too-muchness of legitimacy and hegemony. It tells us something about the mysterious spell of modern power and its sublimity. It tells us that there is something in political ideas that governs us more than we can govern them.

We need, then, to confront two different but interrelated questions. What does it mean that there is a *sublime* side of the political? And, what does it mean to interpret our current global reality in terms of the haunting presence of the ghost of the *Dominus*?

If the model of the *Dominus Mundi* represented a compact model of world sovereignty, both legitimate and universal, enlightened by the metaphor of a manifest god and the liturgy of his presence in the world order, we must acknowledge that this metaphor was fragmented and inverted, and that a dark side emanated from the disjunctures created by modernity. The dark side of a haunting ghost still governs our political imagination, inscribed, as it is, between the melancholy of a return to an equilibrium between great continental blocs,[109] and a utopian desire for salvation, either in the form of a pastoral and peaceful neoliberal order,[110] or in that of a revolutionary messianism from below.[111] Irenic dreams and a sort of dreadful realism alternate on the stage, together with mixed feelings of melancholy and condemnation of the political and the sovereign.

Now if a ghost is a remnant of what has been, we think that we must acknowledge that we are at the same time haunted by a memory and unaware of the deep disjuncture from which it sprang. Haunting is irreducible to the apparition.[112] The spectral or uncanny effect is not simply a matter of seeing a ghost. There is as much the experience of an absence in the loss that the ghost introduces or causes to return. There is something summoned to come back, to dwell again in the places haunted by its absence.[113]

This *surplus* of immanence that we try to capture via the sublime in political, artistic and legal discourse can be multifarious. For example, Fredric Jameson has suggested a reformulated vision of the sublime focused on technology rather than nature.[114] As we have seen, Kant defined nature as sublime because it consistently exceeds the capacity of human concepts to grasp either its particularity or its generality. Such a definition singles out both what we have called a surplus of immanence as well as the too-muchness, or the excessiveness that we are prone to perceive in facts and our surrounding world. This too-muchness is normally expressed in the metaphorical use of language employed both in poetical and political expressions. It is in this way that we may see the daylight dying as a dolphin[115] or describe the King of England as a *mortal god*. Jameson's theory is important not only to grasp our attitude toward technology and its eventual *dominium mundi*,[116] but also to grasp the core mechanics of the Marxian approach to economy, intended as the great process by which nature is captured and transformed through the *magic*

[109] In the same sense, see the parallel conclusions of both Kissinger, *World Order* 371 and C Schmitt, *The Nomos of the Earth in the International Law of the Jus Publicum Europaeum* (GL Ulmen trans, New York, Telos Press Publishing, 2003) 351.

[110] Leshem, *The Origin of Neoliberalism* 160; A Ong, *Neoliberalism as Exception: Mutations in Citizenship and Sovereignty* (Durham, Duke University Press, 2007) 10.

[111] G Agamben, *The Time that Remains: A Commentary on the Letter to the Romans* (P Dailey trans, Stanford, Stanford University Press, 2005) 3, 6.

[112] J Derrida, *Specters of Marx. The State of the Debt, the Work of Mourning and the New International* (P Kamuf trans, London, Routledge, 1994) 130 ff.

[113] J Derrida, *Of Spirit: Heidegger and the Question* (G Bennington and R Bowlby trans, Chicago, The University of Chicago Press, 2017) 48, 54.

[114] F Jameson, *The Geopolitical Aesthetic: Cinema and Space in the World System* (Bloomington, Indiana University Press, 1995); F Jameson, *Postmodernism, or, the Cultural Logic of Late Capitalism* (London, Verso, 1991); I Buchanan, *Fredric Jameson: Live Theory* (London, Continuum, 2006).

[115] Lord Byron, 'Childe Harold's Pilgrimage' IV, 29.

[116] Legendre, *Dominium mundi: L'empire du management.*

of commodities creating their own value. The pretension of the Marxian discourse to be scientific always prevented, indeed, a full appreciation of its metaphors and its romanticisation of the economic process.

The overarching admiration for nature and the desire to tame its forces easily displays this surplus of immanence intrinsic in our relationship with nature *and* technology, possessing a clear excess residing in the cultural and political reactions that accompanied modern human achievements, beyond our capacity to divine in advance what these reactions could be: on an extreme side, their positive appreciation in a *modernist* aesthetic of speed, skyscrapers, cables and factories; on another extreme side, the fearsome and terrific nightmare of a domain of *technique* that could obscure everything which is truly human.

As Jameson suggested, the actual advent of digital technology put on centre stage a new type of machine or artefact that proved difficult to respond to cognitively. The image of a global matrix[117] of interlocked machines may imply the emergence of *a new form of the sublime* because technology is presented as exceeding human capacities and categories. The awesome capabilities of computers are beyond our capacity to grasp them *as physical objects*. As such, they are rather unimpressive, and we get no sense of what they are capable of by simply looking at them. All of this raises, nevertheless, the same question that Jameson pointed out, namely, the existence of a persistent *representational* problem. But the point for us here is not so much the *magic* quality of objects, but rather our unpredictable political reactions to their emergence. In other words, it represents the excessive nature of the political. What are, then, the consequences of the sublime nature of the political? What kind of a change should we imagine?

What is really at stake in these terms and in relation to our specific matter, is the *image* that we have of the world order. This image shapes our attitudes toward change, as change depends on the perceived image of the locus of power. If we imagine that this locus of power is the Winter Palace,[118] a single symbolic place of command and control where the *Dominus* dwells, we could try to seize it. Only this act could provoke a change. If we imagine that the locus of power is an impersonal and widespread network of interlocked machines or of different agencies we probably should try more decentralised strategies of multiplying struggles and confrontations. If we think that the locus of power lies now in the boardroom of public companies we should try to collect enough shares to vote in corporate meetings. In this sense, the kind of mobilisation that is required by a desire for change, as well as the tasks that we must formulate to reach it, is highly imaginary.

The icon of the Winter Palace leads to a concentrated action focused on a single point. The opposite icon of a soft and diffused but oppressive power quite

[117] For the use of the metaphor of matrix see also G Teubner, 'The Anonymous Matrix: Human Rights Violations by "Private" Transnational Actors' (2006) 69 *The Modern Law Review* 327.

[118] S Newman, *Politics of Postanarchism* (Edinburgh, Edinburgh University Press, 2010) 169.

naturally germinates local, multifarious and probably unexpected strategies of resistance. If we locate the locus of virtue in the compact communities of a lost communal life we would easily fight against new intruders, whether in the form of poor migrants or rich venture capitalists. Hegemony is control over the imagination, and imagination *is* sublime. Imagery is shaping the sort of action to be triggered, a concentred power inspires occupation, and a diffused power incites more resistance than occupation. Imagery is unfathomable, but it is not arbitrary in terms of its consequences. A revolution succeeds only if its imagery is 'right'. When it is wrong a false attack would be launched against false targets, determining its failure.

To the extent that our attempt has been to supersede conventional and unsound theories, their rejection may have important consequences for the historical consciousness of the Western political tradition. The Western political tradition should perhaps no longer be viewed as a continuous uninterrupted tradition from its Greek origins on. A demonological turn created a fracture in the tradition. This implies that the projects of governance based on the conventional picture are untenable and must be abandoned.

We have to create a new outlook on our past, blurring and possibly reversing received ideas. In particular, we need a completely different consciousness of the locus of sovereignty. It is not so much that it ceased to be a royal palace, a fortress, or a factory, or that it eventually became a network of interlocked agencies of a more liquid character. Rather, sovereignty has been, from modernity onwards, a hidden and contrived locus of authority: a *locus absconditus*.

We should take consciousness of the demonological political sublime and its fascination that pervaded the West, whether embedded in economic or public institutions, yet which has been denied. What we need, in these terms, is a new consciousness. Only then can a new and unpredictable form of change start targeting this hidden and mysterious *locus absconditus*: the spectral space where the Ghost of the deceased *Dominus* sits yet, crowned upon his grave.

BIBLIOGRAPHY

[Multiple works by the same author are ordered alphabetically by the first initial. Multiple reprints, editions and translations of the same work are listed chronologically.]

Accursius, *Glossa in Digestum vetum* in *Corpus Glossatorum Iuris Civilis*, vol 7 (M Viora ed, Torino, Officina Erasmiana, 1969)

Addison, J, *The Miscellaneous Works of Joseph Addison*, vol 2 (New York, Harper & Brothers, 1845)

Aegidius Romanus [Giles de Rome], *De ecclesiastica potestate* (Richard Scholz ed, Weimar, Hermann Bohlaus Nachfolger, 1929)

Agamben, G, *Homo Sacer: Sovereign Power and Bare Life* (D Heller-Roazen trans, Stanford, Stanford University Press, 2004)

Agamben, G, *Opus Dei: an Archaeology of Duty* (A Kotsko trans, Stanford, Stanford University Press, 2013)

Agamben, G, *Pilate and Jesus* (A Kotsko trans, Stanford, Stanford University Press, 2015)

Agamben, G, *Profanations* (J Fort trans, New York, Zone Books, 2015)

Agamben, G, *Stasis. Civil War as a Political Paradigm* (N Heron trans, Stanford, Stanford University Press, 2015)

Agamben, G, *State of Exception* (K Attel trans, Chicago, The University of Chicago Press, 2010)

Agamben, G, *The Highest Poverty: Monastic Rules and Form-of-Life* (A Kotsko trans, Stanford, Stanford University Press, 2013)

Agamben, G, *The Kingdom and the Glory: For a Theological Genealogy of Economy and Government* (L Chiesa trans, Stanford, Stanford University Press, 2011)

Agamben, G, *The Sacrament of Language: An Archaeology of the Oath* (A Kotsko trans, Stanford, Stanford University Press, 2011)

Agamben, G, *The Signature of all Things: on Method* (L D'Isanto and K Attell trans, New York, Zone Books, 2010)

Agamben, G, *The Time that Remains: A Commentary on the Letter to the Romans* (P Dailey trans, Stanford, Stanford University Press, 2005)

Agamben, G, *The Use of Bodies* (A Kotsko trans, Stanford, Stanford University Press, 2016)

Alcock, SE, D'Altroy, TN, Morrison, KD and Sinopoli, CM (eds), *Empires. Perspectives from Archaeology and History* (Cambridge, Cambridge University Press 2001)

Allen, JW, *English Political Thought, 1603–1660* (London, Methuen & Co, 1938)

Alpers, PJ, *The Poetry of the Faerie Queene* (Princeton, Princeton University Press, 1967)

Ariosto, L, *Orlando Furioso* (E Bigi and C Zampese eds, Milano, Rizzoli, 2012)

Arquillière, HX, *L'augustinisme politique* (Paris, Vrin, 1955)

Arvidsson, M, Brännström, L and Minkkien, P (eds), *The Contemporary Relevance of Carl Schmitt Law, Politics, Theology* (London, Routledge, 2015)

Ashton, J, *The Religion of Paul the Apostle* (New Haven, Yale University Press, 2000)

Assmann, J, *Herrschaft und Heil. Politische Theologie in Altägypten, Israel und Europa* (Frankfurt, Fischer Taschenbuch Verlag, 2002)
Baillie, J, 'An Essay on the Sublime' in A Ashfield and P de Bolla (eds), *The Sublime: A Reader in British Eighteenth Century Aesthetic Theory* (Cambridge, Cambridge University Press, 1996) 87–100
Baldus, *Commentaria super Codice* (Lyon, Gaspar Trechsel, 1545)
Baldus, *Consilia, sive Responsa* (Venetiis, Nicolinus, 1589)
Baldus, *Commentaire sur la paix de Constance (1183)* (D Gorlier trans, Limoges, Pulim, 2016)
Baldus, *De pace constantie tractatus subtilissimus* (Mediolanum, Johannes, Jacomo & Fratelli De Legnano, 1502)
Baldus, *In Usus Feudorum* (Augustae Taurinorum, Nicolai Beuilaquae, 1578)
Barducci, M, *Hugo Grotius and the Century of Revolutions 1613–1718* (Oxford, Oxford University Press, 2017)
Barnett, M, *Empire of Humanity: A History of Humanitarianism* (Ithaca, Cornell University Press, 2011)
Bartolus, *Commentaria in primam Codicis partem* (Venetiis, Baptista de Tortis, 1493)
Bartolus, *Commentaria in primam Codicis partem* (Venetiis, Iunta, 1570)
Bartolus, *Commentaria in primam Digesti veteris partem* (Venetiis, Iunta, 1570)
Bartolus, *Commentaria in secundam Codicis partem* (Venetiis, Iunta, 1570)
Baxter, CR, 'Jean Bodin's Daemon and His Conversion to Judaism' in JH Franklin (ed), *Jean Bodin* (London, Routledge, 2006) 285–306
Benedict, R, 'The Historical Position of the Rhodian Law' (1909) 18 *Yale Law Journal* 223–42
Benjamin, W, 'Critique of Violence' in W Benjamin, *Reflections. Essays, Aphorisms, Autobiographical Writings* (E Jephcott trans, New York, Schocken Books, 2007) 277–300
Benjamin, W, *The Origin of German Tragic Drama* (J Osborne trans, London, Verso, 2009)
Berman, HJ, *Law and Revolution, I: The Formation of the Western Legal Tradition* (Cambridge, Harvard University Press, 1983)
Berman, HJ, *Law and Revolution, II: The Impact of the Protestant Reformations on the Western Legal Tradition* (Cambridge, Harvard University Press, 2009)
Bernard, GW, *The King's Reformation: Henry VIII and the Remaking of the English Church* (New Haven, Yale University Press, 2007)
Berschin, W, *Griechisch-lateinisches Mittelalter. Von Hieronymus zu Nicolaus von Kues* (Bern, A Francke, 1980)
Bertozzi, M, *Thomas Hobbes: l'enigma del Leviatano* (Ferrara, Bovolenta, 1983)
Besserman, LL, *The Legend of Job in the Middle Ages* (Cambridge, Harvard University Press, 1979)
Blackstone, W, *Commentaries on the Laws of England, Volume 1: A Facsimile of the First Edition of 1765–1769* (Chicago, The University of Chicago Press, 1979)
Bloch, M, *Les rois thaumaturges. Étude sur le caractère surnaturel attribué à la puissance royale, particulièrement en France et en Angleterre* (Paris, A Colin, 1961)
Blom, HV, 'Grotius and Socinianism' in M Muslow and J Rohls (eds), *Sociananism and Arminianism. Antitrinitarians, Calvinists and Cultural Exchange in Seventeenth Century Europe* (Leiden, Brill, 2005)
Böckenförde, E-W, 'The Rise of the State as a Process of Secularization' in E-W Böckenförde (ed), *State, Society and Liberty: Studies in Political Theory and Constitutional Law* (IA Underwood trans, New York, Berg, 1991) 26–46

Bodin, J, *Colloquium Heptaplomeres de Rerum Sublimium Arcanis Abditis* (Paris, Jacques Du Puys, 1588)
Bodin, J, *Colloque de Jean Bodin; des secrets cachéz des choses sublimes, entre sept sçavans qui sont de differens sentimens* (reprint, Paris, L Tenin, 1914)
Bodin, J, *Colloque entre sept sçavans, qui sont de differens sentimens, des secrets cachez des choses relevées* (F Berriot ed, Genève, Droz, 1984)
Bodin, J, *Colloquium of the Seven about Secrets of the Sublime* (ML Kuntz trans, Princeton, Princeton University Press, 1975)
Bodin, J, *De la démonomanie des sorciers* (Paris, Jacques Du Puys, 1580)
Bodin, J, *De la démonomanie des sorciers* (reprint, Hildesheim, Georg Olms Verlag, 1988)
Bodin, J, *On the Demon-Mania of Witches* (RA Scott ed, Toronto, Centre for Reformation and Renaissance Studies, 1995)
Bodin, J, *Les six livres de la Republique* (Paris, Jacques Du Puys, 1576)
Bodin, J, *Les six livres de la Republique* (MA Breslow ed, Paris, Fayard, 1986)
Bodin, J, *The Six Bookes of a Commonweale* (R Knolles trans, London, G Bishop, 1606)
Bodin, J, *Six Books of The Commonwealth* [Facsimile Reprint of the English Translation of 1606] (KD McRae ed, Cambridge, Harvard University Press, 1962)
Bodin, J, *On Sovereignty. Four Chapters from the Six Books of the Commonwealth* (JH Franklin ed, Cambridge, Cambridge University Press, 1992)
Bosbach, F, *Monarchia Universalis. Ein politischer Leitbegriff der fruehen Neuzeit* (Goettingen, Vandenhoeck & Ruprecht, 1988)
Bourdin, B, *La Genèse Théologico-Politique de l'Etat Moderne* (Paris, Presses Unversitaires de France, 2015)
Bourdin, B, *The Theological-Political Origins of the Modern State: The controversy between James I of England & Cardinal Bellarmine* (S Pickford trans, Washington DC, Catholic University of America Press, 2010)
Bredekamp, H, *Thomas Hobbes Der Leviathan Das Urbild des modernen Staates und seine Gegenbilder. 1651–2001* (Berlin, Akademie Verlag, 2012)
Brewer, JS (ed), *Letters and Papers, Foreign and Domestic of the Reign of Henry VIII* (London, Royal Commission for State Papers, 1830–52)
Browne, T, *Religio medici* [1643] (New York, John B Alden, 1889)
Brunnemann, J, *Commentarius in quinquaginta libros Pandectarum* (Coloniae, Fratrum Cramer, 1762)
Buchanan, I, *Fredric Jameson: Live Theory* (London, Continuum, 2006)
Burke, E, *A Philosophical Enquiry into the Origin of Our Ideas of the Sublime and Beautiful* [1757] (A Phillips ed, Oxford, Oxford University Press, 1990)
Burke, E, *Reflections on the Revolution in France* [1790] (WL Arnstein ed, Lexington, DC Heath and Company, 1993)
Burke, E, *Reflections on the Revolution in France: A Critical Edition* (JCD Clark ed, Stanford, Stanford University Press, 2001)
Burke, E, *The Correspondence of Edmund Burke*, vol 6 (TW Copeland ed, Cambridge, Cambridge University Press, 1958–78)
Burke, E, *The Writings and Speeches of Edmund Burke*, vol 1 (TO McLaughlin and JT Boulton eds, Oxford, The Clarendon Press, 1997)
Burns, JH, *The True Law of Kingship: Concepts of Monarchy in Early-modern Scotland* (Oxford, The Clarendon Press, 1996)
Burton, R, *An Anatomy of Melancholy* [1621] (TC Faulkner, NK Kiessling and RL Blair eds, Oxford, The Clarendon Press, 1989)

Calvin, J, 'Sermon CLXI' in E Cunitz, J-W Baum and EWE Reuss (eds), *Joannis Calvini Opera Quae Supersunt Omnia* [Corpus Reformatorum] vol 35 (Brunsvigae, CA Schwetschke, 1863) clm 463–76

Cameron, A, 'The Construction of Court Ritual: the Byzantine Book of Ceremonies' in D Cannadine and S Price (eds), *Rituals of Royalty. Power and Ceremonial in Traditional Societies* (Cambridge, Cambridge University Press, 1987) 106–63

Cames, G, *Allégories et symboles dans l'Hortus Deliciarum* (Leiden, Brill, 1971)

Canning, J, *The Political Thought of Baldus de Ubaldis* (Cambridge, Cambridge University Press, 2003)

Capra, F and Mattei, U, *The Ecology of Law, Toward a Legal System in Tune with Nature and Community* (Oakland, Berrett-Koehler Publishers, 2015)

Cargill Thompson, WDJ, *The Political Thought of Martin Luther* (P Broadhead ed, Brighton, Harvester Press, 1984)

Carile, A, *Teologia politica bizantina* (Spoleto, Fondazione Centro italiano di studi sull'Alto Medioevo, 2008)

Carlyle, T, *On Heroes, Hero-Warship and the Heroic in History* (London, Chapman and Hall, 1840)

Caryl, J, *An Exposition with Practicall Obseruation upon … the Books of Job* (London, L Fawne, H Cripps and L Lloyd, 1647)

Cengarle, F, 'Il Sole ducale (1430): a proposito di una divisa viscontea' in F Cengarle and MN Covini (eds), *Il ducato di Filippo Maria Visconti, 1412–1447. Economia, politica, cultura* (Firenze, Firenze University Press, 2015) 231–46

Chanteur, J, 'Note sur les notions de "Peuple" et de "Multitude" chez Hobbes' in K Koselleck and E Schnur (eds), *Hobbes* (Berlin, Forschungen, 1969) 223–36

Charleton, W, *The Darkness of Atheism Dispelled by the Light of Nature: a Physico-Theological Treatise* [1652] (Bristol, Thoemmes, 2002)

Christie, GC, *Jurisprudence. Text and Readings on the Philosophy of Law* (St Paul, West Publishing, 1973)

Clark, S, 'King James's *Daemonologie*: Witchcraft and Kingship' in S Anglo (ed), *The Damned Art: Essays in the Literature of Witchcraft* (London, Routledge & K Paul, 1977) 156–78

Clark, S, *Thinking with Demons: the Idea of Witchcraft in Early Modern Europe* (Oxford, Oxford University Press, 1999)

Coccej, SLB, *Grotius Illustratus* (Wratislaviae, Johannes Jacobi Korn, 1752)

Conte, E, '"Ego quidem mundi dominus". Ancora su Federico Barbarossa e il diritto giustinianeo' in L Gatto and P Supino Martini (eds), *Studi sulle società e le culture del Medioevo per Girolamo Arnaldi* (Roma, All'Insegna del Giglio, 2002) 135–48

Cowan, B, 'Benjamin's Theory of Allegory' (1981) 22 *New German Critique* 109–22

Cowdrey, HEJ, 'The Peace and the Truce of God in the Eleventh Century' (1970) 46 *Past and Present* 42–67

Cynus of Pistoia, *Lectura super aurea volumine Codicis* (Venetiis, Andrea de Thoresanis de Asula, 1493)

Damrosch, LF, Henkin, L, Pugh, RC, Schacter, O and Smit, H (eds), *International Law. Cases and Materials* (St Paul, West Group, 2001)

Dante Alighieri, *Monarchy* (P Shaw ed, Cambridge, Cambridge University Press, 1996)

Dante Alighieri, *The Divine Comedy* (EH Wilkins and T Goddard Bergin eds, Cambridge, Harvard University Press, 1965)

Davies, J, *The Question Concerning Impositions, Tonnage, Poundage … Fully Stated and Argued from Reason, Law and Policy* (London, H Twyford, 1656)

Dawson, JP, *The Oracles of the Law* (Ann Arbor, University of Michigan Law School, 1968)
De Man, P, *Aesthetic Ideology* (A Warminski ed, Minneapolis, University of Minnesota Press, 1996)
De Vitoria, F, 'De Indis noviter inventis' in JB Scott (ed), *The Spanish Origin of International Law: Francisco de Vitoria and His Law of Nations* (Oxford, Oxford University Press, 1934) Appendix A, i–xlv
Delumeau, J, *La paura in occidente: (secoli XIV–XVIII) la città assediata* (Torino, Società Editrice Internazionale, 1979)
Dennis, J, *The Critical Works of John Dennis*, vol 1 (EN Hooker ed, Baltimore, Johns Hopkins University Press, 1939)
Derrida, J, *Of Spirit: Heidegger and the Question* (G Bennington and R Bowlby trans, Chicago, The University of Chicago Press, 2017)
Derrida, J, *Séminaire: la bête et le souverain* (Paris, Galilée, 2010)
Derrida, J, *Specters of Marx. The State of the Debt, the Work of Mourning and the New International* (P Kamuf trans, London, Routledge, 1994)
Dias Schirm, L, *Omnem e Iurisdictio: Comentários De Bartolus Da Sassoferrato (1314–1357) Sobre Dominium* (Belo Horizonte, Universidade Federal De Minas Gerais, Faculdade de Filosofia e Ciências Humanas, 2011)
Drewer, L, 'Leviathan, Behemoth and Ziz' (1981) 54 *Journal of the Warburg and Courtauld Institutes* 148–56
Dreyer, F, 'The Genesis of Burke's Reflections' (1978) 50 *The Journal of Modern History* 462–79
Duby, G, *The Laity and the Peace of God. The Age of Chivalry* (C Postan trans, London, Edward Arnold, 1977)
Dunning, WA, 'Jean Bodin on Sovereignty with Some Reference to the Doctrine of Thomas Hobbes' (1896) 11 *Political Science Quarterly* 82–104
Dvornik, F, *Early Christian and Byzantine Political Philosophy: Origins and Backgrounds* (Washington DC, Dumbarton Oaks Center for Byzantine Studies, 1966)
Dyzenhaus, D, *Legality and Legitimacy: Carl Schmitt, Hans Kelsen, and Hermann Heller in Weimar* (Oxford, Oxford University Press, 1999)
Dyzenhaus, D and Poole, T (eds), *Hobbes and the Law* (Cambridge, Cambridge University Press, 2012)
Eberle, J, *Die Gedichte des Archipoeta: Lateinisch und Deutsch* (Frankfurt am Main, Insel Verlag, 1966)
Edwards, JJ, 'Calvin and Hobbes: Trinity, Authority, and Community' (2009) 42 *Philosophy & Rhetoric* 115–33
Elmer, P, *Witchcraft, Witch-hunting, and Politics in Early Modern England* (Oxford, Oxford University Press, 2016)
Elton, GR, *England under the Tudors* (London, Routledge, 1960)
Esposito, R, *Bíos: Biopolitics and Philosophy* (Minneapolis, University of Minnesota Press, 2008)
Esposito, R, *Living Thought: the Origins and Actuality of Italian Philosophy* (Z Hanafi trans, Stanford, Stanford University Press, 2012)
Esposito, R, *Persons and Things: from the Body's Point of View* (Z Hanafi trans, Cambridge, Polity Press, 2015)
Falk, F, 'Hobbes' "Leviathan" und die aus dem Blick gefallenen Schnabelmasken' (2011) 39 *Leviathan* 247–66
Fasolt, C, *The Limits of History* (Chicago, The University of Chicago Press, 2004)

Fatovic, C, *Outside the Law: Emergency and Executive Power* (Baltimore, Johns Hopkins University Press, 2009)

Fichera, M, 'Carl Schmitt and the New World Order: A View from Europe' in M Arvidsson, L Brännström and P Minkkien (eds), *The Contemporary Relevance of Carl Schmitt Law, Politics, Theology* (London, Routledge, 2015) 165–78

Figgis, JN, 'Bartolus and the Development of European Political Ideas' (1905) 19 *Transactions of the Royal Historical Society* 147–68

Fishwick, D, *The Imperial Cult in the Latin West: Studies in the Ruler Cult of the Western Provinces of the Roman Empire* (Leiden, Brill, 1991)

Fortescue, J, *De Laudibus Legum Angliæ* [ca 1470] (A Amos trans, London, Butterworth, 1825)

Foucault, M, *The Birth of the Clinic: An Archaeology of Medical Perception* (AM Sheridan Smith trans, New York, Pantheon Books, 1973)

Foucault, M, *"Society Must Be Defended": Lectures at the Collège de France, 1975–1976* (D Macey trans, M Bertani and A Fontanta eds, New York, Picador, 2003)

Frankenberg, G, *Political Technology and the Erosion of the Rule of Law: Normalizing the State of Exception* (H Bauer and G Frankenberg trans, Cheltenham, Edward Elgar, 2015)

Franklin, JH (ed), *Jean Bodin* (London, Routledge, 2006)

Franklin, JH, *Jean Bodin and the Sisteenth-Century Revolution in the Methodology of Law and History* (New York, Columbia University Press, 1963)

Gabel, JB and Wheeler, CB, *The Bible as Literature. An Introduction* (Oxford, Oxford University Press, 1990)

Gagé, J, 'Les pratiques magiques d'épiphanie royale—basileia—et la mystique impériale aux IIe et IIIe siècles' in W Haase and H Temporini (eds), *Aufstieg und Niedergang der römischen Welt* (Berlin, Walter de Gruyter, 1998) 2382–2403

Gallie, WB, 'Essentially Contested Concepts' (1955–1956) 56 *Proceedings of the Aristotelian Society New Series* 167–98

Gibbon, E, *The History of the Decline and Fall of the Roman Empire* [1776–88] 6 vols (Claxton, Remsen & Haffelfinger, 1875)

Ginzburg, C, *Fear, Reverence, Terror* (J Tedeschi and AC Tedeschi trans, Greenford, Seagull Books, 2017)

Ginzburg, C, *Myths, Emblems, Clues* (J Tedeschi and AC Tedeschi trans, London, Hutchinson Radius, 1990)

Glanvill, J, *Sadducismus Triumphatus or, Full and Plain Evidence Concerning Witches and Apparitions* (London, J Collins, 1681)

Godfrey of Viterbo, *Gesta Friderici* in 30 MGH (G Waitz ed, 1870) clm 1–45

Goethe, JW, *Goethes Werke: illustrierte Auswahl mit Einl. und erklär. Anmerkungen im Verein mit mehreren Goethefreunden* (H Steuding ed, Leipzig, Albrecht Seemann Verlag, 1905)

Goldsmith, MM, 'Picturing Hobbes's Politics? The Illustrations to Philosophical Rudiments' (1981) 44 *Journal of the Warburg and Courtauld Institute* 232–37

Goodare, J, 'The Attempted Scottish Coup of 1596' in J Goodare and A MacDonald (eds), *Sixteenth Century Scotland. Essays in Honour of M Lynch* (Leiden, Brill, 2008) 311–36

Gordley, J, 'Humanists and Scholastics' in CM Carmichael (ed), *Essays on Law and Religion, The Berkeley and Oxford Symposia in Honour of David Daube* (Berkeley, University of California, 1993)

Gordon, CH, 'Leviathan: Symbol of Evil' in A Altmann (ed), *Biblical Motifs. Origin and Transformation* (Cambridge, Cambridge University Press, 1966) 1–9

Gramsci, A, *Prison Notebooks* (JA Buttigieg ed, New York, Columbia University Press, 2010)

Greenleaf, WH, 'A Note on Hobbes and the Book of Job' (1974) 14 *Anales de la Cátedra Francisco Suárez* 10–34

Greenleaf, WH, 'James I and the Divine Right of Kings' (1957) 5 *Political Studies* 36–48

Greenleaf, WH, *Order, Empiricism and Politics: Two Traditions of English Political Thought: 1500–1700* (Oxford, Oxford University Press, 1964)

Grewe, WG, *The Epochs of International Law* (M Byers trans, Berlin, Walter de Gruyter, 2000)

Grotius, H, *De Jure Belli ac Pacis* [1625, text of 1646] (JB Scott ed, Washington, Carnegie Institute, 1913)

Grotius, H, *De Jure Belli ac Pacis* [1625] (PC Molhuysen ed, Leiden, Sijthoff, 1919)

Grotius, H, *De Jure Belli ac Pacis* [1625] (R Feenstra and C Persenaire eds, Aalen, Sientia, 1993)

Grotius, H, *Mare Liberum* [1609 text 1618] (R Feenstra ed, Leiden, Brill, 2009)

Grotius, H, *Mare Liberum* [1609] *The Freedom of the Seas* (JB Scott ed, R van Deman Magoffin trans, New York, Oxford University Press, 1916)

Guterbock, F, 'Zur Edition des Geschichtswerks Otto Morenas und seiner Fortsetzer' (1930) 48 *Neues Archiv des Gesellschaft für altere deutsche Geschichtskunde* 116–47

Hano, M, 'A l'origine du culte impérial: les autels des Lares Augusti. Recherches sur les thèmes iconographiques et leur signification' in W Haase and H Temporini (eds), *Aufstieg und Niedergang der römischen Welt* (Berlin, Walter de Gruyter, 1998) 2333–81

Hardt, M and Negri, A, *Empire* (Cambridge, Harvard University Press, 2001)

Hayek, FA, *Law, Legislation and Liberty: A New Statement of the Liberal Principles of Justice and Political Economy*, 3 vols (Chicago, The University of Chicago Press, 1976–1979)

Hayek, FA, *The Counter-Revolution of Science: Studies on the Abuse of Reason* (Berkeley, University of California Press, 1952)

Head, T and Landes, R, *The Peace of God: Social Violence and Religious Response in France around 1000* (Ithaca, Cornell University Press, 1995)

Heidegger, M, *The Question Concerning Technology, and Other Essays* (New York, Harper Collins Publishers, 2013)

Heim, F, *Virtus. Idéologie politique et croyances religieuses au IV siècle* (Berne, Publications Universitaires Européennes, 1991)

Haspels, CHE, *The Highlands of Phrygia. Sites and Monuments* (Princeton, Princeton University Press, 1971)

Henderson, EF (ed), *Select Historical Documents of the Middle Ages* (London, George Bell & Sons, 1905)

Henderson, F, 'Faithful Interpreters? Translation Theory and Practice at the Early Royal Society' (2013) 67 *Notes and Records of the Royal Society of London* 101–22

Henkin, L, *The Age of Rights* (New York, Columbia University Press, 2002)

Henricus Institoris (alias Jacob Sprenger), *Malleus Maleficarum* [1487] *The Hammer of Witches. A Complete Translation of the Malleus Malleficarum* (CS Mackay trans, Cambridge, Cambridge University Press, 2009)

Hertz, N, *The Silent Takeover: Global Capitalism and the Death of Democracy* (London, Cornerstone Digital, 2013)

Hinnant, CH, 'Schiller and the Political Sublime: Two Perspectives' (2002) 44 *Criticism* 121–38

Hobbes, T, *Behemoth* (P Seaward ed, Oxford, Oxford University Press, 2014)

Hobbes, T, *De Cive* (H Warrender ed, Oxford, Oxford University Press, 1984)

Hobbes, T, *Leviathan* (N Malcolm ed, Oxford, Oxford University Press, 1996)

Hofmann, H, *Legitimität gegen Legalität: der Weg der politischen Philosophie Carl Schmitts* (Berlin, Duncker & Humblot, 2010)
Holdsworth, W, 'Sir Edward Coke' (1935) 5 *The Cambridge Law Journal* 332–46
Horkheimer, M and Adorno, TW, *Dialectic of Enlightenment: Philosophical Fragments* (E Jephcott trans, Stanford, Stanford University Press, 2009)
Horton, LF, *The Melchizedek Tradition: A Critical Examination of the Sources to the Fifth Century A.D. and in the Epistle to the Hebrews* (Cambridge, Cambridge University Press, 1976)
Howell, TB (ed), *A Complete Collection of State Trials and Proceedings for High Treason and Other Crimes and Misdemeanors from the Earliest Period to the Year 1783, with Notes and Other Illustrations*, vol 2 (London, Longman, Hurst, Rees, Orme and Brown, 1816)
Huguccio Pisanus, *Summa Decretorum* 6 MIC Series A (U Přerovský ed, 2006)
Huillard-Bréholles, JLA, *Vie et correspondance de Pierre de la Vigne: ministre de l'empereur Frédéric II, avec une étude sur le mouvement réformiste au 13e siècle* (Paris, H Plon, 1865)
Hyde, E, *The True Catholicks Tenure or a Good Christian Certainty which He Ought to Have for This Religion, and May Have of His Salvation* (Cambridge, John Field, 1662)
Instinsky, HU, *Bischofsstuhl und Kaiserthron* (München, Kosel, 1955)
Instinsky, HU, 'Offene Fragen zum Bischofsstuhl und Kaiserthron' (1971) 66 *Römische Quartalschrif* 79–87
Jakobs, HH, *Hugolinusglossen im accursischen Apparat zum Digestum vetus. Studien zur europäischen Rechtsgeschichte* (Frankfurt am Main, Klostermann, 2017)
James I, 'A Speach to the Lords and Commons of the Parliament at White-Hall' [1609] in CH McIlwain (ed), *The Political Works of James I* (Cambridge, Harvard University, 1918) 306–25
James I, 'Basilikon Doron' [1599] in CH McIlwain (ed), *The Political Works of James I* (Cambridge, Harvard University, 1918) 3–52
James I, *Daemonologie, in Forme of a Dialogue, Divided into Three Bookes* (Edinburgh, Robert Waldegrave, 1597)
James I, 'Speech of the Star Chamber' [1616] in CH McIlwain (ed), *The Political Works of James I* (Cambridge, Harvard University, 1918) 326–45
James I, 'The True Law of Free Monarchies' [1598] in CH McIlwain (ed), *The Political Works of James I* (Cambridge, Harvard University, 1918) 53–70
Jameson, F, *Postmodernism, or, the Cultural Logic of Late Capitalism* (London, Verso, 1991)
Jameson, F, *The Geopolitical Aesthetic: Cinema and Space in the World System* (Bloomington, Indiana University Press, 1995)
Jenkins, RJH and Westerink, LG (eds), *Nicholas I, Patriarch of Constantinople. Letters* (Washington DC, Dumbarton Oaks Center for Byzantine Studies, 1973)
Jerome St, *Commentarii in Librum Job* in 26 PL (JP Migne ed, 1845) clm 619–802
Joerges, C, *Darker Legacies of Law in Europe: the Shadow of National Socialism and Fascism over Europe and its Legal Traditions* (Oxford, Hart Publishing, 2003)
Johannes Teutonicus (John Zimeke), *Apparatus Glossarum in Compilationem Tertiam*, 1 MIC Series A (K Pennington ed, 1981)
John of Salisbury, *Policraticus* (CCI Webb ed, Oxford, The Clarendon Press, 1909)
John of Salisbury, *Policraticus* (CJ Nederman ed, Cambridge, Cambridge University Press, 1990)
John of Salisbury, *Policraticus* (JP Migne ed, 1885) 199 clm 379–822
Kahn, PW, *Political Theology: Four New Chapters on the Concept of Sovereignty* (New York, Columbia University Press, 2013)

Kant, I, *Critique of the Power of Judgement* [1790] (P Guyer ed, Cambridge, Cambridge University Press, 2008)

Kantorowicz, E, *Frederick the Second: 1194–1250* (EO Lorimer trans, New York, Frederick Ungar Publishing Co, 1957)

Kantorowicz, E, *The King's Two Bodies: A Study in Mediaeval Political Theology* (Princeton, Princeton University Press, 1998)

Kelsen, H, *Die Staatslehre des Dante* (Wien, F Deuticke, 1905)

Kelsen, H, *Pure Theory of Law* (M Knight trans, Berkeley, University of California Press, 1967)

Kennedy, Da, *The Dark Sides of Virtue: Reassessing International Humanitarianism* (Princeton, Princeton University Press, 2015)

Kennedy, Da, 'The Mystery of Global Governance' (2008) 34 *Ohio Northern University Law Review* 827–60

Kennedy, Du, 'Antonio Gramsci and the Legal System' (1982) 6 *ALSA Forum* 32–37

Kierkegaard, S, *Repetition and Philosophical Crumbs* (MG Piety trans, Oxford, Oxford University Press, 2009)

King, E, 'Quinquennial Terror: Machiavelli's Understanding of the Political Sublime' (2013) 3 *Open Journal of Political Science* 69–75

Kissinger, H, *A World Restored: Metternich, Castlereagh, and the Problem of Peace, 1812–22* (Boston, Houghton Miffin, 1957)

Kissinger, H, *World Order* (New York, Penguin Books, 2014)

Koeppler, H, 'Frederick Barbarossa and the School of Bologna. Some remarks on the Authentica Habita' (1939) 54 *The English Historical Review* 577–607

Koskenniemi, M, 'International Community from Dante to Vattel' in V Chetail and P Haggenmacher (eds), *Vattel's International Law from a XXIst Century Perspective* (Leiden, Nijhoff, 2011) 49–76

Koskenniemi, M, 'International Law as Political Theology: How to Read Nomos der Erde?' (2004) 11 *Constellations. An International Journal of Critical and Democratic Theory* 492–511

Koskenniemi, M, 'Sovereignty, Property and Empire: Early Modern English Contexts' (2017) 18 *Theoretical Inquiries in Law* 355–89

Koskenniemi, M, *The Gentle Civilizer of Nations: the Rise and Fall of International Law 1870–1960* (Cambridge, Cambridge University Press, 2004)

Kuntz, ML, *Venice, Myth and Utopian Thought in the Sixteenth-century: Bodin, Postel and the Virgin of Venice* (Ashgate, Aldershot, 1999)

Latowsky, AA, *Emperor of the World: Charlemagne and the Construction of Imperial Authority, 800–1229* (Ithaca, Cornell University Press, 2016)

Lee, D, 'Sources of Sovereignty: Roman Imperium and Dominium in Civilian Theories of Sovereignty' (2012) 1 *Politica Antica* 79–94

Lee, D, 'Hobbes and the Civil Law. The Use of Roman Law in Hobbes's Civil Science' in D Dyzenhaus and T Poole (eds), *Hobbes and the Law* (Cambridge, Cambridge University Press, 2012) 210–35

Legendre, P, *Dominium mundi: L'empire du management* (Paris, Éd Mille et une nuits, 2007)

Legg, S (ed), *Spatiality, Sovereignty and Carl Schmitt. Geographies of the nomos* (London, Routledge, 2011)

Lenz, JMR, *Catharina von Siena* [1777?] in *Dramtischer Nachlass von J M.R. Lenz* (K Weinhold ed, Frankfurt, Ruten and Loening, 1884)

Lerner, RE, *Ernst Kantorowicz: a Life* (Princeton, Princeton University Press, 2017)

Leshem, D, *The Origins of Neoliberalism: Modeling the Economy from Jesus to Foucault* (New York, Columbia University Press, 2016)
Liverani, M, 'The Ideology of the Assyrian Empire' in MT Larsen (ed), *Power and Propaganda. A Symposium on Ancient Empires* (Copenhagen, Akademisk Vorlag, 1979) 297–317
Luhmann, N, 'Metamorphosen des Staates' in N Luhmann, *Gesellschaftsstruktur und Semantik. Studien zur Wissensoziologie der modernen Gesellschaft* (Frankfurt am Main, Suhrkamp Verlag, 1995) 101–37
Luther, M, 'Der XLVI Psalm' in M Luther, *D Martin Luthers Werke: Kritische Gesamtausgabe*, vol 35 (Weimar, Hermann Böhlaus Nachfolger, 1883–1980) 455–57
Luther, M, 'On Secular Authority: How Far does the Obedience Owed to It Extend?' in H Höpfl (ed), *Luther and Calvin on Secular Authority* (Cambridge, Cambridge University Press, 2005)
Lyotard, JF, *The Postmodern Expalined: Correspondence, 1982–1985* (D Barry trans, Minneapolis, Univeristy of Minnesota Press, 1992)
Mackinder, H, 'The Geographical Pivot of History' (1904) 23 *The Geographical Journal* 421–44
Maiolo, F, *Medieval Sovereignty: Marcilius of Padua and Bartolous of Saxoferrato* (Delft, Eburon Academic Publishers, 2008)
Malmesbury, W, *Historia regum* (W Stubbs ed, London, Her Majesty's Stationery Office, 1889)
Mantey, V, *Zwei Schwerter—Zwei Reiche. Martin Luthers Zwei-Reiche-Lehre vor ihrem spätmittelalterlichen Hintergrund* (Tübingen, Mohr Siebeck, 2005)
Martinich, AP, 'Interpreting the Religion of Thomas Hobbes: An Exchange Hobbes's Erastianism and Interpretation' (2009) 70 *Journal of the History of Ideas* 143–63
Martinich, AP, *The Two Gods of Leviathan: Thomas Hobbes on Religion and Politics* (Cambridge, Cambridge University Press, 2010)
Maschke, G, '"Amigo y enemigo": Kautilya y Álamos de Barrientos, anticipadores del criterio schmittiano' (2017) 1 *Carl-Schmitt-Studien* 111–120
Mattheus de Afflictis, *Praelectio in Constitutiones utriusque Siciliae* (Venice, Guarisco, 1606)
Maxwell-Stuart, PG, 'King James's Experience of Witches, and the 1604 English Witchcraft Act' in J Newton and Jo Bath (eds), *Witchcraft and the Act of 1604* (Leiden, Brill, 2008) 31–46
Maxwell-Stuart, PG, *Satan's Conspiracy: Magic and Witchcraft in Sixteenth-century Scotland* (East Linton, Tuckwell Press, 2001)
McCormick, JP, 'Irrational Choice and Mortal Combat as Political Destiny: The Essential Carl Schmitt' (2007) 10 *Annual Review of Political Science* 315–39
McCormick, JP, *Carl Schmitt's Critique of Liberalism: Against Politics as Technology* (Cambridge, Cambridge University Press, 1997)
McCormick, JP, *Machiavellian Democracy* (Cambridge, Cambridge University Press, 2011)
McGrade, M, 'O rex mundi triumphator: Hohenstaufen Politics in a Sequence for Saint Charlemagne' in I Fenlon (eds), *Early Music History: Studies in Medieval and Early Modern Music* (Cambridge, Cambridge University Press, 2009) 183–219
McIlwain, CH, *Constitutionalism Ancient and Modern* (London, The Lawbook Exchange, 2005)
McIlwain, CH (ed), *The Political Works of James I* (Cambridge, Harvard University, 1918)
Mintz, SI, *The Hunting of Leviathan* (Cambridge, Cambridge University Press, 1962)

Moloney, P, 'Hobbes, Savagery, and International Anarchy' (2011) 105 *The American Political Science Review* 189–204

Moltmann, J, *The Crucified God: The Cross of Christ as the Foundation and Criticism of Christian Theology* (RA Wilson and J Bowden trans, Minneapolis, Fortress Press, 1993)

Mommsen, T and Krueger, P (eds), *Digesta Iustiniani Augusti* (Berlin, Weidmann, 1870). English edition Mommsen T and Krueger P (eds), *Corpus Juris Civilis. Institutiones and Digesta*, vol 1 (Cambridge, Cambridge University Press, 2014)

Monk, SH, *The Sublime: A Study of Critical Theories in XVIII-Century England* (Ann Arbor, University of Michigan Press, 1935)

Morgenthau, HJ, *Politics among Nations: the Struggle for Power and Peace* (New York, AA Knopf, 1948)

Morgenthau, HJ, *Scientific Man vs. Power Politics* (Chicago, The University of Chicago Press, 1946)

Mowinckel, S, 'sahal' in D Winton Thomas and WD McHardy (eds), *Hebrew and Semitic Studies presented to Godfrey Rolles Driver* (Oxford, The Clarendon Press, 1964) 95–103

Muenckler, H, *Empires: The Logic of World Domination from Ancient Rome to the United States* (Cambridge, Polity Press, 2007)

Muldoon, J, *Empire and Order. The Concept of Empire 800–1800* (London, Palgrave Macmillan, 1999)

Munz, P, *Frederick Barbarossa: A Study in Mediaeval Politics* (Ithaca, Cornell University Press, 1969)

Murphy, K, 'The Physician's Religion and "salus populi": The Manuscript Circulation and Print Publication of "Religio Medici"' (2014) 111 *Studies in Philology* 845–74

Murphy, T, 'Law and Revolution, II: The Impact of the Protestant Reformations on the Western Legal Tradition. Book Review' (2006) 69 *The Modern Law Review* 480–84

Neumann, F, *Behemoth: The Structure and Practice of National Socialism, 1933–1944* (Oxford, Oxford University Press, 1944)

Newman, S, *Politics of Postanarchism* (Edinburgh, Edinburgh University Press, 2010)

Nietzsche, F, *Ecce homo* in F Nietzche, *Werke, Complete Critical Edition* (G Colli and M Montinari eds, Berlin, Walter de Gruyter, 1967)

Normand, L and Roberts, G (eds), *Witchcraft in Early Modern Scotland: James VI's Demonology and the North Berwick Witches* (Exeter, University of Exeter Press, 2000)

Nye, JS, *Soft Power: The Means to Success in Foreign Politics* (New York, PublicAffairs, 2009)

Oakley, F, 'Jacobean Political Theology: The Absolute and Ordinary Powers of the King' (1968) 29 *Journal of the History of Ideas* 323–46

Oakley, F, *Kingship: the Politics of Enchantment* (Malden, Blackwell Publishing, 2006)

Oakley, F, *Politics and Eternity: Studies in the History of Medieval and Early Modern Political Thought* (Leiden, Brill, 1999)

Oakley, F, 'The "Hidden" and "Revealed" Wills of James I: More Political Theology' (1972) 15 *Studia Gratiana* 367–75

Oakley, F, *The Watershed of Modern Politics. Law, Virtue, Kingship and Consent (1300–1650)* (New Haven, Yale University Press, 2015)

Ockham, G(uilelmus de), *Opera Theologica*, vol 9 (JC Wey ed, New York, The Franciscan Institute of St Bonaventure University, 1980)

O'Gorman, N, 'The Political Sublime: An Oxymoron' (2006) 34 *Journal of International Studies* 889–915

Ong, A, *Neoliberalism as Exception: Mutations in Citizenship and Sovereignty* (Durham, Duke University Press, 2006)

Orr, DA, "'God's Hangman': James VI, the Divine Right of Kings, and the Devil' (2016) 18 *Reformation & Renaissance Review* 137–54
Ostrogorsky, G, *History of the Byzantine State* (J Hussey trans, Oxford, Basil Blackwell, 1956)
Otto Morena, *De rebus Laudensibus* in 7 MGH (F Guterbock ed, 1930)
Pacchi, A, *Convenzione e ipotesi nella formazione della filosofia naturale di Thomas Hobbes* (Firenze, La Nuova Italia, 1965)
Pacchi, A, 'Una "biblioteca ideale" di Thomas Hobbes: il MS E2 dell'archivio di Chatsworth' (1968) 21 *Acme* 5–42
Padoa Schioppa, A, *A History of Law in Europe. From the Early Middle Ages to the Twentieth Century* (C Fitzgerald trans, Cambridge, Cambridge University Press, 2007)
Pagden, A, *Lords of All the World: Ideologies of Empire in Spain, Britain and France C. 1500–c. 1800* (New Haven, Yale University Press, 1995)
Panofsky, E, *Meaning in the Visual Arts* (Chicago, The University of Chicago Press, 1982)
Pelayo, A, *De Planctu Ecclesie Libri Duo* (Venetiis, Sansovinus, 1560)
Pennington, K, 'The Consilia of Baldus the Ubaldis' (1988) 56 *Tijdschrift voor Rechtsgeschiedenis* 85
Pennington, K, *Pope and Bishops. The Papal Monarchy in the Twelfth and Thirteenth Centuries* (Philadelphia, University of Pennsylvania Press, 1984)
Pennington, K, *The Prince and the Law, 1200–1600: Sovereignty and Rights in the Western Legal Tradition* (Berkeley, University of California Press, 1993)
Peri, C, *Il regno del nemico. La morte nella religione di Canaan* (Brescia, Paideia, 2003)
Perz, GH and Rodenberg, C (eds), *Epistolae saeculi XIII e Regestis Pontificum Romanorum Selectae* in MGH (Berlin, Weidemann, 1883)
Peter Damian, *De divina omnipotentia* [1065] (P Brezzi and D Nardi Firenze, Vallecchi, 1943)
Pettit, P, *Made with Words. Hobbes on Language, Mind, and Politics* (Princeton, Princeton University Press, 2008)
Pfeiffer, S, 'The Imperial Cult in Egypt' in C Riggs (ed), *The Oxford Handbook of Roman Egypt* (Oxford, Oxford University Press, 2012) 83–100
Pierre de Lancre, *Table de l'inconstance des mauvais anges et démons: où il est amplement traité des sorciers et de la sorcellerie, par Pierre de Lancre* [1612] (Bayonne, Impr la Presse, 1938)
Poesch, J, 'The Beasts from Job in the Liber Floridus Manuscripts' (1970) 31 *Journal of the Warburg and Courtauld Institutes* 41–51
Praz, M, *La carne, la morte e il diavolo nella letteratura romantica* (Milano, La Cultura, 1930)
Price, SRF, 'Gods and Emperors: The Greek Language of the Roman Imperial Cult' (1984) 104 *The Journal of Hellenic Studies* 79–95
Ptak, R, 'Neoliberalism in Germany: Revisiting the Ordoliberal Foundations of the Social Market Economy' in P Mirowski and D Plehwe (eds), *The Road from Mont Pèlerin: The Making of the Neoliberal Thought Collective* (Cambridge, Harvard University Press, 2009) 98–138
Quaglioni, D, *I limiti della sovranità. Il pensiero di Jean Bodin nella cultura politica e giuridica dell'età moderna* (Padova, Cedam, 1992)
Quaglioni, D, *La sovranità* (Roma, Laterza, 2004)
Rengger, N, 'On Theology and International Relations: World Politics Beyond the Empty Sky' (2013) 27 *International Relations* 141–57

Richard, JC, 'Recherches sur certains aspects du culte impérial: Les funérailles des empereurs Romains aux deux premiers siècles de notre ère' in W Haase and H Temporini (eds), *Aufstieg und Niedergang der römischen Welt* (Berlin, Walter de Gruyter, 1998) 1121–34

Richardson, J, *The Language of Empire. Rome and the Idea of Empire from the Third Century BC to the Second Century AD* (Cambridge, Cambridge University Press, 2008)

Righi, R, 'Carl Schmitt interprete di Hobbes (1921–1938)' (1980) 2 *Studi di filosofia, politica e diritto* 51–69

Ritter, G, *The Corrupting Influence of Power* (Westport, Hyperion Press, 1979)

Rosenthal, E, 'Plus Ultra, Non plus Ultra, and the Columnar Device of Emperor Charles V' (1971) 34 *Journal of the Warburg and Courtauld Institutes* 204–28

Rosh, G, *ὄνομα βασιλείας. Studien zum offiziellen Gebrauch der Kaisertitel in Spatantinker und Fruhbyzantinischer Zeit* (Wien, Verlag der Österreichischen Akademie der Wissenschaften, 1978)

Rumpf, H, *Carl Schmitt und Thomas Hobbes* (Berlin, Duncker & Humblot, 1972)

Ryan, M, 'Bartolus of Sassoferrato and Free Cities' (2000) 10 *Transactions of the Royal Historical Society* 65–89

Saint-Bonnet, F, *L'état d'exception* (Paris, Presses Universitaires de France, 2001)

Samuel, G, 'On the Beach: What Can Beaches Reveal About Legal Reasoning and Categorisation?' (2017) 12 *Journal of Comparative Law* 187–202

Santner, EL, *The Royal Remains: the People's Two Bodies and the Endgames of Sovereignty* (Chicago, The University of Chicago Press, 2012)

Scattola, M, *Das Naturrecht vor dem Naturrecht* (Tubingen, Max Niemeyer Verlag, 1999)

Scattola, M, *Teologia politica* (Bologna, Il Mulino, 2007)

Schiller, F, "On Naive and Sentimental Poetry" in HB Nisbet (ed), *German Aesthetic and Literary Criticism: Winckelmann, Lessing, Hamann, Herder, Schiller, Goethe* (Cambridge, Cambridge University Press, 1985) 177–232

Schiller, F, 'On the Sublime (Toward a Further Development of some Kantian Ideas)' in F Schiller, *Essays* (W Hinderer and WO Dahlstrom eds, London, Continuum, 1993) 22–44

Schmitt, C, *Constitutional Theory* (J Seitzer trans, Durham, Duke University Press, 2008)

Schmitt, C, *Der Wert des Staates und die Bedeutung des Einzelnen* (Berlin, Duncker & Humblot, 2004)

Schmitt, C, 'Die vollendete Reformation. Bemerkungen und Hinweise zu neuen Leviathan—Interpretationen' (1965) 4 *Der Staat* 68–69

Schmitt, C, 'Die weltgeschichtliche Struktur des heutigen Weltgegensatzes von Ost und West. Bemerkungen zu Ernst Jüngers Schrift, "Der Gordische Knoten"' in A Mohler (ed), *Freundschaftliche Begegnungen: Festschrift für Ernst Junger zum 60. Geburtstag* (Frankfurt, Klostermann, 1955) 135–67

Schmitt, C, *Dictatorship. From the Origin of the Modern Concept of Sovereignty to Proletarian Class Struggle* (M Hoelzl and G Ward trans, Cambridge, Polity Press, 2014)

Schmitt, C, *Die geistesgeschichtliche Lage des heutigen Parlamentarismus* (Berlin, Duncker & Humblot, 1926)

Schmitt, C, *Donoso Cortés in gesamteuropäischer Interpretation: vier Aufsätze* (Berlin, Duncker & Humblot, 2009)

Schmitt, C, *Hamlet or Hecuba. The Irruption of Time into Play* (S Draghici trans, Corvallis, Plutarch Press, 2006)

Schmitt, C, *Land and Sea: a World-historical Meditation* (SG Zeitlin trans, New York, Telos Press Publishing, 2015)

Schmitt, C, *Political Romanticism* (G Oakes trans, Cambridge, MIT Press, 1991)
Schmitt, C, *Political Theology: Four Chapters on the Concept of Sovereignty* (G Schwab trans, Chicago, The University of Chicago Press, 2010)
Schmitt, C, *Political Theology. II. The Myth of the Closure of any Political Theology* (M Hoelzl and G Ward trans, Cambridge, Polity Press, 2008)
Schmitt, C, *The Concept of the Political* (G Schwab trans, Chicago, The University of Chicago Press, 2008)
Schmitt, C, *The Leviathan in the State Theory of Thomas Hobbes: Meaning and Failure of a Political Symbol* (G Schwab and E Hilfstein trans, Chicago, The University of Chicago Press, 2008)
Schmitt, C, *The Nomos of the Earth in the International Law of the Jus Publicum Europaeum* (GL Ulmen trans, New York, Telos Press Publishing, 2006)
Scott McClure, C, 'Hell and Anxiety in Hobbes's "Leviathan"' (2011) 73 *The Review of Politics* 1–27
Scott, RT, *Review to Lise Vogel, The Column of Antoninus Pius* (1975) 69 *The Classical World* 148
Searle, JR, *Making the Social World: The Structure of Human Civilization* (Oxford, Oxford University Press, 2010)
Selden, J, *Mare Clausum; the Right and Dominion of the Sea* (London, Andrew Kembe and Edward Thomas, 1663)
Sennert, D, *Chymistry Made Easie and Useful* (London, Peter Cole, 1662)
Shaw, PA, *The Sublime* (London, Routledge, 2017)
Shelley, PB, *Prometheus Unbound—A Lyrical Drama in Four Acts* (London, C & J Ollier, 1820)
Sherwin, RK, 'Sublime Jurisprudence: On the Ethical Education of the Legal Imagination in Our Time' (2008) 83 *Chicago-Kent Law Review* 1157–96
Shirer, W, *The Rise and Fall of the Third Reich* (New York, Touchstone Edition: Simon & Schuster, 1990)
Smith, TW, 'Between Two Kings: Pope Honorius III and the Seizure of the Kingdom of Jerusalem by Frederick II in 1225' (2015) 41 *Journal of Medieval History* 41–59
Spektorowski, A, 'Maistre, Donoso Cortés, and the Legacy of Catholic Authoritarianism' (2002) 63 *Journal of the History of Ideas* 283–302
Sperling, M, *Visionary Philology: Geoffrey Hill and the Study of Words* (Oxford, Oxford University Press, 2014)
Stach, W, *Salve, mundi domine! Kommentierende Betrachtungen zum Kaiserhymnus des Archipoeta* (Leipzig, Sächsische Akademie der Wissenschaften, 1939)
Stark, RJ, *Rhetoric, Science, and Magic in Seventeenth-Century England* (Washington, The Catholic University of America Press, 2009)
Steinwenter, A, *Nomos empsuchos: Zur Geschichte einer politischen Theorie* (Wien, Anzeiger der Akademie der Wissenschaften, 1946)
Stelzer, W, 'Zum Scholarenprivileg Friedrick Barbarossas (Authentica Habita)' (1978) *Deutsches Archiv fur Erforschung des Mittelalters* 123–65
Sternberger, D, 'Machiavellis "Principe" und der Bergriffs des Politischen' in D Sternberger (ed), *Schriften*, vol 3 (Frankfurt am Main, Insel Verlag, 1980) 29–111
Stolleis, M, 'La reception de Bodin en Allemagne' (1995) 24 *Quaderni fiorentini* 141–56
Strauss, L, 'Reason and Revelation' in H Meier (ed), *Leo Strauss and the Theological-Political Problem* (Cambridge, Cambridge University Press, 2007) 141–79

Strauss, L, *Natural Right and History* (Chicago, The University of Chicago Press, 2008)
Sundet Jones, K, 'Apocalyptic Luther' (2005) 25 *Word & World* 308–16
Taubes, J, *Occidental Escatology* (D Ratmoko trans, Stanford, Stanford University Press, 2009)
Taubes, J, *The Political Theology of Paul* (D Hollander trans, Stanford, Stanford University Press, 2003)
Tedeschi, N, *Lectura super Tertio* (Venetiis, Iohannes de Colonia, 1475)
Teubner, G, 'The Anonymous Matrix: Human Rights Violations by "Private" Transnational Actors' (2006) 69 *The Modern Law Review* 327–46
Thompson, CJS, *Royal Cramp and Other Medycinable Rings* (London, Wellcome Historical Medical Museum, 1921)
Ullmann, W, 'De Bartoli sententia: Concilium repraesentat mentem populi' in D Segoloni (ed), *Bartolo da Sassoferrato. Studi e documenti per il VI centenario* (Milano, Giuffrè, 1962) 707–33
Ullmann, W, *Medieval Political Thought* (London, Penguin Books, 1965)
Ullmann, W, *The Carolingian Renaissance and the Idea of Kingship* (London, Methuen Publishing, 1969)
Ullmann, W, 'The Development of the Medieval Idea of Sovereignty' (1949) 64 *English Historical Review* 1–33
Vogel, L, *The Column of Antoninus Pius* (Cambridge, Harvard University Press, 1973)
Walther, HG, *Imperiales Königtum, Konziliarismus und Volkssouveränität: Studien zu den Grenzen des Mittelalterlichen Souveränitätsgedankens* (München, Fink, 1976)
Watt, G, 'Hard Cases, Hard Times, and the Humanity of Law' in J Bate (ed), *The Public Value of The Humanities* (London, Bloomsbury Academic, 2011) 197–207
Watt, G, *Trust and Equity* (Oxford, Oxford University Press, 2016)
Weber, M, *Economy and Society: An Outline of Interpretive Sociology* (Berkeley, University of California Press, 1978)
Weber, M, *The Protestant Ethic and the Spirit of Capitalism* (S Kalberg trans, Oxford, Oxford University Press, 2010)
Weinrich, L (ed), *Quellen zu deutscher Verfassungs-Wirtschaft und Sozialgeschichte bis 1250. Ausgewallte Quellen zur deutschen Geschichte des Mittelalter* (Darmstadt, Wissenschaftliche Buchgesellschaft, 1977)
Weyer, J, *De Praestigiis Daemonum et Incantationibus ac Venificiis* (Basileae, ex officina Operiniana, 1568)
Whiston, W, *An Account of the Daemomaniacks, and the Power of Casting Out Daemons* (London, Boyle's Head, 1737)
Wieacker, F, *A History of Private Law in Europe* (T Weir trans, Oxford, Oxford University Press, 1996)
Wilks, M, *The Problem of Sovereignty in the Later Middle Ages: the Papal Monarchy with Augustinus Triumphus and the Publicists* (Cambridge, Cambridge University Press, 2008)
Wittgenstein, L, *Tractatus Logicus-Philosophicus* (London, Kegan Paul, 1922)
Woolf, CNS, *Bartolus of Sassoferrato: His Position in the History of Medieval Political Thought* (Cambridge, Cambridge University Press, 2012)
Wormald, J, 'The Witches, the Devil and the King' in T Brotherstone and D Ditchburn (eds), *Freedom and Authority: Scotland, c. 1050–c. 1650: Historical and Historiographical Essays Presented to Grant G. Simpson* (East Linton, Tuckwell Press, 2001) 165–80
Yates, FA, *Astraea: the Imperial Theme in the Sixteenth Century* (London, Pimlico, 1993)

Yates, FA, *The Occult Philosophy in the Elizabethan Age* (London, Routledge & K Paul, 1979)

Zarmanian, T, 'Ordnung und Ortung/Order and Localisation' in S Legg (ed), *Spatiality, Sovereignty and Carl Schmitt. Geographies of the Nomos* (London, Routledge, 2011) 291–97

Zimmermann, R, *The Law of Obligations: Roman Foundations of the Civilian Tradition* (Oxford, Oxford University Press, 1996)

INDEX

www.ingramcontent.com/pod-product-compliance
Ingram Content Group UK Ltd.
Pitfield, Milton Keynes, MK11 3LW, UK
UKHW020816290926
15470UKWH00003B/1191

9 781509 911752